What Works?

A Practical Guide for Teacher Research

Elizabeth Chiseri-Strater &
Bonnie S. Sunstein

HEINEMANN
Portsmouth, NH

Heinemann
A division of Reed Elsevier Inc.
361 Hanover Street
Portsmouth, NH 03801–3912
www.heinemann.com

Offices and agents throughout the world

The authors and publisher wish to thank those who have generously given permission to reprint borrowed material:

"Chasing Friendship: Acceptance, Rejection, and Recess Play" by Karen Wohlwend was originally published in *Childhood Education* (volume 81, no.2, Winter 2004–2005). Reprinted by permission of the Journal of the Association for Childhood Education International.

Library of Congress Cataloging-in-Publication Data
Chiseri-Strater, Elizabeth.
    What works? : a practical guide for teacher research / Elizabeth Chiseri-Strater & Bonnie S. Sunstein.
        p. cm.
    Includes bibliographical references and index.
    ISBN 0-325-00713-6
    1. Education—Research—United States—Handbooks, manuals, etc.
2. Teachers—United States—Handbooks, manuals, etc.   I. Sunstein, Bonnie S.
II. Title.

LB1028.25.U6C47 2006
370.7′2—dc22   2005034451

EDITOR: Lisa Luedeke
PRODUCTION: Vicki Kasabian
INTERIOR AND COVER DESIGNS: Jenny Jensen Greenleaf
TYPESETTER: House of Equations, Inc.
MANUFACTURING: Louise Richardson

Printed in the United States of America on acid-free paper
10 09 08 07 06 RRD 1 2 3 4 5

To imitate speech is easy: an entire nation can do it:
to imitate judgment and the research for your material
takes rather more time.

—MICHEL DE MONTAIGNE,
"On the Education of Children"

For Tom Newkirk

who introduced us to Montaigne and taught us to take the time
to research, judge, question, and interpret our data
and to always trust our teaching intuitions.

Contents

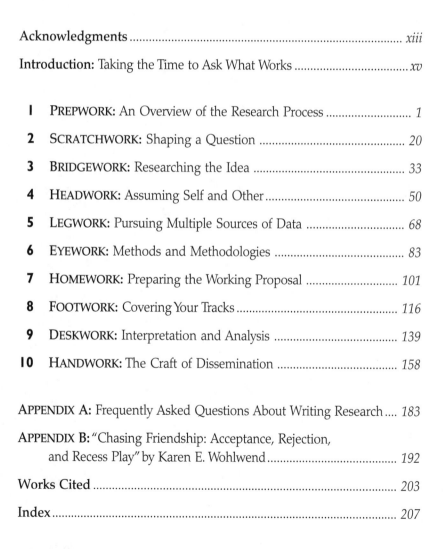

Contents

Teacher Inquiry as Resistance
  Why teachers?
  Inquiry about what?
  Resistance to what?

A Story About Beth: One Teacher Inquires
  What's her situation?
  What's her research question?
  What prompted her question?
  What are her options?

Taking the Time
  How do we fit research into our schedule?
  How do we fit our schedule into research?
  How much or how little time does research require?

Praxis: Connecting Theory and Practice
  Why bother doing research?
  What's in it for me?
  What am I going to learn?
  What are my students going to learn?

  PREPWORK: Write about what bothers you.

About Chapter 2: SCRATCHWORK: Shaping a Question
  PREPWORK: Make a list of research questions that interest you.
  When you cluster them, what themes or topics appear?

Acknowledgments

*E*nriching and refreshing one's teaching is certainly not a solitary act. A good teacher research project, hewn from experience and knowledge, can have an important place in print despite an uncertain political climate in schools. And so it is with this book. With it, we recognize a valuable archive of people and programs who've had enthusiastic, loving, and patient interest in the questions we've asked.

As our book shifted slowly from collegial conversations into the form you're holding, we were lucky to have help from them. For Bonnie, this book would not exist without the University of Iowa Career Development Award and a Spring 2005 Affiliate Professorship from the University of New Hampshire's Center for the Humanities and Department of English. Elizabeth thanks her colleagues in the English department, especially Hephzibah Roskelly and Nancy Fogarty at the Jackson Library of the University of North Carolina at Greensboro, and all the students in her graduate Research Methods and Pedagogy class who read two versions of this book.

Together, we are so grateful for Northeastern University's Martha's Vineyard Summer Writing Institutes, particularly directors Tim Donovan and Susan Wall, as well as eight summers full of teacher-researchers from around the country. In February 2004, Julie Cheville of Rutgers University, Betsy Rizza of Princeton Day School, and an auditorium full of New Jersey Writing Project teachers helped to craft an early conception of the book's framework.

And as this book developed, we indulged in collegial conversation, received detailed reading, and took crucial suggestions from a few long-time colleagues and friends: Deborah Appleman, Burt Feintuch, Danling Fu, Arthur Hunsicker, Jim Marshall, Donna Qualley, Linda Rief, Hepsie Roskelly, Jeff Wilhelm, and Sarah Townsend. Both our 2004 and 2005

Vineyard Case Study Design students read and responded to our drafts: Summer McLin, Rene Caldwell, Kristen Ziegler, Katie McKiernan, Michelle Navone, Kelly Richards, Nancy Steen, and Ellen Mangiamele.

Because of the miles that usually lie between us, our collaboration has required not only opening our homes and families to each other, but it's relied on three special friends who have opened their homes and minds to us in Massachusetts. Judy Rosenwald offered us specific ideas and a lifetime of broad reading during daily breakfasts, and allowed us two uninterrupted weeks to spread our data on her ping-pong table. Ginni and David Spencer's five months' generosity ranged from a fish-shaped notepad, a crate of Tootsie Pops, the sounds of slapping halyards, and the gong of a mariner's clock in their cozy winter hideout by a footbridge over Lobster Cove. As transplanted lovers of New England, we found deep refreshment. Most important, we thank these three people for the constant reminders of what lifelong friendship is about.

We are both lucky, together and separately, to have worked for many years with Heinemann–Boynton/Cook Publishers. For this book, we had our "dream team." From our earliest ideas, Lisa Luedeke gave us courage to write what we believed, kept us focused and realistic. And then, with a flash of professional competence, Vicki Kasabian, Eric Chalek, Melissa Wood, and Maura Sullivan offered us their expertise and humor in just the right proportions.

And, of course, we thank our families. Elizabeth thanks her two insightful and artistic daughters, Tosca Chiseri and Alisha Strater. Bonnie's family, Janet Stone, Amy Sunstein, Stephen Sunstein, and Mike Wright offer constant lessons about the nature of growth and unconditional love.

Introduction
Taking the Time to Ask What Works

> Any encounter with actual human beings who are trying to
> learn how to learn requires imagination on the part of
> teachers—and on the part of those they teach.
>
> —MAXINE GREENE, *Releasing the Imagination*

Our classrooms are under siege. We feel the flames. And as teachers, we're afraid our students will become the casualties. We're bombarded by national educational policies, state assessment mandates, regional curriculum demands, and community competition about competencies and for resources. We recoil from the backlash against pedagogies we've worked hard for decades to refine and implement. We're bruised from the kickbacks of current battles: student-centered learning versus standardized curricula, secular- versus religious-based instruction, process versus postprocess approaches, phonics versus whole language, charter schools versus homeschooling, public schools versus private schools, and scores of other competing forces. Like war correspondents from the front, educators have written books over the years with titles suggesting that all is not well in our schools: *Teaching as a Subversive Activity; Pedagogy of the Oppressed; Savage Inequalities; Teaching Is Not Testing; One Size Fits Few; The End of Education; Punished by Rewards; Standards, Grading, and Other Follies.*

But like all useful comparisons, this war metaphor breaks down when we think it through. Although many of us wish that we enjoyed budgets like the military, we know education is not war. Schools, like all cultural institutions, experience ideological battles in cycles of agreement and dissent. Mandates and curricular shifts are not necessarily acts of oppression;

in fact, they sometimes help us define our broadest goals and expectations. As teachers, we'll never surrender what we believe. Nor will we simply shut the classroom door and ignore what seems like crossfire outside. We need to make our voices speak through the fire and invite the noisy public to listen.

Teacher Inquiry as Resistance

- ☀ Why teachers?
- ☀ Inquiry about what?
- ☀ Resistance to what?

How do we validate what works in our classes? How can we explain *why* it works to the people who care: our students, their parents, our colleagues and administrators, and the embattled and often uninformed public? Our response: we can conduct teacher research. When we speak as teachers informed by our own research, we can control the fires and inform the noisy public about what works in our classrooms. Teacher inquiry is a form of resistance against both authoritarian mandates and professional or public apathy. It allows us to rebuild our educational independence in the pursuit of authentic, nonmandated change.

> ⚙ How do we validate what works in our classes? How can we explain *why* it works to the people who care?

We often hear our colleagues, in teacher's lounges and at local TGIF gatherings, bemoan change and turn down opportunities to take part in all kinds of educational reform:

"This is just a recycled version of what I saw in the seventies, and it wasn't any good then."

"We don't have time to have our students do math, science, read, write—we're too busy doing safety education, drug awareness, diversity integration."

"That may work for you, but it won't work for me."

"My kids won't be able to write again for two months, because I have to get them ready for the writing test."

"You university people don't know what it's like down here in the trenches. You should try our job just for one day."

But we also hear complex stories and reflections about what *does* work in teaching—and how teachers found it out. The process of swapping stories, trading strategies, and asking questions is the foundation for systematic teacher inquiry. How can teachers describe what works? understand what doesn't work? turn stories, questions, and strategies into research? First, pose the questions: What constitutes "failure"? Why does that kid sit in the back of the room, always have the right answer, draw diagrams all the time, but never open his book? Why do my eighth graders need to write only a five-paragraph essay—with five sentences in each paragraph?

Teachers are lifelong learners, continual questioners; otherwise, we wouldn't have chosen to spend our adulthood in school. Our intention is to show that systematic inquiry is both a form and a method for teacher resistance and for teacher agency. As teachers and researchers ourselves, we write to you (in a single voice although we are two authors) with almost four decades apiece of teaching and researching in public and private schools, colleges, universities, and other sites in which people learn. We've each asked millions of questions about our classrooms and our students. Some we've never been able to answer. Others we've transformed into research. Bonnie studied how three teachers experienced their own writing in a summer program; Elizabeth documented a group of kindergartners doing "invented reading" to a stuffed red bear; Bonnie tracked a class of special-needs students circumnavigating their own IEPs; Elizabeth tracked two college students for two years to see how they gained literacy skills across the curriculum. Among other projects, Bonnie designed a program for doctors who write about pharmacological research studies; Elizabeth created a writing curriculum for soil scientists. We've used our research to write books and essays, revise curriculum, develop community-based projects, and change standards for assessment. Although we both like to think that others have benefited from our work, our research has, more important, enabled us to become better teachers—over and over again. Research feeds our natural curiosity and sustains the ongoing conversation that makes a professional life grow.

Systematic inquiry, often called "action research" or "teacher research," offers the opportunity to answer questions for ourselves about our classrooms, our curriculum, and our students' learning. Classroom studies help us resist prepackaged, laminated, hole-punched, "teacher-proof" curricula, attitudes about "teaching-to-the-test," and so many of the administrative mandates that oppress us. As we carry out research plans with our students, we sharpen our powers for understanding them and ourselves as learners. With systematic inquiry, we can ask questions and re-form them, we can observe our classes and document what we see and hear, we can design our studies and disseminate our findings for colleagues and communities. We can claim our own agency and assume control of ourselves as professionals.

Each time we wonder what works, we're setting the stage for inquiry. We care about our subject matter, and we care about how we and our students learn. Teachers make ideal researchers because we're always asking, "What's going on here?" We ask teaching questions to discover whether our hunches have any merit and whether our practices are connected to our theories. We ask learning questions to find out whether our students absorb the ideas we think we deliver. We ask questions about context to better understand the environments and conversations that influence our students and ourselves. We form solid research questions when we pay attention to the ideas in the corners of our minds.

A Story About Beth: One Teacher Inquires

- ☀ What's her situation?
- ☀ What's her research question?
- ☀ What prompted her question?
- ☀ What are her options?

Beth Campbell is a "lateral entry" teacher hired on an emergency basis in an understaffed school considered undesirable by its own community. When she accepts her job, Beth promises to begin the certification process in secondary English. Beth already has a BA degree in U.S. history and secondary education, an out-of-state certification in social studies, an MA in folklore, and teaching experience (student teaching in a rural school, lots of substitute teaching, some university courses). She has considerable experience as a museum curator and writer but has never taught full time in an inner-city public school. Two months after the school year has begun, Beth takes over three block-schedule high school English classes abandoned by a popular substitute teacher who's decided to go to law school. Beth's school is one year away from probation.

Her principal and her colleagues are under fire. The school has not met current academic criteria, and its standardized state test scores are too low. The local paper writes frequently about violence in this school; after a few students were accused of making a "peer hit list," students in other schools in the area imitated them. With such a bad reputation, the teacher turnover rate is exceedingly high; this year, four teachers have walked out during the first month. By January the school will have experienced a 20 percent faculty turnover and the principal, the third in three years, will announce that he'll be leaving in March.

Beth's teaching experience serves as her practicum for state emergency certification purposes, but unlike many teachers, she has neither a supervisor nor a cooperating teacher. The principal hands her a stack of prepackaged lesson plans to use with her ninth graders; in the spirit of supporting uncertified and untenured teachers, the state educators purchased "teacher-proof" materials. Beth receives a heavy pile of worksheets, CD-ROMs, textbooks with instructors' manuals that give directions for what to say and do. ("Anyone can teach with this stuff," the product salespeople say. "This is what teachers want. That's why we make them; they're comfortable.") At first, Beth is relieved to have the predesigned plans. She hasn't been in a public school since her own adolescence. For her first month or so, managing what looks like unruly classes takes priority over the English curriculum's content.

But one mild October day, she finds herself following the guide's directions for teaching "The Gift of the Magi," with its focus on irony. When a student asks, "Why are we reading a Christmas story in October?" Beth stops in her tracks, steps away from her packaged curriculum, and asks herself the same question, along with a few others: Why *am* I teaching O. Henry in October? Is there another ironic short story out there that might be more suitable for these minority students? Is there a different way to discuss irony with students whose own lives are so filled with irony, whose everyday language reveals their understanding of irony, whose music is fundamentally based on irony? None of these questions is raised in the teacher's guide. It is time for her to claim agency for herself, resist the mandated curriculum, and find out what might work.

Like many teacher-inquirers, Beth lets her student's question shape her research: why teach a Christmas story in October? She considers the available materials. Rather than refusing to use the school's curriculum, or walking out altogether, Beth employs her expertise to discover what is already working—and design what might work better—to teach irony.

Together Beth and her students learn about irony by drawing on experiences from their own lives. The students grasp the concept quickly and easily expand on it in class. Beth abandons the planned discussion questions and worksheets; instead, the class "freestyles," coming up with raps that explore ironies in the stories, plays, and poems they have read so far; in the failing school of which they are a part; in their own lives. These students have a hard time identifying with the man in the O. Henry story who can't afford a hairbrush, since even though they are quite poor, they live in the age of Wal-Mart. But they know irony. In one boy's rap song, an uncle who finally gets the car of his dreams goes to prison. Another boy's decision to live with his mother in poverty dooms his chances of escaping from this cycle. While administrators further up the institutional chain celebrate "success," these students watch their own school fall apart.

> ⚙ Like many teacher-inquirers, Beth lets her student's question shape her research.

Taking the Time

- ☀ How do we fit research into our schedule?
- ☀ How do we fit our schedule into research?
- ☀ How much or how little time does research require?

Many projects begin with the tension over what's *not* working in a classroom. Beth faced a battalion of forces causing tension. Both the state's testing mandates and the materials she was handed made her feel unqualified and incompetent. The prepackaged materials seemed to assume that she knew nothing about either students or literature and that her students had neither experience nor ideas. But Beth decided to look closely at what she and her students *did* know, what she *could* teach, and what her students *could* learn. She turned her nagging thoughts about what wasn't working into a focused question about what might work.

> ⚙ Many projects begin with the tension over what's not working in a classroom.

Beth's situation may seem extreme, but many of our questions do emerge from the tension between external mandates and our own common sense. We believe that all teachers should take the time to examine what works in their own classroom. We admit, of course, that our time is already too filled with department and all-school meetings, inservice requirements, parent conferences, consultations about pull-out programs, disciplinary documentation, website management, lesson plans, grading, and assessment. We can't design a study or a project for every question we ask. But we can choose the questions that nag us the most.

Most of the time, we don't have the hours to follow our hunches, extend our questions, track our learning or teaching processes—or those of our students. Our best pedagogical intentions dissipate when the class ends, when we can't find the hall pass, when the public address system sounds, or when it's the day before the big test. The intentions disappear under piles of student papers, within the clutter in briefcases, bookshelves, and plastic tote trays. We worry and wonder as a student leaves our class for an athletic event, ESL support, band practice, or special ed. But our questions remain there, caught in the corners of our minds.

This book is an invitation to pay attention to the corners of our minds, to allow ourselves the luxury and creativity of conducting inquiry on a few focused topics. Research time is not the same as teaching time. The habits of mind we use to ask and answer our classroom questions don't end with a grading period or a buzzer. Scholarship about our teaching reveals itself gradually.

Our ways of paying attention, our rhythms of observing and recording, require another kind of time, more like that spent brainstorming and mapping. The questions in the corners of our minds need to percolate and brew until we understand them enough to articulate them to ourselves. Only then can we can design a research project, choose a method for collecting data, interpret and analyze the information we've gathered, and eventually decide on a way to share it with others who can benefit from what we've learned.

> ☼ *This book is an invitation to pay attention to the corners of our minds, to allow ourselves the luxury and creativity of conducting inquiry on a few focused topics.*

Creating a time line for a project means superimposing your research upon your school's calendar. Planning a research project with an already full schedule is a challenge; like writing or designing anything, it is also messy and chaotic. We know teacher-researchers whose plans have been interrupted by job-assignment changes, construction delays, hurricanes, family crises. Semesters and whole school years can come and go. But the questions remain, and eventually teacher-researchers can return to them. Since each question is unique, it demands an intellectual rhythm that might not synchronize with administrative or family rhythms. Taking the time to plan our time, our internal clock slowing or quickening with the pace of our research, the external clock regimenting the other parts of our lives, is the most creative challenge in systematic inquiry.

Praxis: Connecting Theory and Practice

- ☀ Why bother doing research?
- ☀ What's in it for me?
- ☀ What am I going to learn?
- ☀ What are my students going to learn?

As successful teachers, we engage in "praxis" many times a day—when we ask what works and try to explain why. Praxis—connecting our ideas with our actions, deriving theories from our practices—gives us the power to understand teaching as a kind of scholarship and resist ideas that confuse our common sense. We reclaim internal agency for ourselves as inquisitive, successful professionals when we take the time to ask what works and then try to answer it.

Sadly, the term *praxis* brings chills to our newest teachers because it has become a name for one national standardized entrance test instead of a pedagogical idea. In letting this happen, we've diminished the power of a very important concept. It takes courage to ask questions of our teaching, to challenge ideas we hold, and to doubt our own established teaching patterns and practices enough to question them.

This book expands the definition of teacher research by stretching the potential genres that people traditionally accept as "research." Certainly, studies over time, written up for journals or books, "count." But so do projects that result in curriculum revisions, carefully crafted assignments, interactive websites, library and museum displays, public performances, inservice workshops, booklets, brochures, and portfolio projects. The dissemination of teachers' knowledge to a public hungry for "the truth" is one key reason for doing teacher research. Using our own voices and the voices of our students to influence and affect public educational policy ought to be part of our mission as teachers.

> ⚙ The dissemination of teachers' knowledge to a public hungry for "the truth" is one key reason for doing teacher research.

But another key reason—the simplest but also the most profound—is to affirm our own self-confidence and keep us learning about what we love to do. Sharing our findings enables us to trust our teaching practices. Our practices will vary. We may hold on to a routine like reading aloud for a half hour every day. We may link a state standards-mandated skill to a creative poetry unit. Perhaps we will implement response journals in our literature classes. Whatever our goal, we need to interpret what works—and why it works—for a larger public. Teacher research invites voice, freedom, and

> ☼ *When we let ourselves pay formal attention to students and learning . . . we grow as teachers.*

autonomy without relinquishing guidelines or mandates. When we let ourselves pay formal attention to students and learning, use the tools of systematic research, trust our pedagogical intuitions, and remain politically brave, we grow as teachers and provide meaningful education for our students. To us, systematic inquiry is the essence of professional development, reflective practice, and imagination.

Prepwork
An Overview of the Research Process

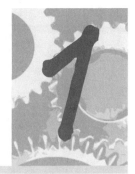

A teacher-researcher is an observer
   a questioner
      a learner
         and a more complete teacher.

       —GLORIA BISSEX AND RICHARD BULLOCK,
Seeing for Ourselves

*W*hether you are part of a formal group of teacher-researchers, a student in a university course, or a teacher undertaking a project for yourself, this book is a suitable guide. You may dip in and out of the chapters and exercises at will or follow the order in which we present these methods and designs.

But first, let's preview *What Works?* using the story of teacher-inquirer Holly Richardson to bring to life the strategies and theories you might use to undertake your own project. Your questions and research will differ from Holly's, but the process of close investigation, observation, and interpretation will follow a similar pattern.

This first chapter includes some "prepwork"—focused, guided quick writes that will help you tap into your own knowledge, interests, goals, and ideas. Each prepwork exercise corresponds with the topics and skills you'll find later in Chapters 2 through 10 (along with more detailed exercises we call "mindwork"). Doing these short exercises will help you prepare for a longer research project of your own. We and our student-colleagues find them helpful and, as we like to say, "on task." Try them. We think you'll find our prepwork and mindwork more formal versions of the intuitive thinking teachers and students engage in regularly.

Reading about research can seem more daunting than doing it. (We assure you that writing about research seems daunting as well!) Our years of working with teacher-inquirers have proved to us that all purposeful teachers have the built-in classroom data, the intellectual oomph, and the professional energy to conduct a project while teaching at the same time. As Bissex and Bullock write in the epigraph to this chapter, classroom inquiry makes us more "complete" as teachers and, of course, as learners.

To see the process of inquiry in action, let's look over the shoulder of Holly Richardson, a veteran high school English teacher, as she completes a research project while teaching in Alaska. Holly was a member of a teacher-research group we led while this book was taking shape, and she used our guidelines to initiate a community oral history project for Aniak High School. Holly's story begins with the questions every teacher faces at the outset of a project:

- How do I initiate ideas?

- How do I shift the chaos of my everyday teaching into organized thinking?

- What kind of writing will help me identify a research topic?

Research questions usually emerge from your everyday teaching life. Maybe you've told a story in the teacher's room and can't get it out of your head. The anecdote haunts you. The more often you tell the story, the more you know about it and see how it implies bigger issues. You begin to sketch out some questions and think about what you'd need to know to answer them. You're on your way to shaping a possible study.

> ☼ *Research questions usually emerge from your everyday teaching life.*

Holly is about to begin her third year teaching in Alaska and is bothered by the tension between her students' low scores and their rich oral storytelling abilities. She knows that some of her students' stories, handed down from their elders, are an important part of the heritage that shapes their learning processes. The school district is placing an emphasis on literacy because 50 percent of the students' reading and writing scores are below the national average. Holly begins to shape her ideas in writing during the summer:

> ☼ *Holly is bothered by the tension between her students' low scores and their rich oral storytelling abilities.*

I think the upcoming school year is the perfect time for my students to use their written accounts of oral history and myth to generate a school-wide interest in reading and writing. Louise Rosenblatt writes about the importance of students "living through" a piece of writing in order to develop a connection to the text, the world, and the individual. With this idea in mind, I'd like to focus on the importance of Yup'ik story and mythology to the overall literacy of students at Aniak High School.

Holly couples her informal thoughts about her students' strengths with her school's literacy goals as she begins to prepare for formal research. In doing so, she calls upon her knowledge of Louise Rosenblatt's reader response theory to support her teaching plans. She links theory to practice by recording her thinking on the page.

◈ *Prepwork:* Write about what bothers you.

What tensions do you see in your classroom?

◈ Between your students in school and their lives outside of school?

◈ Between yourself and your administration?

◈ Between your educational background and the curriculum?

Or: What do you want to do in your classroom that you're not now doing?

◈ What's preventing you?

◈ What support would you need to be able to carry out a new strategy, curriculum, or project?

◈ How could you help your students connect more with their own community—its strengths and its heritage?

◈ How could you help your students see connections between their community and its history or between their local community and a broader regional or global community?

Try writing about one or two (or all) of these ideas. It's not important now to elaborate on or "solve" your problems and desires; simply articulate them to yourself.

About Chapter 2: Scratchwork: Shaping a Question

☀ Can I ask some questions that will lead to a more focused research question?

- ☀ How can my trial questions sort themselves into a main question and related subquestions?

- ☀ What are the key terms I use in this question, and how do I understand the language of my question enough to make it clear to others?

- ☀ Can I describe my position in relationship to this question?

- ☀ What are the practical and ethical consequences of answering this question? How do I plan the research? get permission?

"Scratchwork" refers to the way a teacher follows a hunch or, as we've come to describe it, "scratch an itch" about a pedagogical problem or question. Chapter 2 shows you how to move from a broad general topic of inquiry toward manageable, focused research questions and subquestions that will scaffold your study.

Holly's preparatory writing—her observations and early notes—and her decision to focus on a small number of students (four) lead her to these questions:

- ☀ In what ways does telling their cultural stories connect four native Alaskan high school students to literacy?

- ☀ How can these students capture the essence of the oral story in written words to be shared with the larger world?

- ☀ How do students react to reading and writing when their own stories are a primary learning tool?

- ☀ Does the use of cultural stories, beliefs, and practices generate student interest in reading and writing?

Like making a working outline, these focusing questions provide a framework for your research design (even though as you build your research project, your focus might change). Holly writes:

Since my research questions focused on the cultural stories that connect four native Alaskan high school students with their community and to the way literacy works in their lives, I knew that a successful study had to be taken outside the classroom walls. The participants tested below the state average on exams, and their comfort levels rose once they left the school building. Instead of listening to their stories in a sterile educational setting, we had dinner meetings. Each week I'd make dinner for the kids, and with food, good company, and a comfortable setting, the stories flowed. As I learned more about the oral history of the community and the ways my students use their stories to interpret the world around them, my research questions became more defined and new questions arose.

The questions Holly begins with may or may not be the same questions her final study will answer. During the course of her research, as her knowledge accumulates, she refines the project as well as its final outcome. The *This Is My Story* anthology and the response of Aniak's community are not things she can predict at the outset. What she knows all along, though, is her hunch that stories are ways of knowing—even though as forms of literacy they aren't conventionally measurable.

◈ *Prepwork for Scratchwork: Make a list of research questions that interest you. When you cluster them, what themes or topics appear?*

What ideas do you have about:

◈ Student learning?

◈ Curriculum?

◈ Teaching strategies?

◈ Evaluation or grading or reflection?

◈ Subject matter?

◈ The culture at large or the culture of the school?

Share these ideas with an interested colleague or friend. Does he or she have questions about the language you use in your questions—or how you'll answer them? Have your partner make notes on what words need sharpening or defining. Together, try to locate key terms or single words within your question that may have unclear or multiple meanings. Rewrite the main question. Think about how subquestions might fit in and what process you might use to answer them.

☀ How do I inventory the knowledge I've gained from experience and from my professional development?

☀ What sources of information can I tap about my topic?

☀ How do I use bibliographic material creatively so that I can discover who the experts are on this topic?

☀ What constitutes a reliable source about this topic—and how do I know it?

"Bridgework" means locating the already available materials connected with your topic in an attempt to span the gap between your own knowledge and that of others. As teachers, we well understand that any study involves inventorying our prior knowledge, as well as that of others, to build a bridge to new inquiry. While we may discover something new for our own students in our classrooms, our goal is not to discover new intellectual territory but to confirm what works within our own setting. To do this, we must be familiar and conversant with the work of others.

> ☼ Any study involves inventorying our prior knowledge, as well as that of others, to build a bridge to new inquiry.

As Holly thinks in retrospect about the notion of "myth" with which she began her work, she writes about how her students helped her to reconceive her own prior knowledge:

As a beginning researcher, one of the most important lessons I learned was in regard to my use of the word "myth." I originally set out to collect the "mythology" of a culture and ended up, instead, collecting their beliefs. The difference was quickly pointed out to me by one of my student storytellers, who graciously informed me that "these aren't myths; these stories are what we believe really happened." From that point on, I became conscious of my word choice, of the vernacular of the culture.

Holly had researched much about Alaska before going to teach there. Her early reading had introduced her to other teacher-researchers who had taught in settings that were culturally different from their own, as well as books about storytelling and about Alaska.

Before I started collecting my own research, I wanted to learn about what others had already done and how they began collecting stories from an area. Shirley Brice Heath's anthropological look at Appalachia in *Ways with Words* was immensely helpful to me. So was Richard Meyer's book *Stories from the Heart: Teachers and Students Researching Their Literacy Lives*. In addition to reading research, I read collections of stories. The *Foxfire* books not only entertained me, they kept me ever mindful of maintaining a speaker's authentic voice. I also read books of poetry, novels, reference texts, anthologies of short stories—anything that would help me keep my mind on the land and the people of Alaska while I was working on this project.

◈ **Prepwork for Bridgework:** Write about what you already know about your topic, and brainstorm what you might want to find out.

◈ Where would you go to answer your questions?

◈ Who among your colleagues and friends might know about this topic?

◈ Aside from books or websites, what would you consider to be potential sources to learn more about your questions (video or radio documentaries, newspapers, magazines, brochures, archives, historical accounts, informed people)?

About Chapter 4: Headwork: Assuming Self and Other

☀ How do I understand my own assumptions when I "assume" them and don't consciously know what they are?

☀ How can I adapt an outsider's stance in a culture (school) in which I participate?

☀ How can I uncover how certain personal features like age, race, gender, ethnicity, and regional and local alliances affect my ways of seeing?

"Headwork" refers to the difficult but important task of climbing into the heads of the "others" we study. As teachers, we're used to that. We're constantly trying to envision how our students see us and to assume the perspectives of our students. Chapter 4 introduces the ideas of understanding and articulating your assumptions as part of your research. It discusses how to position yourself in relationship to others and offers three key questions for monitoring your positions and assumptions—and those of the others—as they shift during your study.

Holly assumes, going into her study, that if her students can write about their own oral culture, it will enhance their literacy and perhaps their writing and reading scores, too. Though she is an insider to the culture of a high school, Holly is an outsider to the culture of Aniak. One challenge she faces is to represent her own double perspective (as insider and outsider) as well as the many perspectives of the community members she is studying: her students, their parents, the elders, and the oral storytelling tradition they all hold. In order to represent such multiple vantage points, Holly needs to reveal her position in relationship to the culture, and to do that, she writes about it:

> In August of 1998, I was hired as the only English teacher in Aniak High School. Aniak is a small island town (population 600–650) on the Kuskokwim River, approximately 300 miles west of the city of Anchorage, known to all out here simply as "town." The student population at AHS varies between 45 and 55, and the teens are fondly nicknamed "the Halfbreeds." While this nickname is considered to be politically inappropriate by many, to the people of this community it represents who they are. Indeed, the majority of my students are of mixed blood— Yup'ik Eskimo and European American.
>
> The racial mix is important to my study, as represented by the high school's "Halfbreed" mascot. On the gymnasium wall is a painting of two men. A white man is holding a gun in his hand and a Yup'ik Eskimo is holding a fishing pole. The two men are shaking hands and smiling. Hence, Aniak symbolizes what can at times be a volatile clash of cultures.

Notice that Holly uses the painting on the gymnasium wall and the school's mascot "the Halfbreed" to illustrate how the culture represents itself to itself. Rather than simply stating the tension between the two populations and her opinion of it, she's using details from her field notes to write about the place she's studying. The above paragraphs illustrate her demographic research about Aniak, her careful notes documenting the school's physical features, as well as her years spent teaching in the school. (Field notes and demographic research are discussed in Chapters 5 and 8.)

◈ **Prepwork for Headwork:** Think about yourself as a researcher.

◈ Who are you to be doing this research?

◈ Where did your own ideas/strategies come from?

Map your heritage as a learner, and contrast it with that of your students. Consider your community background and contrast it with that of your students, too. Choose an artifact that represents the school you're teaching in—or the town. Describe it as a symbolic representation of something you know or see about the school's culture. How might this symbol either constrain or enable the students and their learning?

About Chapter 5: Legwork: Pursuing Multiple Sources of Data

☀ Where and when should I begin collecting data? What kinds of data can I collect?

☀ How do I know when I have enough of any one kind of data? How does one kind support another kind?

☀ What data are important, and how do I determine that?

☀ How do I organize data—what do I do with all that stuff so that it will be useful for my project?

Almost everything in our classrooms can be data: bulletin boards, notes in the wastebasket, graffiti on the desks, our plan books, the students' notebooks, even the arrangement of the room. But all data are not equal; using data sources depends on the questions you are asking. Collecting data both in and out of the classroom—in the local and educational communities at large—involves considerable legwork.

Data flood our daily lives, always; we work with data all the time. But until

> ⚙ *All data are not equal; using data sources depends on the questions you are asking.*

we consciously organize, systematize, and analyze information around some purpose, it remains without context. Chapter 5 shows how to locate useful data from both print and nonprint sources: student work, student histories, formal and informal interviews, archival records, public print and library resources, and material artifacts.

In Holly's case, she knows that her students' test scores are way below the national norm, and she may have continued to collect data on this fact alone: newspaper accounts, administrators' documents, parents' conversation, state reports, and students' opinions. But she also knows that with an expanded, broader definition of "literacy" that includes storytelling genres, she can show her students and the school that the test itself is unable to tap into the students' literacy strengths. For instance, when Holly prompts her students to write about storytelling's influence in their lives, one of her students, Julia Pletnikoff, writes fluently about her passion for storytelling, and it eventually becomes the epigram for the community anthology:

> Have you ever heard a story that you didn't believe in because it sounded so unreal, so fictional, or so supernatural? But then . . . you step outside into the crystal clear cold air when the night couldn't be any darker and all the stories you've heard come to life. Every story has truth, and the legends have knowledge. Every time you hear a story that is so hard to believe, just find a way to relate to the story or the story will find a way to relate to you.

Holly's data and her project may not change her students' scores on their literacy tests, but Julia's extended response shows Holly that the project will help answer her question about the gap she discerns between the curriculum's demands and her students' special competencies.

❖ **Prepwork for Legwork:** List for yourself the data sources you already have that could support your question.

❖ What would count as evidence?

❖ How do you as a teacher create data sources (journal, plan book, notes to parents, etc.)?

Continued on next page

Continued from previous page

◈ What among your students' records, materials, and class work constitute appropriate data?

◈ Which people might you interview?

◈ Which public or private archives might you consult?

◈ To what professional experts might you turn—authors, inservice facilitators, documentarians or filmmakers, website voices?

◈ What material artifacts might contibute more texture and information to your data?

About Chapter 6: Eyework: Methods and Methodologies

☀ What choices do I have in terms of research methods?

☀ What's the difference between "method" and "methodology"?

☀ How do I answer questions about validity and reliability when I'm only one teacher in one school?

☀ How does one case study tell me something about a whole class?

☀ Will my research study be coherent if I apply more than one research method?

"Eyework" is about looking through and surveying methodologies to identify and understand possible methods you might use to conduct your research. Teacher research is pragmatic, a hybrid methodology that uses whatever methods it needs to answer a question. You need to know what's available before you can choose. And then you need to understand the most appropriate methods in order to see what works.

Holly knows she is going to gather stories—those of Aniak's townspeople and those of her students. She calls upon linguistic or text-based analysis because most of her information will come from people's words in interviews and tape recordings. She employs quantitative methods when she considers the town's demographics, the test scores in relation to standard definitions of literacy, and how much time her students spend telling stories rather than reading. She knows she will be looking at her students in context—as they gather the stories told in their town and analyze them in her classroom. So she will be using ethnographic methods along with the linguistic and quantitative ones. When she gathers all her data, she decides to present her material as case studies. Holly uses cultural critique, too, when she documents the tension between two distinct groups of townspeople and also how alcohol influences the community.

Overall, then, Holly creates a hybrid methodology to analyze and interpret the storytelling traditions of Aniak High School in their own context. In turn, the project offers her and her students an opportunity to give back to their community. Together, they publish an anthology, a booklet of community stories, legends, myths, recipes, and advice, and they present it as a gift to the townspeople. Holly reminisces:

> The process itself was rewarding for all of the participants. The village elders enjoyed working and sharing stories with the high school students. Many times, my students had heard the story told by the elder, but some of the details were changed. This led to discussions about how and why our stories change. The finished product, a book called *This Is My Story*, represents the handiwork of the entire community. Parents wrote down stories for our book, a computer class helped with the formatting, and I was able to secure a grant offered through the local health clinic that funded the bookbinding and copying.

◈ **Prepwork for Eyework:** *Think about your process for solving problems in your daily life. What methods—and combinations of methods—do you use?*

The following exercise reveals differences between long-term and short-term problems and what both kinds of problems suggest with regard to our research processes. It mirrors the pragmatic decision-making process we use in busy, chaotic, complicated contexts like classrooms.

◈ Think of a short-term problem you solved in the last day (how to remove snow when you have no shovel, how to find a parking spot close to where you want to be, how to behave at a department meeting in which you've brought the wrong materials). Write about your thinking and actions as you solved this problem. Make lists, diagrams, or drawings in addition to prose. Analyze the methods you used, not worrying about technical language. Did you solve this

Continued on next page

Continued from previous page

problem with more than one strategy? How would you describe your process?

❖ Think of a long-term problem you've had to solve over the last year (buying a car, handling child-care arrangements, caring for a sick relative, implementing a new grading system). Write about the processes you used—and the steps you took—to solve the problem. How long did you spend on each process? What did the overall problem-solving "map" look like for you? for the others involved in the problem? What hybrids of methods did you call upon to solve it?

❖ Compare your approaches to solving long-term and short-term pragmatic problems. Where and how do they differ? Why was it important to use more than one method as you solved your problems? What implications do you see for school-based research projects?

About Chapter 7: Homework: Preparing the Working Proposal

☀ What is a proposal and for whom am I writing it?

☀ What permissions—and whose permission—do I need in order to conduct this study?

☀ How can I design a realistic time line that fits into my busy school and home schedule?

☀ Will my project cost any money to carry out, and how can I solicit sources of support?

Just as you write lesson and unit plans that cover varied blocks of time, you'll need a detailed outline, a plan for fitting your study into your teaching life. We call this "homework" because you need to design a plan that fits into your professional and personal commitments. This plan culminates in a working proposal that includes a time line, a

> ☼ *Just as you write lesson and unit plans that cover varied blocks of time, you'll need a detailed outline, a plan for fitting your study into your teaching life.*

list of data sources, a budget, contact people, time for drafting and revising, and ideas for ways to share your project.

Holly's five-page proposal, drafted as she begins her year of research and writing, starts with a brief background description of herself in relationship to her community and a rationale for what she plans to study. She lists her research questions, her data sources, and the methods she plans to use to analyze her data and provides a monthly time line that includes planned interviews, writing assignments, meetings with her four focal students, and published work to share with the community. She ends the proposal with a paragraph about possible findings. Here is Holly's plan for November:

Continue collecting stories and editing stories
Send tape of student reading to radio station
Have lunch meeting with participants
Prepare a reflective writing assignment for all student participants
Write in my journal

◈ **Prepwork for Homework:** It's sometimes easier to begin a project by working backward. Think about the outcome. What do you want to accomplish?

◈ A completed website?

◈ A curriculum guide?

◈ An article for a your favorite professional journal?

◈ An exhibit of student work?

◈ A community heritage or civic engagement project, like a fair or an exposition?

◈ A professional development product or workshop for colleagues and administrators?

◈ A portion of a professional portfolio designed specifically for a national or regional board certification?

Take a calendar and fill in the busiest times of your year so you don't create unrealistic deadlines. On this calendar, sketch out possible times for observing, interviewing, gathering materials, reading, writing, analyzing, and revising. Adjust your calendar so that it meets your needs, and decide whether you want your deadlines to correspond to months, semesters, report periods, or other frames.

☀ How can I discipline myself to keep a journal of everything I do in my project?

☀ How will I plan to take field notes while I'm teaching?

☀ When will I make time each day to write up my field notes?

☀ I'm good at talking to people; how is an interview different from that?

☀ I know that how students use space in my room is important. How do I find a way to "map" it and use it as data?

☀ Even if I do have time to collect all this data, when will I have time to reflect, interpret, analyze, write, and revise?

Obviously, carrying out a project is different from planning it. Teachers know better than anyone that a lesson plan we expected to take a day may stretch into a week. The lonely footwork that follows good planning is the greatest challenge of doing a research project, but it is also the most exciting part because it is your own. You have put yourself in charge of carrying out—and adjusting— one focused piece of inquiry. Footwork is a long and arduous but rewarding hike. As we trek, we closely observe our classrooms and ourselves, listen to language and interpret it, note elements of our familiar classroom environments (sometimes for the first time), and see our own questions from the perspectives of others, which enhances and shifts our own perspective.

> ⚙ The lonely footwork that follows good planning is the greatest challenge of doing a research project, but it is also the most exciting part because it is your own.

Holly keeps a daily journal during the year she conducts her research. In it, she reflects on what she is learning about myths, legends, and folklore as she teaches some of it, notes important ideas about teaching from the reading she is doing (she reads widely), and keeps a conversation going with herself. Here's an excerpt in which Holly plays with a suspicion about gender roles in storytelling:

There's a common thread that seems to be woven throughout the tapestry of stories being told. Females are portrayed in a passive, stealthy, or manipulative role. The antagonists are usually female. Also, when listing characters, the females are last. I wonder how this really impacts my students' lives? I wonder how many other cultures are similar?

Had Holly not kept this daily journal, she would have no way of following her interest in gender and storytelling. Whether she uses this excerpt or not, her journal provides her with important data as her personal knowledge continues to develop during the course of her project.

⬦ **Prepwork for Footwork**: *Imagine yourself during the course of your project by thinking about what you might need to circumnavigate (events, conditions, people, policies). What can you do to help yourself prepare?*

Make a double list:

1. On one side of a paper, inventory your strengths. Who are your biggest fans, with whom you can share your work? What contacts might you use for interviews or resources? What research or writing skills do you bring to this project? What would be your dream result? What kind of changes might your work institute?

2. On the other side of the paper, list some of the drawbacks or insecurities you have as you enter this project. What institutional constraints do you face? What personal obligations might interfere? Which research skills have you never fully developed? What resources would you like to gather but have no idea how to get? What is the most disastrous result you can imagine as an outcome of your project?

As you read through the two lists, try to make a realistic assessment of your strengths and weaknesses as a teacher-inquirer. During the course of your work, you'll be able to return to this list and reassess your growth and the project's progress.

About Chapter 9: Deskwork: Interpretation and Analysis

☀ How do I sort through my mass of data?

☀ What is triangulation? Why and how do I do it?

☀ What do I do when I get stuck or blocked?

☀ Where do I put data that don't fit?

☀ How do I analyze emerging themes?

☀ What is a "finding"? How do I find it?

"Deskwork" is just that, spreading out your data on a table or desk (or even a floor or bed) and looking for themes and patterns that offer possible interpretations. Looking for data that relate to your question means grieving for the material you can't use and finding multiple ways to confirm what seems to fit.

Holly creates three end products for her study: one is an essay describing the literacy of the four case-study students, another is a conference presentation to her colleagues, and the third is the anthology *This Is My Story*, written by the Aniak High School students and published for and distributed to the entire community. By studying the interviews with her four key students and linking their insights and stories with her journal notes and other sources, she's able to determine how gathering stories from townspeople affected the reading and writing skills of her students. Holly also finds subthemes about their lives and their families' lives that leak into her study. Her challenge of interpretation and analysis is to sort out the information about literacy from the cultural information that interests her but is not directly relevant.

◈ **Prepwork for Deskwork: Inventory your potential as a working researcher.**

◈ What kinds of organizational habits do you have as a teacher? Do you use a lot of sticky notes? three-ring binders and hole-punched paper? index cards? plastic ware?

◈ What kinds of adjustments might you need to make in your classroom in order to accommodate a study? Do you need to clean out a cabinet? buy or borrow a tape recorder? a camera? a plastic hanging file folder?

◈ How do you usually visualize a complicated array of tasks? Do you make a flow chart? a map? an outline?

◈ Where in your day will you find time to review your data? How and when can you carve out an hour per day or week to review what you've collected and decide how it fits with what you already have?

Make a list of things you'll need to do in order to organize yourself before you start: things to buy or borrow, spaces to clean, time to

Continued on next page

Continued from previous page

manage. Check yourself against this list as your project progresses. Good organization is often the key to good teaching—and you'll find that it's the key to good research, too.

About Chapter 10: Handwork: The Craft of Dissemination

- ☀ What do I already know about writing?

- ☀ How might I write for the audience and in the genre I've chosen?

- ☀ What does research say about the nature of writing about research?

- ☀ In what ways is research writing different from other writing I've done?

- ☀ How can I apply what I know about teaching writing to my own project?

- ☀ What kinds of questions about writing do teacher-researchers face?

Obviously, "handwork" refers to writing, the connection between the mind and the hand. Chapter 10 discusses the common issues researchers face as they begin to turn data into text, as they face the blank page or screen. Our rich heritage of research on writing helps us understand where our own writing strategies fit in and how to handle the challenges of writing about research.

> ☼ *Good organization is the key to good teaching—and to good research.*

Holly has to think about writing for at least three different audiences and purposes. Her plan from the beginning has been to create an anthology of her students' stories for their community. She also wants to write a reflective essay about her research for other teachers, as well as prepare a twenty-minute presentation for the annual convention of the National Council of Teachers of English.

She comes to her project having studied about oral and written storytelling techniques and about how authors capture oral language in written texts. In her coursework, she has read books about the teaching of writing and, of course, she has been teaching writing herself for several years. With this background, Holly understands her students' own writing struggles and is able to help them shape the stories for their anthology—teaching them to slow down, understand their audience, learn to use the library, get help from one another, and collect information from their families.

Mainly, she has learned to teach her students about the power of revision: "Once students slowed down to think about their writing, they produced better writing. Once better writing was produced, the students felt proud and wanted to create even better writing." Since Holly's research project is about writing, she sees that some of her own struggles mirror the struggles of her students: to be clear, to revise for a particular kind of audience and purpose, and to retain the soul of the people she is trying to represent.

◈ *Prepwork for Homework*: Try some prompted brainstorming, the writing teacher's traditional method for getting ideas on paper.

◈ What do you already know about your own writing process?

◈ What kinds of audiences have you written for? In what genres have you written?

◈ What questions do you have about writing research?

◈ How would you like to disseminate your research?

As you start the writing phase of your project, return to each of the "prepwork" exercises from this first chapter. If you've completed them, you already have a systematic record of your early thinking and some of your initial questions about the research process. Revisit them when you try the "mindwork" exercises in the chapters that follow. These quick writes are valuable, and you may even be able to integrate what you've written into your final study, no matter what form it ends up taking. Readers are always interested in the journey as well as the outcome.

The last words in Holly's essay reveal traces of the anxieties that remain (ones she had when she began her study) as well as the deep insights she has gained from her time in Alaska and the project she and her students have undertaken together: "I left Aniak with a heavy heart and a mind that worries about the future of my students. It is my wish that they continue to explore their fascinating world through the use of their own stories and that they allow their words to illuminate the darkest nights and give warmth to their souls on the longest summer days."

Scratchwork
Shaping a Question

[W]e don't enter a setting deciding ahead of time what events will mean, but we allow the meaning to emerge from our observations and repeated reflections. We may enter with certain guiding questions, but don't impose our answers. We allow them to emerge from the process of looking.

—SONDRA PERL, "Reflections on Ethnography and Writing"

As teachers, we're not afraid of questions. We are active inquirers, constantly challenging our curriculum, our school culture, our colleagues, and our students. We use questions to frame our lessons, evaluate our students' learning, and assess the worth of our own teaching. Posing a research question is nothing new. It often begins as a small, nagging idea, an intuition that needs following or a hunch that begs further attention. Shaping a research question is like scratching an itch that bothers us. As Sondra Perl says in the epigraph above, we don't impose our answers on a project (or in a classroom, for that matter), but rather we allow them to emerge as we look.

We might ask questions like these:

☀ Could I get students to collaborate better if I rearranged my room?

☀ Has this team of student-athletes developed a secret language?

☀ Can I internationalize my curriculum to include global perspectives?

☀ Do girls and boys experience adventure stories in the same ways?

- What if I introduced double-entry notebooks to my math classes?

- What kind of talk goes on in student-led book clubs?

Following our intuitions is the beginning of shaping a *guiding* research question. As we learn more about our topic, we will shape and reshape and revise our question many times.

Much of what we refer to as "science-based research" in our culture involves testing hypotheses, confirming probabilities, or quantifying outcomes for large numbers of people—in medicine, consumer reports, political polling, and, of course, schools. We do rely on quantitative methods in our schools (grading and assessing, demographic information, tracking, scheduling, etc.).

> ✿ *We will shape and reshape and revise our question many times.*

But that's not the full research story. The teaching and learning that happens in our classrooms is often more qualitative than quantitative. We interact within cultural settings, more like parenting, coaching, or mentoring. To study these complicated school contexts, we can borrow qualitative research methods from the social sciences. When we study people inside their own culture, we don't try to generalize from a large population. We don't look for what's replicable, reliable, or statistically valid. Rather, we look for what's singular, particular, and unique. As researchers, we want to include as much of our situation as we can, rather than strip the context or "control" it somehow. In qualitative teacher inquiry, our goal is to capture particularity, to create a richly detailed, sharply focused snapshot of the students in our classes and their work, of ourselves and our teaching. Shaping, reshaping, and revising the question as the research accumulates is the natural thing to do.

Others can learn from our classroom studies, just as we learn about teaching from characters and themes in literature, movies, and TV. We all are familiar with (and have opinions about) stories that involve teachers, and our friends and relatives love to ask what we think of teacher-characters like Mr. Holland, Mr. Kotter, Miss Jean Brodie, even Mr. Peepers. We think of ourselves and our colleagues when we encounter characters like Ichabod Crane in *The Legend of Sleepy Hollow* or Miss Grundy in the *Archie* comics or when we see Miss Reilly in *October Sky*. Popular images of schools and teachers clutter our bookshelves and TV and movie screens. Careful teacher inquiry based on detailed research and well-crafted questions from professional insiders adds important voices to our culture's ideas about schooling.

Gaining an Insider-Outsider Perspective

At times, it's the outsiders, the nonteachers, who help us see the tangles and complexities of our profession in new ways. A neighbor who sees us lug piles of student papers home every day may ask, "Do your students *really read* those comments you spend all that time writing?" This obser-

> ⚙ *At times, it's the outsiders, the nonteachers, who help us see the tangles and complexities of our profession in new ways.*

vation strikes a chord: "Is there a more efficient method for responding to student writing?" we wonder. Eventually it may lead to a research question: how can teacher comments be made most helpful for student writers? Our sympa-

thetic neighbor's question, triggered by obvious everyday rituals that have become invisible to us, has pushed us toward sharper inquiry than we would have undertaken on our own. Similarly, in the teacher's room, at staff meetings, during parties and Friday after-school gatherings, our colleagues, too, can help us consider other points of view and offer a collegial "insider-outsider" perspective. It's always easier when there's an actual person seeing what we cannot, but as researchers, we can train ourselves to take the position of an outsider.

On the other hand an insider perspective is equally valuable. We will not waste our time on an obvious or popular question to which we already know the answer. For example, well-seasoned language arts teachers have long rejected the eternal phonics/whole language debate. They see it as useless, because they know that most students need both approaches to succeed and that phonics instruction alone will not get anyone "hooked"

> ⚙ *We will not waste our time on an obvious or popular question to which we already know the answer.*

on lifetime reading habits. When we're inside the classroom every day, we want to find timely pragmatic answers that lead to real actions: How much time do I spend preparing my kids for state testing? In what ways could I share

these terrific student projects with the local community and with their parents? If this student's going to be a business major, how are my writing assignments preparing her? It's critical to couple the insider and outsider perspectives as we design our teacher-research questions.

Generating Trial Questions

Let's return to the neighbor's question: "Do your students *really read* those comments you spend all that time writing?" Perhaps our first response is defensive: "Geez, *of course* they read my comments. Why else would I write them?" But then we remember seeing our students' backs as they toss their papers into the wastebasket on the way out of the classroom, savoring not one bite of our insightful commentaries or astute marginalia. We immediately replace this unpleasant image with that of the earnest student who returned after college to report that one comment we don't even remember kept him going throughout his years as an English major. Nevertheless the nagging question remains: how can teacher comments be made most helpful for student writers? We know there is a large cache of useful formal research on this topic, but none of it will tell us about our own ways of responding with our own students and assignments. What kinds of informal trial questions might we generate around the idea of teacher response? How do we begin to scratch our itch?

Like carving wood, practicing the piano, running daily laps, or testing a recipe, each pass through the material gets us closer to our destination. Generating trial questions, even though it may seem counterintuitive, broadens our scope and allows us to explore our chosen territory before we narrow the topic. Here are a few questions we might ask ourselves if we were exploring the many dimensions of teacher response to student writing:

- ☀ In what ways do my assignments determine the extent to which students pay attention to my comments?

- ☀ Do my students read email comments more often than paper comments?

- ☀ What if I write my comments on a separate piece of paper?

- ☀ Are my comments to my students about their writing primarily positive or negative?

- ☀ To what extent do my students really understand my comments the way I mean them?

- ☀ Are there gender-related differences in my students' responses to my comments? What are they?

- ☀ Do students revise more when I respond to earlier drafts rather than to later ones?

- ☀ Is asking students to respond to my comments in writing useful? How?

☀ What happens when students receive peer response as well as teacher response?

☀ What if I find a way to hold conferences instead of writing comments on student papers?

To make the hypothetical real, let's examine the story of teacher-researcher Gail Russell, who also wants to study her students' writing. In three separate snapshots, we'll watch Gail as she does her essential "scratchwork," shaping, refining, and using research questions for her study.

SNAPSHOT I: Gail Russell Shapes a Question

Gail teaches ninth-grade "standard track" (a new term for what her school once called "low-achiever") English/language arts in a public North Carolina high school. For the second year in a row, her county's schools have failed to meet the annual yearly progress required by the *No Child Left Behind* legislation. Gail feels she didn't need outsiders to tell her this. In her research journal she writes, "But I don't need the outside admonishment of *No Child Left Behind* to tell me that many of my students are failing. I see it in their writing, behavior, and overall school disposition." Gail wants to shape a research question that focuses on the students who resist her curriculum and have trouble in her classes. She doesn't believe in "dumbing down" the content of her courses; she teaches the same curriculum in her standard track as she did in her previous honors sections.

Gail is also getting her master's in education and is enrolled in a course in which she must design a classroom research study. Having recently taken a postcolonial theory course, she decides to write about her most marginalized and disenfranchised students, who are mostly African American males. At the same time, she is almost angry at them for not trying to succeed. She writes:

> I find it difficult to value someone who doesn't take his work seriously, no matter the line of excuses I make for him. It is also difficult for me not to define myself by the work I do. I care about the kids. I have a strong work ethic. And I love teaching and learning for their own sake. Those things are fruitful, but what meaning ripens as I place them within the context of a belabored postmodern setting? My goal has been to learn how to negotiate the paradox of efficiency: resisting the "machine" while nurturing students.

Gail's first pass at her research question is: how can I apply postcolonial theory to my writing curriculum to help empower these African American males to write self-consciously?

Gail's colleagues in her university course ask her to define her terms so that they (and others) will understand her question better. What does she mean by "apply postcolonial theory"? What is her current "writing curriculum"? What does "empower" mean and how do students "write self-consciously"? Is she talking about African American male students everywhere or just the population in her class?

It's helpful to begin the task of understanding your questions by defining the key terms. When someone asks you to articulate key words and phrases you use, don't be discouraged. Over time, as one of our mentors liked to say, your question should feel like a favorite pair of old shoes. You wear them again and again because they fit, they feel right no matter how stretched out they are, and they've taken you many miles (their soles replaced as necessary). They're *your* shoes, and you treasure them.

> ⚙ *It's helpful to begin the task of understanding your questions by defining the key terms.*

◈ Mindwork: Explore Trial Questions

List some possible trial questions, like the ten we wrote about student response to teacher comments. Look back at the first two prepwork exercises you did in Chapter 1. Ask questions of your questions. Try a little analysis. Do these exploratory questions fit into categories, groups, clusters? Look for common themes. What do you seem most interested in? What resources do you have for answering them? Even at the outset, try to underline a few key terms that you might further define. Always, always ask yourself for which question you have the most passion. What feels right? Which itch needs a good, long scratch?

Try another method of categorization. Make four columns on a piece of paper or on the computer:

◈ Teaching Practices

◈ Student Learning or Outcomes

◈ School Policies or Politics

◈ Curriculum

Continued on next page

Continued from previous page

Arrange your questions under these headings to get a better idea of where your interests lie. Many may blur or overlap, but you may be able to identify which questions lie outside your scope, which might help you or your students, which will best serve your school or department, and, most important, which are your driving passions. Once you discover the heart of your research interests, all other questions will branch out from it.

Narrowing the Question

Many questions, like Gail's original one, are too clumsy to become a working question. Consider your relationship to the question as you narrow it down. Think about your fixed positions (your nationality, race, age, class, gender, geographic location) and subjective influences (your specific life experiences). Consider, too, the ethics of conducting teacher research. (For more detailed ways of thinking about positions and ethics, see Chapter 4.) This kind of thinking should help you identify the project you are in the best position to conduct, the one most comfortable in relation to your students and your colleagues.

The comfort boundary is very real. You may wonder about your students' home lives. For example, a student in your class who is often absent but manages to get her work done tells you her mother wants her to stay home with the younger children several times a week. Your question might be, what happens to one student's academic progress when her home life demands she be absent half the time? It would be ethically unfair to study only her progress at school—yet without the full consent and cooperation of the student and her family, it would be difficult to capture a fair perspective of her home life.

Sometimes personal loyalties interfere with the ability to conduct a study. To prepare a study of your own students' behavior in book clubs, you decide to visit another colleague's class for several months during your daily planning period. He is your mentor and close friend. In the course of your research, you interview the students and the teacher. Students say they hate their book clubs, hate reading their books, and think the teacher is using this curriculum to keep them busy while he does his own paperwork. You interview your friend. He complains that the students aren't independent readers, they can't read like they used to, that this is the worst class he's ever had. If you're a good colleague and friend, this data, which might have enriched your own study, will remain forever in a file. You don't want to write negative things about your colleague and his class; no study is worth the breakdown of a collegial friendship. You can still study book club behavior, but you'll rely on different data, from somewhere else.

We hope these anecdotes won't scare you or steer you away from your passions. But it's important at the outset to think through a question in its many ethical implications and refractions. There are so many questions, so many possible projects.

Gail is keenly aware she is approaching her African American male students from her newly acquired postcolonial perspective: they are part of an oppressed group, what researcher/writer John Ogbu (1974) calls a "subordinate minority." As a white middle-class woman, Gail considers whether she should single out her African American students to study or target all her "low-tracked" students. Her background reading helps her better understand minority students, but it doesn't need to be the only focus. She writes:

> For my purposes, understanding at least in part *why* some of my students flatly chose not to try can help me begin to address their needs and see the value and reward in the work they do accomplish. Surely I need to pay attention to the structure of American education and the popular idea that it addresses and fails to address the needs of all its students. But while reforms come and go, I can concentrate some pedagogical energy into creating an ethos of shared value for all the students in my classroom.

Gail decides to expand her study to include all her "standard" ninth graders.

◈ Mindwork: Position Yourself in Relation to the Question

Here's another exercise for narrowing an early trial question, and considering its ethics. First, ask,

◈ Who am I in relation to this idea? Do some quick private writing as you think about this question.

◈ How does my position (professional background, experiences as a teacher, history with this topic, race, class, gender, age, geographic location, etc.) affect the way I approach and/or understand it?

Continued on next page

Continued from previous page

Second, ask these tougher questions:

◈ What ethical issues might I raise?

◈ Who will be best served by this study?

◈ Who might be affected or hurt by it, and how?

◈ What are my hidden biases and assumptions?

◈ Could I change my question to avert ethical difficulties, or should I face these difficulties directly?

Taking into consideration your answers to these tough questions, rewrite and narrow your topic, your question, and whatever subquestions you sense might fit under the main one. Your narrowed topic reflects your professional interest, political agenda, student needs, and whatever audience you've chosen to address. Although the topic can sound like a title, the question itself is best when you phrase it as a full interrogative sentence. How you shape your question determines what you'll see, how you'll look, and what you'll contribute to others. As you continue to revise and reshape, you're helping yourself make future decisions about data, method, and dissemination.

SNAPSHOT II: Gail Defines Key Terms and Language

Gail's goal is to democratize her classroom, to provide equity for the students who have less power than she does. And she wants to do this without "colonizing them" into her admitted middle-class work ethic and value system. Conversely, she wants her smart low-tracked students to see literacy as a way to gain social access and economic and social mobility. Big goals, for sure. She suspects that many of her students hide their intellectual abilities because it isn't "cool" to be smart. She keeps a journal and asks her students to keep daily learning logs. She wants to locate her research question through thoughtful informal writing—hers and her students'. Gail writes, "I can't change a system that seems to create more problems for African American males than it relieves. But I can locate my own best teaching practices and help these students improve inside an unfriendly public institution. I am concerned with recognizing practical ways I can engage my low-tracked writers, especially those already oriented toward improving academically."

Once Gail decides to invite her entire class of students to become co-researchers, she reworks her question, incorporating a strategy more specific to her writing classroom. She's recently discovered Kathleen Yancey's *Reflection in the Writing Classroom* and is impressed with the simplicity of Yancey's approach: to ask students to write about writing. As she writes about her own journal, she realizes that reflective writing may be valuable for her students. Gail's newly minted question—in what ways does reflective writing encourage students to appropriate their writing?—drops the postcolonial lens as well as her identification with African American students. At this point, although she has explored a lot of territory, Gail returns to some elements of her original question. She discovers it isn't really about postcolonial theory at all. She just wants to be a better writing teacher.

After drafting her new question, the challenge for Gail is to identify the key words in her question that may need further refinement, that may not be clear to others. She needs to define the terms "reflective writing" and "appropriate." Yancey's book helps her define and describe "reflective writing." Gail has drawn the word "appropriate" from her postcolonial vocabulary. Cautious about the term, she offers a dictionary definition: "It is often a way to describe what marginalized people do when they have been robbed or violated: they take back for themselves something previously used against them or taken from them." Eventually, she defines her use of the word as "to take to or for oneself, take possession of": she wants students to *own* their *own* texts by connecting to and taking possession of them through reflective writing. Gail also realizes she has a tendency to romanticize the concept of appropriation. She will need to guard against that. Defining her terms leads her at this point to create subquestions, further refining or defining the overall question as well as hinting at methods and data sources.

Creating Subquestions

It is both the joy and the despair of conducting research that the more you look, the more you see. Researchers like to tell stories about how one simple focused research question opens the floodgate to hundreds of other studies and questions. We worry about all the studies we can't conduct as we design the one we're going to conduct.

As a passionate teacher, you want your hard work to matter to your students, to their communities, and to your colleagues. But you know, too, that less is more, that a more focused study will yield more focused results, and that you can learn a lot from studying one small sample in intricate detail.

> ⚙ *It's important to create subquestions early— the auxiliary statements that will guide you.*

So it's important to create subquestions early— the auxiliary statements that will guide you.

From Gail's larger research question—in what ways does reflective writing help students appropriate their writing?—the following subquestions emerge:

1. Do the ways students talk and write about writing ("reflect") suggest they know their own texts?

2. Are students finding what is good about their writing?

3. Are students able to critique their writing?

4. Are students reflecting with greater depth (do they have more to say) over time?

5. Do the ways students approach writing tasks change as a result of reflection?

6. In what ways does reflection work to discourage students from appropriating their writing?

7. In what cases are students unable to find something good about their work? In what cases are students unable to critique their work? In what cases are students unable to reflect with great depth over time?

8. In what ways are my teacher observations and reflections helping me develop as a teacher? Do the ways I reflect on my teaching suggest that I am able to understand students' growth as reflective writers?

9. Do the ways I am teaching writing and reflective writing change over time?

10. Do my own reflections show an ability to critique my teaching?

These questions become a template for Gail's research study, drive her on.

Like Gail's, your question and subquestions will guide you as you choose your methods, confirm your methodologies, locate and collect your data. Your research question may shift as you learn. You may redraft the version you put on your wall. Sometimes it seems counterintuitive to widen your lens in order to narrow it, shift your focus from your students to you and back again, use theory for the "why" of your practice, or crank out subquestions from a main question to reveal blind spots in your thinking. But that's why we ask questions.

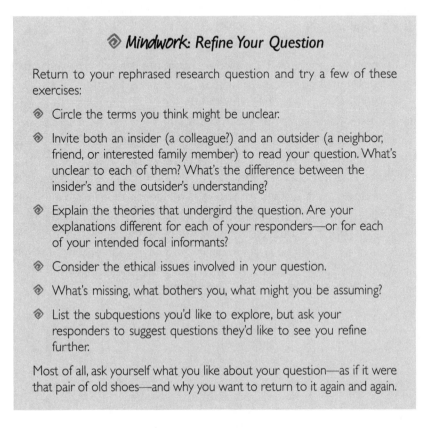

◈ *Mindwork:* Refine Your Question

Return to your rephrased research question and try a few of these exercises:

◈ Circle the terms you think might be unclear.

◈ Invite both an insider (a colleague?) and an outsider (a neighbor, friend, or interested family member) to read your question. What's unclear to each of them? What's the difference between the insider's and the outsider's understanding?

◈ Explain the theories that undergird the question. Are your explanations different for each of your responders—or for each of your intended focal informants?

◈ Consider the ethical issues involved in your question.

◈ What's missing, what bothers you, what might you be assuming?

◈ List the subquestions you'd like to explore, but ask your responders to suggest questions they'd like to see you refine further.

Most of all, ask yourself what you like about your question—as if it were that pair of old shoes—and why you want to return to it again and again.

SNAPSHOT III: Gail Revises Her Study

Gail conducts her study in the spring of 2004 and writes about her findings in a course paper the following fall. She doesn't discover that her students' writing is transformed by the process of reflecting on it. She doesn't find that students' reflective abilities help them pass their end-of-course writing exams any better than other strategies that have helped them in the past. She doesn't learn that reflective writing empowers her disenfranchised students.

She does learn, though, that when she grades writing, she is not responding merely to the work but to "how the student frames and understands the work." Reflective writing represents "a new uncharted genre in which writing is everywhere and sometimes students don't even know they are writing reflectively because they are writing so much." Reflective writing has its rewards for Gail because "it takes some of the weight off of me and allows students to become more responsible for their work." Gail finds that

> ⚙ *Don't be afraid to narrow or widen your lens; what you'll see will be sharper for the process of looking.*

what Kathleen Yancey suggests is true: students can learn to theorize about their own work and make it a habit of mind through the process of reflecting on it. In Gail's words, "Doing research in my classroom has changed the way I think about my teaching and my students' learning."

We conduct teacher inquiry for the reasons Gail suggests—to examine the personal assumptions that might affect our teaching and to become better classroom teachers. Gail's research questions show a dramatic shift in emphasis over the time she works on this project. She moves from a focus on one subset of the student population to the wider group of an entire class and finally back to herself as a teacher. Your initial question may remain the same throughout an inquiry project. It may shift focus even more than Gail's does. But your thinking will certainly change in the course of your research. Don't be afraid to narrow or widen your lens; what you'll see will be sharper for the process of looking and therefore of the most value to you as a teacher.

Bridgework
Researching the Idea

> Research is the name we give to the activity of writing . . . ;
> whatever it searches for, it must not forget its nature as
> language.
>
> —ROLAND BARTHES, "Writers, Intellectuals, Teachers"

- ⚙ Collegial Snooping
- ⚙ Creating a Google-ography
- ⚙ Creating an Annotated Bibliography
- ⚙ Using Keywords to Find Key Works
- ⚙ Bibliography Hopping
- ⚙ Exploring Archives

Y ou find yourself a little restless in your classroom, a little impatient with your teaching. You can't quite put your finger on it. Nothing is really wrong, but you put yourself on alert. You watch yourself teach, observe your students closely, and note surprises or thoughts that disturb you. You begin to ask questions:

If my students wrote more often, maybe in journals like the students in that book I read, would they become more fluent writers?

Is there some way I can take my students on a walk in their town so they can see how geometry pervades the landscape?

What would students need to know in order to look back and see how the immigrants in their neighborhoods have changed over time?

Why do these kids always sigh and roll their eyes when I ask them to pull out a piece of paper? Do they hate writing or fear it?

What if I supplemented the textbook with multimedia?

Somewhere in the corner of your mind lurks a research project. Your thoughts interest you, but the main idea is still unformed. You know other teachers have asked similar questions about their classrooms. For heaven's sake, you've read some of those very ideas in books and articles and encountered them in professional development workshops and conferences. You know you haven't invented these questions. On the other hand, this is your own idea, based on your own kids and your understanding of them and feelings about your classroom.

When you begin to ask yourself "what if" questions, you may be ready to begin your "bridgework," the research that connects your classroom to other classrooms. You've formed a tentative research question and some subquestions that go with it. You're ready to roll. But you'd never ask your students to begin a research project without first seeing what others have done, so you need to take your own advice. The combined resources of trusted colleagues; curriculum guides; and published print, online, or archival resources are a sturdy bridge between your classroom questions and those of other interested colleagues.

Much of the power of teacher inquiry comes from the fact that you explore your own problems. You want to answer your own question, find out "what works" or what might work with this subject and with your students. Doing research in your own classroom creates knowledge; it doesn't simply report on the knowledge of others. But background research bridges what you already know—and the questions you're asking—with what others know and what you want to learn more about.

❖ Mindwork: Discover What You Know

Even before you go to the library or log online, you'll first want to inventory what you already know about your topic. For example, if you're curious about using classroom journals because of your own experience with journals, you might list or freewrite about that experience:

❖ What is my history as a journal keeper?

❖ What do I know about the differences in types and uses of journals?

❖ Whose published journals have I read and liked?

❖ What have I noticed in my students' writing behavior that might make them embrace (or resist) journals?

❖ To what assignments might I add some kind of journal requirement?

Continued on next page

Continued from previous page

◈ Which of my curriculum goals might journals help develop?

Consult the bridgework prepwork you did in Chapter 1 and, using your now more refined topic, do a "brain dump": list, map, outline, diagram, brainstorm, freewrite. Form your topic into questions and subquestions:

◈ What sources do I know already that I might consult?

◈ What people might I ask or contact as resources?

◈ Where would I go to find out more?

Reread what you have written and highlight the parts you think are worth further exploration.

Collegial Snooping

You may feel a bit embarrassed to blurt out to a colleague, "So have you ever used journals in your classroom?" But take the plunge. You'll no doubt discover some pretty strong ideas and helpful professional resources. It may take some snooping to find out who is onto something new. Most often, when a colleague knows you are genuinely interested, you'll get the help you need, from someone who knows the culture of your school and your students. As all teachers know, there is no better way to learn about teaching than a good conversation with another teacher.

Any source you consult is a potential reference, so it's always a good idea to include all your snooping in a working bibliography—one that reflects your work in progress (for example: Colleague, Carol F. 2006. Personal interview. March 30). Your final, more formal bibliography (or works cited or references) should include all the print, online, archival, and interview sources you've used in the written version of your research project.

> ⚙ It's always a good idea to include all your snooping in a working bibliography.

Another kind of collegial snooping is soliciting the insights of a long-distance partner who is interested and supportive of your project. (Email comes in extremely handy here!) Kelly Richards, a high school teacher whose project you'll read more about in Chapter 9, returned home from a summer seminar fired up to begin her research. She had a solid proposal about student involvement in evaluation, and she had enormous energy. But suddenly she was back at school and quite alone. She emailed high school history teacher Katie McKiernan, who lived in a distant state and was feeling isolated herself. Katie had come across a relevant professional book by Anne Davies, Kathleen Gregory, and Caren Cameron, *Setting and Using Criteria for Use in Middle and Secondary Classrooms*, which became one of the centerpieces of Kelly's study and took her further in her research.

Learning from colleagues is how we make knowledge and grow as teachers and why we stay in the profession. Our most important colleagues don't necessarily teach in the classroom next door. We nurture our "academic kinships" at conferences, over the Internet, through published professional literature, in summer institutes and graduate seminars. We are our own best resources. No teacher ever minds a little collegial snooping. It goes a long, long way toward lightening a stressful career.

Creating a Google-ography

After taking inventory of what you know and doing some collegial snooping, you're ready to launch your bibliographic research—seeking out good books, articles, brochures, and electronic resources. As one does so often for so many purposes, you may find yourself at your computer. The Internet is a kind of miracle, in the way a telephone or a television was a miracle to our ancestors. What once required opening and closing many wooden card-catalogue drawers, lumbering through aisles of books, noting long codes of numbers on little slips of paper, can now be done in a few minutes without leaving your desk.

Electronic resources blur the traditional boundaries between primary and secondary resources. There are at least three good reasons for beginning a search on the Web:

1. Basic information, much like the materials in a reference room: facts, histories, descriptions, and ideas for the research path you're planning;

2. Lots of potential contacts: people who have shown interest in your topic, agencies and advocacy groups related to it;

3. An array of potential downloadable material—the aggregate of available "stuff" related to your topic.

Hopping online and typing keywords into your favorite search engine sets you off on a rapid-fire research journey. Although most Internet servers offer a limited history of your most recent Web searches, it's important to keep a careful chronological list of your trail of sources—your "Google-ography"—as you find them: you don't want to lose track of the places you've visited as you're investigating an idea.

As you cruise the Web, you'll have some initial ideas about narrowing or expanding your topic. A Web search also helps you locate and think about new keywords. You'll probably find that your Google-ography includes not only articles and books but also conference presentations, speeches, and even course syllabi that might prove valuable and timely.

For example, if you are researching the use of in-school journals, everything you find about the topic becomes an artifact, something someone values. You gain some understanding of the educational worth and currency of this writing practice by investigating the array of materials available on the Internet for public scrutiny. Some of this material will not be useful—items for sale, for example—but there are websites devoted exclusively to journal writing in the classroom that include bibliographies arranged both categorically and alphabetically. Because there is so much material on this topic, you would begin by sorting through the sources, deciding what best fits with the idea you plan to pursue.

When it comes to evaluating the credibility and worth of your electronic source material, remember that what you tell your students applies to you, too. The Web, unlike the library, has neither a board of overseers nor a librarian to help you assess the value of what you find. You set the criteria for the worth of the resource material you find. Most librarians agree that there are four basic criteria for evaluating any source, but particularly Internet sources.

> ⚙ *When it comes to evaluating the credibility and worth of your electronic source material, remember that what you tell your students applies to you, too.*

Evaluating Sources

1. Authority/Reliability: Is the site maintained by a government, educational, or professional organization?

2. Currency: When was the site last updated? Are the links available and accurate?

3. Quality/Accuracy: Is it based on unbiased, accurate, or well-documented material? If it's not, what problems are evident?

4. Audience: Who is the intended audience? Is this site persuading readers toward a particular point of view or advertising a product?

Although many websites may not meet your professional criteria, they can still offer a glimpse into how this topic functions inside the culture. The existence—even simply the numbers—of websites related to your topic can tell an interesting story. Finding over five million hits on journal writing, you can intuit that it continues to be a popular teaching strategy. You Google your way through school home pages, teachers' individual Web pages, lesson plans, educational articles, and book companies' ads. As you narrow your search by adding more keywords (*journals*, *middle school*, *English*, *response*), you discover that journals and writer's notebooks are used in elementary science and math classes, in foreign language classes, and as a strategy for encouraging fluency among speakers of English as a second language. You also see that electronic journaling (under headings like diarist.net and blogger.com) has become very popular with thousands of people worldwide. While fascinated, you're picky. And you're focused. You notice only a bit of useful information for researchers thinking about using journals or writer's notebooks in their classroom. Continued references to Ralph Fletcher's two books appear. An interesting nonprofit site for writers and teachers called "Writing Fix" offers a testimonial on the value of Fletcher's approach to journaling. You realize after an hour or so of surfing the Web that you have verified the continued significance of journals but have not found many new resources for your project. You end your search by looking at a new book called *The Complete Idiot's Guide to Journaling*.

◈ Mindwork: Try a Google-ography

Create a Google-ography for your topic. After mapping your online trail, stop and review what your journey has shown you about your topic:

◈ How many options do you have for further, more focused search?

◈ What do you know now that you didn't know before?

◈ Are there alternative keywords that might help you find more information?

◈ Do you need to consult another electronic source? try another search engine?

◈ What would you want to download or print?

Continued on next page

Continued from previous page

◈ What experts' names crop up again and again, and how might you make use of their work?

Keep track of the chronology of your search in whatever kind of chart or list you find comfortable. That document alone will imply interesting things about what's out there for you or anyone else who's interested in your topic. Your analysis of your search may help you revise, rethink, or refine your research question.

SNAPSHOT: Michelle Gioseffi Finds Key Terms

Michelle is a very new teacher beginning a research project: "When I began teaching sixth grade I felt as though I were running with no direction. I knew I could use my limbs, I felt the strength of my lungs, I knew the impact of my mind, yet I could not unite and find one place to go." Michelle has kept a journal herself for many years, and thinks she may want to use some form of journal in her classroom.

Her initial Web cruise (using *journals* and *school* as keywords) shows over nineteen million entries on this topic, everything from advertisements for designer diaries to professional journals such as *The Elementary School Journal* to online blogs for high school students. Using the terms *journal keeping* and *high school*, Michelle again finds an amazing array of information (over three million entries), from Holocaust writing activities to journal keeping for homeschooled students. Wishing to narrow her search still further, Michelle tries using four keywords: *journal keeping, secondary school, English,* and *response.* This takes her to a number of good sources, among them a school website that uses the terms *journaling* and *writer's notebooks* in the sixth-grade curriculum. Michelle adds *writer's notebooks* to her keyword search.

Inventorying her own personal experiences helps Michelle narrow her direction even more. Having taken a professional workshop at Teachers College, Columbia University in New York, she realizes that a "journal" and a "writer's notebook" are different tools for writers. She also does some collegial snooping as she remembers the workshop leader: "I will never forget her—lady in white, notebook in hand. She flipped through, delicately removing restaurant receipts and magazine clippings. I remember the possibilities I saw in her notebook. Writer's notebooks were a place to collect more than one's own thoughts and daily happenings and feelings. They seemed a place to collect every possible thing, a place to save all that strikes us in life."

Michelle's third initial resource is *Time for Meaning*, a professional book by former high school teacher Randy Bomer. Michelle has read and reread this book until it has became "a very close companion," helping her show her students how to use a writer's notebook to explore their topics: "Athletes have bodies. Painters their canvases. Singers their voices. Writers have their notebooks." Following her students as they create writer's notebooks, Michelle learns how to talk with them about their writing and their notebooks. Among her other sources, her bibliography cites Bomer's book, of course, along with seven other books that define and describe the use of writer's notebooks.

Using the Web first, herself second, and her professional reading third, Michelle evaluates the worth of her sources, narrows her topic, and comes to a far more precise definition of *journal* when she begins to use the term *writer's notebook*.

Creating an Annotated Bibliography

Sometimes we fool ourselves into thinking that we have located good information just because we have accumulated piles and piles of it. As writers ourselves, we know that less often means more: a few good specific sources can work far better than piles of indiscriminate sources. It's useful to assess the worth of source materials as you locate and collect them rather than just stacking them up in a corner. One way to do this is to write a short summary, or *annotation*, of each source as you encounter it. This summary should include the basic bibliographic information (author, title, date, and place of publication) as well as a two- or three-sentence assessment of how it fits into the idea you're investigating. It's a great investment in the writing life: a file of annotated sources, either on your computer or in a cabinet, can support a large range of projects over many years.

> ☼ It's useful to assess the worth of source materials as you locate and collect them rather than just stacking them up in a corner.

Annotating your sources saves time because writing about a source forces you to articulate your understanding of it and its overall importance to your topic. Many researchers depend upon annotated bibliographies to help them sort through masses of materials without having to read each and every source each and every time. So, in addition to creating your own annotated source material, you may want to look for other researchers' annotated bibliographies. The following is how some information on journaling might look in an annotated bibliography.

Bomer, Randy. *Time for Meaning: Crafting Literate Lives in Middle and High School.* Portsmouth, NH: Heinemann, 1995.

This book is a good curriculum resource for secondary-school writing teachers. Based on his own classroom experiences, Bomer describes his challenging writing curriculum, which asks teachers to think about how they use time in their classrooms, since time is the medium of both our teaching and our everyday lives. Bomer includes information on writer's notebooks, writing workshops, conferencing, connecting writing and literature, and using story in memoir and fiction.

Fletcher, Ralph. *Breathing In, Breathing Out: Keeping a Writer's Notebook.* Portsmouth, NH: Heinemann, 1996.

This short book (under 100 pages) provides inspiration for starting (or restarting) a regular notebook, journal, or log. Fletcher guides the writer toward creating a space and a reason for keeping a notebook. Each instructional chapter culls quotes from a range of classic writers (Didion, Sarton, Woolf, Cheever, Updike, Stafford, Irving) and contemporary writers (Nye, Olds, Allison, Lamott, O'Brien). Dedicated to Donald Murray, the book is well written and includes many fine examples from Fletcher's own notebooks.

Rief, Linda. "Reflections on Teaching Writing in 8 Workshops." *URL: www.learner.org/channel/workshops/middlewriting expert_audio.html#1.*

This website is sponsored by Annenberg/CPB, a free satellite channel for schools, colleges, and libraries. Middle school teacher and author Linda Rief provides accessible and practical advice (via audio clips) about having students keep writer's notebooks and engage in quick writes to help them with their writing.

Using Keywords to Find Key Works

Once you narrow the key terms and do some online research about what is available, it's time to make a trip to the library. Finding material there is no longer as arduous as it once was, either, because today's libraries are also geared to systematic retrieval of documents. If you have not been using the library regularly, you'll find contemporary librarians very savvy about using electronic databases in ways that are unique, impressive, and helpful. Don't hesitate to consult a reference librarian in your local or university library; helping patrons is his job. Librarians are eager to show you how to use the library's computer catalog system, its specialized reference materials, and its electronic databases (which index periodical articles from both general and academic journals).

Two specialized electronic databases are particularly helpful for anyone doing teacher research: ERIC (Education Resource Information Center) and the Education Index. Most state library systems make these databases available to their patrons. Since they both deal with educational resources, they can help you locate the types of classroom studies that will be most helpful to you. ERIC includes not only journal articles but also government documents, speeches, conference papers, curriculum guides, and lesson plans. The Education Index has the advantage of sorting by subject as well as "life stage" (preschool, middle school, etc.). Some of the listings in the Education Index provide an abstract of the article; many include the full printable article. There are many discipline-specific research tools, too, of course, that you may find helpful for your search. Consult your reference librarian to find out what computer resources are available. The resources change regularly, but there are general places to do education research in fields such as science (Science Online) the social sciences (Social Science Information Gateway) and the humanities (H-Net: Humanities and Social Sciences Online).

Finding the citation for an article or journal is only half the trip: you also need to locate the places it is housed. Standing by a reference desk with a number on a scrap of paper is not the same as holding the article in your hand. Asking a librarian (head for the signs indicating *Help, Information,* or *Reference*) where a particular resource is located is exactly the right thing for a busy teacher doing classroom research to do. Become familiar with your library, its vast array of newly organized information, and its staff. Not only will it make you more comfortable as a researcher, you will be able to help and encourage your own students to use the library's resources as well.

> ☼ *Asking a librarian where a particular resource is located is exactly the right thing for a busy teacher doing classroom research to do.*

Bibliography Hopping

One good book, a key article, or a rich website on your topic will offer up a long list of sources to pursue as you explore ways to sharpen your focus. When you use one person's bibliography (in a book or article) to "hop" to another source, you're on your way to uncovering a new set of resources unique to your own study. "Bibliography hopping"—perusing works cited lists and looking for the names that occur again and again, indicating they are the likely major players relative to your topic—makes the work of tracking down sources easier. By jumping from one resource to another, checking it against your research question, jumping back to more resources, and noting the useful ones, you will locate the materials most helpful to your topic. Eventually, you will have a pile of actual books and journal articles filled with exactly the information you need.

No one would want to design a classroom inquiry project about journals without citing some of the most important already-published work on this topic, like the three we've cited. When reading the acknowledgments in Randy Bomer's book, Michelle sees that he has been both a student and an instructor in the Teachers College Writing Project, working with Lucy Calkins, whose support he mentions. So Michelle's first hop is to look for books by Calkins listed in Bomer's bibliography. She finds two: *The Art of Teaching Writing* and a book written collaboratively with Shelly Harwayne, *Living Between the Lines*, both published by Heinemann.

Another way to hop from one bibliography to another is for Michelle to skim the section on writer's notebooks in Bomer's book to see what thinkers and writers he mentions. Chapter 3, "Writer's Notebooks: Tools for Thinking and Living" cites the work of Calkins and Harwayne but also discusses Nancie Atwell and Mary Ellen Giacobbe, along with Peter Elbow, Donald Murray, Toby Fulwiler, William Stafford, Natalie Goldberg, and Virginia Woolf, all writers and journal keepers cited in Bomer's bibliography. She may recognize all these people as "process writers" or "expressivists," or she might not recognize them at all. What she wants at this point is not an analysis or a category or even a value judgment about their work. She wants to know what they know about in-class journal keeping. From a single reference, Michelle has lots of names and book titles in mind. She can go to these resources and review their acknowledgments, prefaces, and bibliographies to begin to understand who has done classroom work on writer's notebooks. If she pursues the scholars who write about the values of journals at the college level (Elbow, Murray, Fulwiler), she'll find further justification for using writer's notebooks. Or she could pursue the professional writers who offer firsthand accounts of writer's notebooks (Stafford, Goldberg, Woolf). The more she hops, the more choices she'll find and the closer she'll be to finding the right material.

Still another way to hop around in search of source materials is to go to amazon.com, key in the title of a book you've found valuable, and see what other books are recommended. This strategy, although driven by consumer rather than academic incentives, is surprisingly effective. If Michelle enters Randy Bomer's book, Amazon's website offers these suggestions: *The Art of Teaching Writing*, by Lucy McCormick Calkins; *In the Middle*, by Nancie Atwell; *After The End*, by Barry Lane. If, however, Michelle enters the title of Ralph Fletcher's book on keeping a writer's notebook, *Breathing In, Breathing Out*, she's given many recommendations for books about yoga. The moral here is to use discretion!

Michelle gains confidence during her bibliography hopping when certain thinkers and names recur in each source she consults. Like many researchers, she enters the realm of focused bibliography junkies, experts at getting the most out of each bibliography they encounter.

Exploring Archives

The Web is a giant archive that gathers together information from a dizzying array of sources all over the globe and organizes it with letters and numbers; it is usually the first archive you'll visit. But there are other archives, in places like museums and historical societies, ready for you to explore as well. Not every research project will require you to visit these archives, but don't forget about them. Your school district, for example, may have archives of data about school policies and procedures, even old student papers, journals, school newspapers, or yearbooks connected to your topic. A town's historical society may have archived a collection of educational textbooks that provide insights into how your topic has been viewed over time. If there is a local museum near your school, it too may have an archive that could prove useful to your project. For example, if you are researching a curriculum unit on the immigration patterns of your town over time, the local museum may have documents that will help you build such a unit. There are rich sources of information even in very small places.

Anthropologists and folklorists use the term *material culture* to designate objects loaded with special meaning within the history of a culture. When you collect an array of documents, maps, or drawings related to your research topic, you create your own material culture. Schools are filled with material culture that is often not recognized as such: student writing, student projects, bulletin boards, displays, cartons of old papers, special furniture, mascots, files relative to a curriculum program or a test, public relations brochures,

> ☼ There are rich sources of information even in very small places.

newspaper articles, student records, demographic data. Any relevant collection of "stuff" can be an archive for your study if it contains important information.

Material culture also includes the kinds of plans and maps that teachers create every day to organize their classrooms, curriculum, and lessons. If in the course of doing your project, for example, you arrange your chairs differently to prepare for a new way of doing things and then make a map of how you did it, you are documenting your research. Both your product (the rearrangement of furniture) and the pro-

> ⚙ *Material culture also includes the kinds of plans and maps that teachers create every day to organize their classrooms, curriculum, and lessons.*

cess (your reason for change and the students' reactions to it) are ways of expressing the beliefs and values of your classroom culture. They become archives about the material culture relative to your study. How you use space and organize your materials for teaching gives you clues to your own teaching philosophy, particularly when you make changes as you conduct your inquiry. You become your own archivist as you collect this material and think about it, even when you've designed it yourself.

◈ Mindwork: Shape Your Working Bibliography

Choose a bibliographic format (MLA, APA, *Chicago*, etc.). Create a working bibliography of all the sources you've collected so far: from the Web, from the library, and from archives. Experiment with clustering sources, either thematically, historically, or by genre. Recluster them a different way. See what themes you discover as you rearrange your source materials.

◈ Do you need more current articles or books?

◈ Can you eliminate some sources you initially thought were valuable? relevant?

◈ Have you included enough different types of materials (book chapters, articles, websites, curriculum units) in your bibliography? Or are they all part of the same genre?

◈ Where do you need to go next? What do you wish you'd found?

◈ Is this a time to revise or refine your research question? If so, what would it look like?

SNAPSHOT: Luke Flynn Writes a Bibliographic Essay

Luke Flynn is a Florida middle school teacher who is curious about his students' distaste for writing. When he takes Elizabeth's graduate course on composition methods and theories, one assignment is to write a bibliographic essay to prepare for the classroom investigation that is part of his master's program. (In a bibliographic essay, a writer examines a number of books and articles related by topic or theme, interpreting, analyzing, and even personalizing the connections among the sources and the influences they have on his own interests.)

The only thing that Luke knows for sure about his inquiry project is that it will center somehow on students' self-expressed negative attitudes about writing. Luke himself is a fluid and prolific writer who composes long emails daily to family members and generally loves the freedom that personal writing provides: "I'm interested in this subject because I cannot fathom resisting writing. I have always loved to write. I realized when I started my teaching career that many of my students would not share my enthusiasm for writing, and I feel I owe it to those students to try and understand this so that I may better work with them."

Luke's bibliographic essay formalizes his hunt for relevant resource materials to help him design a classroom project about his students' distaste for writing. While not all researchers need to compose a bibliographic essay, Luke's organizational strategy for presenting his resources is a good one: he positions himself in relationship to the topic, defines the key terms, summarizes the historical background, and clusters sources of similar ideas under relevant subheadings. His bibliographic essay ends with the most important section of all, "Why Does This Research Matter?"

As Michelle does with her general topic *journals*, Luke starts with what he believes is his key term, *writer's block*. This takes him to the early work of Mike Rose (1984) on this topic (*Writer's Block: The Cognitive Dimension*), at which point he discovers that he isn't really interested in *blocked* writers but in *apprehensive* ones. Luke defines his terms at the outset of his bibliographic essay:

> I need to make a distinction here; it is important to understand what writing apprehension is not. I am not talking about what Mike Rose and others refer to as "writer's block." Writer's block affects us all; a writer can struggle with writer's block and not be an apprehensive writer. In *Writer's Block: The Cognitive Dimension*, published in 1984, Mike Rose defines writer's block as "an inability to begin or continue

writing for reasons *other than a lack of basic skill or commitment*" (emphasis added, 3). It is possible that writer's block can lead to writing anxiety (also known as writing apprehension). However, Rose is very careful to point out there is not necessarily a relationship between the two:"blocking and apprehensiveness . . . are not synonymous, not necessarily coexistent, and not necessarily causally linked." (4)

After Luke clarifies the terminology related to his project, he does some historical research prompted by references found in Rose's book. This look backward takes him to a measurement of writing anxiety developed by two researchers working in the 1970s, John Daly and Michael Miller. In his essay, Luke describes the importance of the Daly and Miller writing inventory, an instrument he can use to assess his own students' anxieties:

> When talking about writing apprehension there is no better place to start than with the instrument developed by John Daly and Michael Miller to measure writing apprehension. When the study of writing apprehension was in its infancy, Daly and Miller realized the importance of assessing students' own attitudes; the best way to learn about writing apprehension is to work with the students themselves. With that in mind, Daly and Miller created an inventory to measure students' anxiety toward writing. They wound up with a list of twenty-six statements about writing; students rate themselves on a scale ranging from 1 (strongly agree) to 5 (strongly disagree). Using the numbers that are generated from those statements, a teacher can assess students' anxiety toward writing. Though this measurement was first developed in 1974, it remains the most widely used instrument to measure writing apprehension. Writing apprehension, then, is a measurable reaction of how students view themselves as writers.

As a middle school teacher, Luke of course realizes that just knowing that his students are highly apprehensive about writing is not enough. He has undertaken his bibliographic search with that understanding in mind. What interests him more are the underlying causes of writing apprehension. After defining his terms and positioning the topic historically, Luke heads the next section of his bibliographic study "What Causes Writing Apprehension?" and describes a range of research from the seventies through the twenty-first century that underscores similar conclusions, including a particularly useful summary article written in 2001 by a community college writing instructor named Lynda Holmes:

Lynda Holmes arrives at the same essential conclusion: students' attitudes toward writing are shaped heavily by teachers' reactions to their writing. Relying heavily on the works of Mike Rose, Donald Murray, and J. W. Thomas and W. D. Rohwer, Holmes purports that there are three distinct reasons for student anxiety toward writing (172). The first is a "negative belief about education." Typically, but not always, such negative beliefs can be traced back to bad experiences early in the students' schooling experience. A second reason is "problems regarding communication . . . with their writing educators." "A severe feeling of disappointment due to lack of control over the writing process" is the third. All three reasons can be traced back to teachers and students having differing beliefs and expectations about student writing.

Baker, Gee, Powell, and Holmes seem to believe, as I do, that students, and indeed all humans, have an inherent desire to communicate. Included in that desire to communicate is a desire to write. However, many people become fearful of writing as they progress through school. Many students are not supported enough in their writing endeavors, and this lack of support can and does lead to students becoming apprehensive writers.

On the basis of his bibliographic search, Luke realizes that his own methods of responding to his students' writing will be a major factor in their attitudes and apprehensions toward writing. When he contemplates the research he has done, Luke asks what he can do with the understanding he has gained in order to alleviate his students' negative attitudes. Drawing on the combined work of Mike Rose, Miller and Daly, and many other authorities cited in his study, Luke concludes that as a teacher he must take responsibility for helping his students develop more positive attitudes about writing:

As I said in the introduction, compiling this information was very useful to me; I learned a great deal about an area of writing that affects many of our students yet is seldom discussed. But it would seem a shame to stop here. That is why I plan to conduct research in my own classroom. By administering the Daly-Miller writing inventory at the beginning, middle, and end of the academic year, I hope to chart the anxiety of my students. There are several reasons for doing this. Perhaps the most obvious is to see what effect my teaching strategies have on the anxiety of my students. Will I be able to make my students less anxious writers? In addition, I am interested in determining if there are gender differences with regard to writing anxiety. I am also very interested in how the topic affects the anxiety level of the writer. Lester Faigley and John Daly have suggested that personal writing causes higher levels of anxiety, yet the personal narrative is seen by many writing teachers as a way to ease students into a writing course. Does this thinking need to be reevaluated? It is my sincere hope that by searching for (and I hope finding) the answers to these questions I will be able to help my students be comfortable with their ability to write. Like Robert Boice and many others, I wonder what society is losing by the silence of so many.

These short excerpts from Luke's much longer bibliographic essay show how helpful it is to organize your research findings under clear categories even when no one is requiring you to complete an extensive search. Luke's works cited page provides a good range of bibliographic sources, from books to journal articles, written over a thirty-year period. It was important that he find the first mention of writing anxiety and how it was measured. While his working bibliography included all the resources he found, his formal works cited list includes only the source material he has cited. Luke writes his paper and enters his references in the MLA (Modern Language Association) documentation format required by his English department. Each style not only requires its own citation format, it also specifies how to approach a citation within running text. Notice that Luke includes references to his source material—author's last name and page number—within his own discussion (a feature of the MLA style) rather than putting reference information in footnotes or endnotes (as you would in many social science academic citations). Looking up the author's last name in the list of works cited, the reader finds the full title, publisher, and date and place of publication.

> ⚙ *Organize your research findings under clear categories even when no one is requiring you to complete an extensive search.*

Two other commonly used and accepted academic formats are the *Chicago Manual of Style* (used by many publishers) and the American Psychological Association (APA) style (accepted in most journals and colleges of education). Each organization has a handbook and a website. After checking the differences in citation styles, choose the one that best fits your topic, or ask what style your potential publisher or department expects.

Headwork
Assuming Self and Other

> I felt both dread and joy, like the seeker after the treasure who suddenly sees the flower of the fern. . . . [T]his art called for new demands, a whole world of desires, which stood in no relation to the surroundings of the pupils, as I thought in the first moment.
> —LEO TOLSTOY,
> "Are the Peasant Children to Learn to Write from Us?"

Every now and then, a glance out into the classroom brings with it the thought, *I wonder what they're noticing about me?* Our surface fears have to do with our appearance—hair out of place, zipper inadvertently open, lingerie peeking out from our clothes. But far more deeply, we wonder how much our students know about our politics, our parenting, our pets, our love lives—and we wonder what and what not to tell them. When we meet students in the local supermarket, at the movies, or at a ball game, their surprise surprises us. We are, from their point of view, stepping outside our context. "You actually go to the *store*?" "You're seeing *this movie* with *him* and I'm seeing it *too*?" "What's a teacher doing at a *game*?"

How much of our privacy is appropriate to share? Each of us has a different level of tolerance—and of disclosure—and we often look to our colleagues to learn, compare, laugh, and tell stories about those moments when our private selves bump into our public selves. Our students see us as "the other" everywhere except in the classroom, the one spot where we belong: in our place, for their purposes. It's always a matter of perspective.

Teachers understand the issue of perspective all too well. It's a strong thread in the fabric of our routine. Watching students learn is like burrowing through a mound of multifaceted, multipurpose case studies, day in and day out. We're constantly trying to jump into our students' heads, envision what they see, anticipate what they think, understand their reasons for doing what they do, wonder what their lives are like outside school. Understanding our students' perspective is part of our daily business. In research, we need to be equally sharp at understanding and articulating our own.

"Headwork" involves the complicated issues of perspective in teacher inquiry. Who are you, anyway, as you conduct research in your class? an insider? an outsider? an objective observer? a subjective participant? What are your assumptions as you enter a research project? How can you know your assumptions when you "assume" them unconsciously? How can you lay bare personal features like age, race, gender, ethnicity, and regional and local alliances that affect your own ways of seeing? Is it appropriate to adapt an outsider's stance in a culture in which you participate? Why bother trying to do that when you've worked so hard to position yourself as an insider in your own classroom and among your students?

> ⚙ *Understanding our students' perspective is part of our daily business. In research, we need to be equally sharp at understanding and articulating our own.*

In the story from which this chapter's epigraph is taken, Tolstoy is able to see his "conscious creation" in his own teaching. He feels both joy and dread—as teachers so often do—joy that his students are learning, not by accident, and dread that he will be responsible for repeating whatever he has done to make it happen. Were he not functioning both as outsider and insider, as teacher and learner, he would not be able to make this observation. Understanding what's in your own head—and finding ways to try to understand what's in the heads of others—will pave the way for you to describe, interpret, and analyze your research.

Stepping In, Stepping Out

The idea of *stepping in* and *stepping out* of the researcher stance is borrowed from Hortense Powdermaker, who, like the novelist Zora Neale Hurston, was one of the first American anthropologists to study her own culture. In her book *Stranger and Friend: The Way of an Anthropologist*, she writes, "Long before I ever heard of anthropology, I was being conditioned for the role of stepping in and out of society. It was part of my growing-up process to question the traditional values and norms of the family and experiment with behavior patterns and ideologies. This is not an uncommon process of finding oneself. . . . Why should a contented and satisfied person think of standing outside his or any other society and studying it?" (1966, 55). As Powdermaker observes, what seems ordinary in one context may seem extraordinary in another.

When our students say, "That's awesome," or "Hey, Homeboy!" or "That dude just plain doesn't get it," they assume an insider stance in order to call attention to others' outsider status. When we conduct research in our own classrooms, we must "step in" and "step out" simultaneously. Over time, classrooms certainly do take on the characteristics of a culture, "an invisible web of behaviors, patterns, rules, and rituals of a group of people who have contact with one another and share common languages" (Sunstein and Chiseri-Strater 2002, 3). As teachers and researchers ourselves, we embrace the idea that classrooms develop themselves as cultures and that it's both interesting and appropriate to use anthropological ways of looking at them.

Stepping into a culture involves taking what researchers call an *emic* stance, assuming the position of insider. Stepping out of a culture is the *etic* stance, that of an outsider. Conducting research in our own classrooms, we must continually combine and recombine both of these roles. Although this seems complicated, it's what gives our studies color, texture, and power. In lots of ways, we are insiders. Our classroom culture revolves around rituals, language, and habits we've created and established over much time and with much care. In some ways, a teacher is the key insider in this culture—the "chief," the "tradition-bearer" in her own classroom, his own classroom. Yet in other ways, because of this very position, a teacher will never be the same kind of insider in the classroom as the students are. They, too, have rituals, language, and habits as insiders, some they share with us and some they don't. It's no surprise, then, that the view we have when we teach is tricky. We are outsiders stepping into and insiders stepping out of the culture we study. Detachment and involvement, subjectivity and objectivity—insider and outsider stances should speak to one another in classroom inquiry the same way they speak to one another in our work with students.

> ⚙ Detachment and involvement, subjectivity and objectivity—insider and outsider stances should speak to one another in classroom inquiry.

SNAPSHOT I: Deanna Stoube's Dilemma

Deanna Stoube is an elementary teacher who is also a teacher of teachers in a regional college of education. A student in one of Deanna's classes of preservice teachers, Tricia, describes a moment that eventually becomes the focus of Deanna's own research project. Tricia's son Adam has spent weeks at home writing a story called "The Journey," influenced by his personal reading (of John Scieszka and J. R. R. Tolkien, his favorite writers at the time). When Adam and his siblings tell their father they want to see the movie version of Tolkien's *Lord of the Rings*, Tricia's husband Jack retorts, "No, I think you've seen quite enough violent movies. Especially after reading what Adam wrote." From this, Tricia and Adam learn that Jack has read his son's story, which has been sitting on the family coffee table. In Tricia's words, "My husband goes on and on about how many people were killed and how violent Adam's story was. Well, Adam's face turned white, he got very upset, grabbed the top page of his story, crumpled it up, and ran upstairs in tears."

Tricia's "So what do you think?" sobers Deanna even more than the incident intrigues her. As Tricia's university teacher, Deanna is neither ready with a response nor willing to "be guiding my students' beliefs, goals, and decisions."

"I retreated," Deanna admits, "behind the role of researcher and asked Tricia whether she minded if I studied this incident. She agreed, and my study was born." Taking the incident on as a research project, Deanna recognizes the multiple perspectives and ethical dimensions it will include. The most immediate one involves her role as a teacher of teachers:

> Too often I get caught up in the righteousness of my profession. I sit in a classroom with soon-to-be elementary teachers, facilitating discussions on how to teach language arts. No matter how much I encourage co-learning, we all know that ultimately I'm the teacher. Four words prove this time and time again. "What do you think?" The minute I respond to this, I know that I have made an impact on my students. Learning is never really free. It is influenced and guided by schools and teachers and parents—all who have beliefs, create goals, and make decisions.

Deanna also knows that she is not at all "objective" as she begins this study, nor does she need to be. As a teacher, a parent, a reader, a moviegoer, and a person who reads professional literature about children's reading and writing, Deanna's opinions influence her position in relation to her study. Much later in her project, having collected a lot of data, she describes her positions to herself in her research journal:

I wanted to know what impact a family's reactions to a child's writing has on the child's next writing experience. Tricia told me that she felt Jack just didn't get what he had done. "My husband seemed kind of clueless as to what had transpired." Was this the case? What impact does Jack think this incident will have on Adam's writing development?

Jack says, "It's been a long time and I don't really remember the paper that much. It wasn't a big deal to me." As I transcribed these words from Jack's audiotape, I cringed. "It wasn't a big deal to me"? I wanted to *scream* at him, "What do you mean, it wasn't a big deal to you? Look what you've done to your son!"

The sad fact was that I couldn't honestly do this. It wasn't Jack's fault that this happened. It wasn't Tricia's or Adam's, either. A larger issue was at work here.

Uncovering Multiple Perspectives

At the outset of her project, before she explores larger issues (violence in children's writing, influences from reading and movies, parents' attitudes toward children's stories), Deanna needs to understand her own positions and the positions of the key players in the incident. In her journal, Deanna writes with an emic perspective. She captures her own anxieties, uncovers her assumptions, and explores her multiple positions in relationship to researching one moment in one child's literacy as it plays out in his home.

But in order to carry out the research project, she needs to assume an etic stance, too, documenting the perspectives of the other people involved in the incident: mother Tricia, father Jack, and Adam's current classroom teacher. Most of all, of course, Deanna has a responsibility to document Adam's voice, who confesses to her, "I felt upset when Dad said there was too much violence in my story. I didn't really want to write after that. I don't write stories anymore unless I have to at school."

Checking Assumptions, Positions, and Tensions

Asking questions about your own reactions enhances your ability to step in and step out of the culture you're wanting to study in your classroom. From your earliest freewriting as you explore and define your topic, through the notes you take to your reflections as you look back, as you question, and as you add to what you have written—draft to draft—writing regularly provides you with the details, language, perspectives, and perceptions that will eventually grow into useful "findings." Although you may not realize it, your notes are a primary source that no one has recorded in the same way you have, at the site you've chosen, about the people you've studied.

Asking the following questions many times during the course of a study, and keeping a record of your answers, opens a window into your thinking and paves the way for analysis:

1. *What surprised you?* (Monitor your assumptions.) How do you know your thinking has changed? In what ways does each new piece of evidence confirm or fail to confirm your hunches? Articulating your assumptions as they change helps you understand your preconceived notions and watch yourself as your learning deepens and your assumptions shift.

2. *What intrigued you?* (Become aware of your personal stances—your positions.) You as the fieldworker/inquirer are a key instrument (recorder and presenter) of the research process. What interests and attracts you will always influence what you record and how you write about it. In turn, it will inform what you share with your readers/observers.

3. *What disturbed you?* (Expose your tensions, reveal yourself to yourself.) In research writing, you need to be honest about your blind spots, stereotypes, prejudices, and the things you find upsetting, no matter how small or big they are. Focusing on what bothers you about a research project is not always comfortable, but it almost always leads to important insights.

These three questions, developed over many years of working with students and colleagues, are the heart of our book *FieldWorking: Reading and Writing Research* (2002). Asking them regularly throughout a project, either in a research group or alone, is a powerful and an accurate way to see how your thinking develops and therefore to track the progress (and increase the intricacy) of your analysis as your knowledge accumulates.

> ### ◈ *Mindwork:* Use the Three Questions for Analysis
>
> 1. Looking back at their early thinking about a topic offers researchers the clues they need. Try your hand at these questions early in your work as a researcher. If you're using the exercises in this book, you've
>
> *Continued on next page*

Continued from previous page

already had two opportunities. First, lurking in the ten "prepwork" sections of Chapter 1 are probably some important insights about your assumptions, positions, and tensions. Arrange them in front of you, with a blank paper or screen to write on, and try to find evidence for these important elements that will both help and hinder your research. When you look at your evidence, ask:

- What surprises you?
- What intrigues you?
- What disturbs you?

Write more about the challenges you think you'll have as you shape your project in classroom inquiry. Later, as you learn more, you'll want to look back at this writing.

2. Reexamine the "stepping in" and "stepping out" statements you wrote in the earlier mindwork section of this chapter. Perhaps your writing holds more assumptions, positions, or tensions than you think. Ask all three questions of the paragraphs you wrote, or better yet, answer the questions in conjunction with a partner.

SNAPSHOT II: Deanna Distinguishes Data

Deanna wants to try her hand at classroom inquiry, and she is particularly interested in issues of perspective and of influences on students' writing. How does one person's story support or conflict with another's? How many people's stories enter into one incident involving someone's writing? How do both reading and media viewing influence writing? Hiding in this one moment in the life of a family are at least three stories: Adam's, Jack's, and Tricia's. But there are more data, too: Adam's writing, his reading, his viewing preferences, and an apparent conflict between his parents. Deanna writes:

Tricia's account of the incident was fascinating in and of itself. I wondered, however, about how her husband and son viewed the incident. How did Adam feel about this? What did Tricia do? Why did Jack make these comments? I was curious, too, about what happened after the incident. Did Adam continue writing? Was Tricia able to convince Jack that violence was okay in Adam's stories? Ultimately, I wanted to know what impact a family's reactions to a child's writing have on the child's next writing experience.

Deanna begins her study by collecting data:

- ☀ Three audiocassettes, on which Jack, Tricia, and Adam separately and privately describe the incident to her and how it made them feel.

- ☀ Photocopies of Adam's story "The Journey" and, a few weeks later, a copy of Adam's next piece of writing, "The Adventures of Froggy and Frogger."

- ☀ Several books by John Scieszka and *The Lord of the Rings*, Adam's favorite reading material at the time.

- ☀ Relevant reading she's done about cultural influences on children's writing.

- ☀ Formal, signed "informed consent" notes from Jack, Tricia, and Adam that they will have additional conversations with her during the course of her semester-long study.

- ☀ Her own research journal, in which she documents her thinking as it deepens and changes over time.

Planning for Analysis and Interpretation

Unlike research that relies on measuring devices ("tools" or "instruments," as we often hear in education), in a qualitative study of your own classroom, you are the most important instrument of your research. Neither your research nor your topic needs to be objective, but you do need to own up to your own assumptions, positions, and tensions in order to analyze what you've seen and in order to make sense to anyone who wants to learn from your study. You are taking your readers (or observers) by the hand and honestly telling them who you are—to see what you see, think what you think, and do what you do.

> ⚙ *In a qualitative study of your own classroom, you are the most important instrument of your research.*

By keeping a journal or creating some other system for documenting your thoughts while you collect data, you set the stage for later analysis by being able to follow your research tracks. Many researchers write their notes "in the field," but some situations allow only minimal note taking on site. For teachers studying their own classrooms, this is a hard truth. We cannot observe and participate at the same time—do our job as teachers and watch ourselves doing it. So we need to find ways to return to the quiet of our desks (some people prefer their cars) to flesh out and expand the scanty notes we have taken "in the field." As we all know from observing our colleagues in the classroom, there is so much activity, triggering so many memories and emotions, that it's impossible to write it all down. When we do fieldwork in schools, we follow the advice we give our students: before you go back to your busy life with all its distractions, take time to sit quietly and write in your notebook. Expand your field notes by adding details of conversations, sensory impressions, contextual information, by noting your own reflections and (yes!) your opinions about what you've seen, and by jotting down possible questions and hunches. Analysis begins with reviewing your notes.

> ⚙ *We cannot observe and participate at the same time—do our job as teachers and watch ourselves doing it.*

Analysis is the "headwork," the essential thinking that separates a formal, focused research study from informal classroom impressions. Analysis combines your impressions, the data you've collected, and the perspectives of relevant others. Field researchers, like teachers, create many systems for note taking. They invent, develop, and devise strategies for organizing, coding, and retrieving data. Colored folders, highlighters, sticky notes, hanging folder boxes, and three-ring binders—any and all of these are a researcher's best friends. Computers, too, have organizing features that can help you label and find particular sections of your field notes when you need them. Accumulating a solid and well-organized set of field notes is only one step in the process of creating a research project, but like organizing your lesson plans, class lists, and seating charts, you want to develop a scheme that makes sense to you.

> ⚙ *Analysis is the "headwork," the essential thinking that separates a formal, focused research study from informal classroom impressions.*

A last-minute blitz through a set of notes isn't a good way to master information. Cursory reading does little good when we want to understand a concept thoroughly, invite an idea into our long-term memory, or understand it enough to connect it to another idea. The same holds true for research projects. Your notes will speak to you when you read them regularly and often. As you review them, you will begin to see recurring themes, images, metaphors, and they will suggest patterns. The patterns you notice will help you form your

> ⚙ *Your notes will speak to you when you read them regularly and often. . . . The patterns you notice will help you form your beginning interpretations—and test them against more information as you accumulate it.*

beginning interpretations—and test them against more information as you accumulate it. Some fieldworkers write weekly memos to themselves culled from their field notes, pulling together pieces of data around an emerging idea. Others like to write their memos to a writing or research partner as an extra check and a way to keep track of their own research goals.

SNAPSHOT III: Deanna Considers Ethics and Perspective

Questioning real-life situations, especially those that happen in classes, and pushing them toward our own informed analysis, is not without ethical dilemmas. Deanna's study eventually becomes a course essay, "I Don't Write Stories Anymore: Exploring the Impact of Family Reactions on Students' Writing," that she has presented to colleagues in two different classes and hopes to publish in a professional journal.

In her essay, the voice, of course, is hers. But it is her responsibility as a researcher to represent the voices of the others in her story as specifically as she can—and to represent the home and school settings she describes without judgment. When she includes a value judgment, she must let her audience know whose it is. For Deanna, the ethical issues in this project sit at the intersection of school literacy, university literacy, and home-based literacy. Her idea comes from a university class of preservice teachers' private conversation, the incident comes from the privacy of one family's home, and the child's writing in question is connected to his schooling and his school.

Considering Ethics

Conducting a project in the environment in which you teach involves serious and tricky ethical issues. No one can be fully "objective"; that is not even the point in classroom inquiry. But all those involved directly and indirectly must be fully informed and in agreement, at least, that they will be a part of your study. Before you begin to collect data, you must plan for what researchers call "informed consent." You can never assume you have people's consent to collect the products of their work or to represent their spoken or written words on paper—any more than you'd assume a parent's consent to take a class full of students on a field trip. Whether you work under the supervision of a university's Human Subjects Review Board, according to a public school's privacy and permissions policies, or on your own, you are legally

> ☼ All those involved directly and indirectly must be fully informed and in agreement, at least, that they will be a part of your study.

liable and ethically responsible to have written consent from all of your subjects before you make any of their words—or your own—public.

Here are some things we know from experience. There are different sets of ethical protocols for different kinds of publications and research projects. No publishers will accept printed email messages as "permissions," nor as "informed consent." There are currently different rules for publishing on the Web than there are for publishing in journals or books. The form you develop for informed consent will depend on who is funding your project, where it's taking place, and what you plan to do with your results.

All the teachers we mention in this book have given us formal permission to write about their work. We keep copies of the signed permission slips in a manila folder in Bonnie's office file cabinet, and we have submitted the originals to Heinemann, our publisher. Deanna, whose research is used as an example in this chapter, has received informed consent from Tricia, Jack, Adam, and Adam's teacher. She has obtained permission from the students in her university class to write about their discussion, and she has given us signed permission to use the materials that led to her essay as well as the essay itself. Before this book was published, Deanna had an opportunity to review what we've written about her and the excerpts from her own writing that we've included. That is our ethical obligation to her, to the subjects of her study, and to our readers.

An informed consent form can be as simple as a little permission slip like this one, which we asked the participants in a summer workshop we taught together to sign:

Informed Consent
July, 2004

I, _____, give my permission to Elizabeth Chiseri-Strater and Bonnie Stone Sunstein to share my research proposal, portfolio, or my finished essay with other students in the Northeastern University Summer Writing Program. I understand that they will keep my work in their files and they may want to use excerpts, fully cited, as authors of *FieldWorking: Reading and Writing Research, What Works?* or another publication about teacher research. I understand, too, that I have a right to see and comment on their work in progress as they develop drafts of these books.

Date:
Signature:

We designed this form knowing that each person who signed it would be a teacher-inquirer and would understand why we needed their permission and knowing, too, that we were preparing material for this book.

In other instances, the informed consent must describe the project in more detail (so that the reader/informant can understand what it is you want permission for), as well as offer an opportunity for changing informants' names to protect their anonymity. We've found that many informants enjoy the chance to invent their own pseudonyms. If a student is under eighteen years old, you must obtain informed consent from both the student and a parent/guardian.

However you write an informed consent form, it is essential that it be straightforward, concise, and respectful of your informants' knowledge and level of interest. The large-scale details of your research are certainly important to you, but what your informants need to know is what you plan to do with their words and their work. Take an emic stance here. Think from their perspective, and write an informed consent form that describes what your research plans are, how it will affect them, and what control they'll have over what you say.

Figure 4–1 is a general form that Heinemann suggests for obtaining permissions relative to the books they publish.

For university projects, and often for grant-related projects, you will need to apply for approval from a Human Subjects clearance office (sometimes called the IRB, or Institutional Review Board), the details of which differ from institution to institution. What doesn't differ, however, is the legal and ethical importance of obtaining informed consent. Although you are not conducting experimental research, nor do you have any intentions of "making guinea pigs" of your students and colleagues, nor are you changing any environmental conditions in order to describe what you see, you *are* intending to represent people in their everyday situations, their work, and their words.

University informed consent forms usually cover many different kinds of research, including clinical trials for new medicines and large-sample quantitative studies in every field of research. These forms are sometimes daunting or annoying, including questions like these:

Project Title:
What is the purpose of this study?
How many people will participate?
How long will I be involved?
What will happen during the course of this study?

STUDENT PERMISSION REQUEST LETTER

For any student material, you will need to get signed student release forms. Be sure to get the student's parent/guardian to sign the form if the student is under age eighteen. We cannot publish student work without a signed release form, even under a pseudonym. The requested information (below in italics) must be inserted by you before the form is signed.

[date]
[student/parent/guardian's name and address]

Dear *[student/parent/guardian's name]*,

I am preparing a book tentatively entitled *[working title of the book, and editor's name if you are a contributor]*, to be published by *[Heinemann or Heinemann-Boynton/Cook]* in or around *[month and year]*. *[Insert a brief description of your book, e.g., "It is a book on teaching writing at the elementary level. Its audience is teachers and teacher educators."]* We would appreciate your permission to include the following material by *[student's name]* in this and future editions of this work and in all languages and in all media and excerpts of the material, including use for advertising, publicity, and promotional purposes.

[Provide a description of the student's work. It helps to include a copy of the material for which you are requesting permission.]

The student's real name may or may not appear in the finished book. *[If you plan to use a pseudonym instead of the student's real name, you may want to state what it is here.]*

Two copies of this request are enclosed. Please sign both copies and return one to me, keeping the other one for your files. Thank you for your consideration.

Sincerely,
[your name and address]

I (we) grant permission for the use of *[student's name]* material described above in this and future editions of *[working title of book]*.

_____

Signature of student *(or parent/guardian of student under age 18)*

_____

_____

Printed Name and Address

_____

Date

Fig. 4–1   *Sample Heinemann student permission request letter*

What are the risks of this study?
What are the benefits?
Who is funding this study? Will I be paid?
What about confidentiality?

Many eyes have rolled at the thought of obtaining Human Subjects clearance, but the point is to cover many kinds of research and to protect research subjects from harm.

Often, for classroom-based research, you can obtain a waiver for the long form for experimental research. Institutions differ in their policies about waivers, but again what never differs is the reason for this protective policy, at least for research conducted in the United States. In 1974, The National Research Act established the National Commission for the Protection of Human Subjects of Biomedical and Behavioral Research. Members of the commission came from diverse disciplines, including medicine, law, religion, and bioethics, and their job was to identify the basic ethical principles that should underlie research with human subjects. Prior to this, there had been far too many cases of research that harmed its subjects (itself a fascinating but ugly part of the history of human subjects research). Five years after their first meeting, in 1979, the Commission published what's commonly called the Belmont report, "Ethical Principles and Guidelines for the Protection of Human Subjects of Research." The report identifies three basic principles relevant to the ethics of research involving human subjects. We excerpt them for you here:

> *A. Respect for Persons.* The principle of respect for persons means respecting an individual's autonomy (his right to make decisions for himself). Individuals should participate in research voluntarily and be given enough information to make an informed decision about whether or not to participate. Three elements crucial to the informed consent process are information, comprehension, and voluntariness. . . . The way in which information is provided to the volunteer is as important as the information itself. The investigator should adapt the presentation of information to the subject's level of understanding. . . . Consent must be given under conditions that are free of coercion and undue influence. . . . Consent is valid only if the agreement to participate in the research is given voluntarily.

> *B. Beneficence.* The principle of beneficence requires that the investigator not only protect individuals from harm, but make efforts to secure

their well-being. . . . Risks to subjects may be balanced against the benefits to subjects directly, or to society as a whole. Risk may include consideration of psychological, physical, legal, social, and economic harm. Benefit, on the other hand, is the anticipated positive value of the research to either the subject directly or to society in terms of knowledge to be gained. . . . Beneficence thus requires that we protect against risk of harm to subjects and also that we be concerned about the loss of the substantial benefits that might be gained from research.

C. Justice. The principle of justice means that the benefits and burdens of the research are fairly distributed. For example, during the 19th and early 20th centuries the burdens of serving as research subjects fell largely upon poor ward patients, while the benefits of improved medical care flowed primarily to private patients. . . . In this country, in the 1940s, the Tuskegee syphilis study used disadvantaged, rural, black men to study the untreated course of a disease that is by no means confined to that population. . . . The principle of justice requires that there be fair procedures and outcomes in the selection of research subjects . . . at two levels: the social and the individual. . . . Social justice requires that distinction be drawn between classes of subjects that ought, and ought not, to participate in any particular kind of research, based on the ability of members of that class to bear burdens and on the appropriateness of placing further burdens on already burdened persons. (Human Subjects Office 2005, Chapter 2)

Professional organizations have their own ethical statements about research, and it's always interesting to see not only the similarities but also the differences, which vary with the purpose and interests of the sponsoring group. Among the organizations our students have consulted are the American Psychological Association, the American Folklore Society, the Museum Ethnographers Group, the Association of Internet Researchers. There are many others. Most national and international organizations' ethics statements are available in their printed material as well as on their websites. No matter who sponsors your research or whether you design a project entirely on your own, the three important themes of respect for persons, beneficence, and justice should govern your thinking about how you collect data, conduct interviews, talk about your research to others, and offer some return benefit to the people you involve in your study.

As one of our colleagues has observed, perhaps it would be useful for teachers to have such precisely articulated ethical statements about our

> ☼ *No matter who sponsors your research or whether you design a project entirely on your own, the three important themes of respect for persons, beneficence, and justice should govern your thinking about how you collect data, conduct interviews, talk about your research to others, and offer some return benefit to the people you involve in your study.*

practices with students in schools. Although we don't take an oath upon teacher certification (as doctors take the Hippocratic oath when they graduate from medical school) and we have no specific slogan like "first, do no harm," our choice to teach professionally brings with it an obligation and responsibility for the growth and well-being of the many people within our scope. We hope your research, and its accompanying headwork, will bring growth and well-being to you, your informants, and your school. And we certainly hope the ideas in this chapter will assist you.

◈ Mindwork: State Your Ethics

Most professional groups who engage in research and publishers who publish it have their own ethics statements. Go online and find a few ethics statements from different associations. Compare them, and then try to write an ethics statement for your own project, considering the three features of the Belmont report. It might be interesting, too, to attempt an ethics statement for teachers in your region, at your grade level, or in the discipline in which you teach. Writing your own ethics statement will help you write an informed consent form, in language your research subjects can understand, that will best explain your work and give you the information you'll need for any possible documentation or dissemination of your work.

SNAPSHOT IV: Deanna's Headwork Bears Fruit

In her study of Adam's writing, Deanna finds out—and demonstrates—that home literacy affects school literacy, at least for one child at one critical point in his life. She is able to document his mother's awe at the concentration Adam held while writing, his ability to name the authors and books that had influenced his story. She locates themes in his story and compares them to those in *The Lord of the Rings*: good versus evil, heroes as underdogs, kid heroes, action/excitement/danger, and friendship. She links these findings to the work of other literacy scholars (Anderson, Labbo, Martinez-Roldan, Dyson, Graves, Schneider, Newkirk).

After "The Journey" incident, Adam stops writing at home and begins writing simpler stories at school. Deanna wonders:

> Does Adam want to write? Does Adam feel free to write what he wants? "Oh, I wrote another story . . . it was called 'Froggy.' I haven't finished it. Daddy would like it better than the other." Adam's probably right. Has Jack read "Froggy"? Not according to Adam. "Since Daddy got upset I don't like letting people read my stories."

She goes on to describe the differences she sees in the "Froggy" story, and cites scholarship about the powerful influences television has on students' lives, that it is "the terrain of the student," and that educators can benefit from recognizing its presence in their work at school. She ends her essay with an "Implications" section that begins:

> I can only relate this one incident to you and share with you how parent reactions influenced one child's writing development at one time. We haven't begun to address the impact or influence that parents have on children's writing.

Deanna reminds us that her study details only one incident in one child's writing life. But, by taking multiple perspectives and positioning herself honestly, she delves into the hunches and intuitions many teachers and parents have.

Her study makes us question the stereotypes we have about how home literacy affects school literacy: sometimes in very literate homes, not unlike this one, incidents and family attitudes can temper a child's motivation and voice. She suggests that her research offers a chance for us to think further about the influence of home literacy on school literacy, of media on composition, and of parents' comments as they are filtered through children's experience.

Deanna's headwork—and her essay and presentation—will not make sweeping changes in any school's curriculum or anyone's home. But it does encourage many teachers to think carefully and fairly, perspective by perspective, about influences on children's writing. It enables Deanna herself to allow more discussion of this topic in her classes of preservice teachers. And it offers her a chance to pursue her hunches further in other projects.

Legwork
Pursuing Multiple Sources of Data

> We are far more dependent on the people we study than we can know or say. The rub, of course, is that by such an admission we must recognize that we are flying by the seat of our pants much of the time. There is risk here, but there is also truth.
>
> —JOHN VAN MAANEN, *Tales of the Field: On Writing Ethnography*

Researchers' data are like any other collector's "stuff": sports autographs, European dolls, 78 LP records, antique spice tins, vintage cars, plastic action figures. The more the stuff accumulates, the more collectors want to learn about its history and culture. They read books on related topics; cruise websites; talk to other collectors; buy and sell on the Internet; visit shops and museums that specialize in their interest; and even attend conventions to network and exchange information with others who have similar stuff, perhaps making trades or purchases. Their purpose is to expand and refine their collection—sometimes for others, sometimes for themselves—whether for display or investment. The more they learn, the closer they get to what they think they know.

The passion we see in collectors is also evident in determined researchers. They are always on the hunt. They look for unusual data in unusual places, limited only by their imagination. They empty trash cans to retrieve student writing, scribble interview notes on napkins, draw maps of playgrounds, and copy graffiti from bathroom walls. School researchers find themselves compelled to seek out data at field sites outside school, too, to confirm or dispel a hunch or to follow a lead. A student who may seem shy or disengaged at school might be a star somewhere else, like the daycare center, the uneven parallel bars, the wrestling mat, the church choir, the poetry slam, or the local diner. It's important to think broadly when you're planning your data collecting. Of course, not all data sources are equally useful, but the more places you think to look and the more data you collect, the more data you'll have from which to choose.

Once you've shaped a question, you see data everywhere and everything looks like a data source. The research lens is hard to take off once you put it on. Like a passionate collector, you're obsessed with your project. Eventually, your personal research journal and your boxes of data will bulge with field notes, student work, artifacts, relevant publications, transcripts from taped interviews, surveys, whatever your mind alerts you to collect. And of course you'll feel,

> ✿ *Of course, not all data sources are equally useful, but the more places you think to look and the more data you collect, the more data you'll have from which to choose.*

as Van Maanen does in this chapter's epigraph, as if you're "flying by the seat of your pants" as you watch it all accumulate. But as he also notes, although there is risk in this process, there is also truth. Researchers are tempted to collect widely like collectors do, but their ethical allegiance is to analyze and interpret, casting off extraneous information and following up on what's relevant to their research topic and its questions.

The risk and truth begin with you. As your project grows, you'll keep notes about your process, track your thinking as it changes with your ever-growing pile of evidence. But unlike a collector who simply accumulates, as a researcher you have a focused purpose: to answer the question you've developed using the information you've gathered. You hold on to your question with the same tenacity the collector does his possessions. Your study is relevant to you, to your school, and to your students. No one

> ✿ *Researchers are tempted to collect widely like collectors do, but their ethical allegiance is to analyze and interpret, casting off extraneous information and following up on what's relevant to their research topic and its questions.*

else could or would replicate it in quite the same way. It's in its particularity that your study will resonate with others. Like a particular musical theme, a poem, or a scene from a novel, a reflective research study helps other teachers identify with your situation and make their own connections within it.

So, how do you begin collecting your data? Try starting with the source that brought you to your question in the first place. Perhaps it's a note to yourself about something that puzzles you, a reminder to check on someone's cumulative record, a colleague's suggestion that you try lab notebooks, an article you read or a workshop you attended, an administrator's mandate that everyone should adapt a textbook you hate, or even, as we'll illustrate in our next chapter, the language a student uses when she speaks to you. Start with something you already have that might take you to another source. In Chapter 4, Deanna's research project came out of one perplexing question from Tricia, a student in her class who was sharing her frustration as a parent.

> ☼ Like a particular musical theme, a poem, or a scene from a novel, a reflective research study helps other teachers identify with your situation and make their own connections within it.

"Legwork" comprises the steps you take and the paths you follow to gather different types of data as you think about the range of artifacts and situations that provide evidence related to your study. We've identified seven useful categories of data sources teachers depend on for inquiry projects: yourself, student work, student histories, surveys and inventories, interviews, archives, and artifacts. Of course, these aren't the only kinds of sources. Your project, the people you study, and your imagination will lead you to others specific for you.

SNAPSHOT: Jan Reeder Collects Data About Book Clubs

Jan Reeder, a high school teacher in Missouri, is fed up with teaching novels to whole classes at a time. But as a reader herself, she loves book clubs. She decides to experiment with "literature circles," a book-club arrangement in which small groups of students select, read, and discuss one novel together. Jan chooses one student from each of two junior classes to follow closely as she implements her new approach. They are very different students: a high achiever who loves to read and a reluctant reader who often receives failing grades. During the study, Jan becomes very aware of how literature circles are changing her own teaching: "What if I had been given a few choices in my own education and blossomed before I was thirty? At my age, I still see that major growth is possible for me."

In addition to her research journal, Jan's data sources include regular interviews with the two focal students, their written responses to the novels, and classroom field notes, which she takes while the literature circles are meeting. Her study is strong as it stands. It answers her question, and enables her to continue to implement literature circles in subsequent years.

But if Jan were to extend this study further, she might choose to include several other kinds of data sources. To determine baseline information about her students, she might conduct an informal reading inventory to find out what kinds of reading they do—novels, stories, poems, magazines, newspapers, 'zines, websites, manuals—and thus get an overall portrait of all her students' reading preferences. Or she might assign a short reading biography, in which students tell their own stories of themselves as readers—when they first began to read; what their favorite childhood books were; what their all-time favorite piece of literature is; where they like to read; what their reading habits are; whether they have library cards, belong to nonschool book clubs, or share books with relatives or friends. Standardized reading scores, of course, would also provide information for Jan about students as readers.

To understand how the focal students interact within their literature circles, Jan might record the circle sessions, transcribe them, and analyze them for patterns. Verbatim records like this may reveal information she might miss while taking notes as she "listens in."

Should Jan want to know more about book clubs, she could research their history as they developed from early in American culture through the more contemporary incarnation of TV book clubs and "all-community reads."

Yourself as a Data Source

* Research journal

* Teacher logs

* Reflective notes

As we saw with Deanna in Chapter 4, using yourself as a data source is essential. However you choose to note your initial and ongoing thinking, you'll need to have some kind of record about how your understanding of the question changes as your research progresses. Whether you key in notes on your laptop, write them in a notebook next to your bed, or talk into a recorder while you're commuting, your own thoughts are a continuous inventory of your process. These reflective notes become particularly important when you review them in light of other data you collect. Keep a record so you won't forget your initial ideas as your understanding deepens and newer ones form. Chapter 4's three questions for reflection are useful ways to document your changing thinking: what are your assumptions? your positions? what tensions do you perceive?

Here's one example. Collyn Rybarczyk's younger brother was in her high school English class. She assumed he would resist her assignments, because she'd always thought of him as a lazy student. To her surprise, she found he was one of the most articulate co-researchers in her study about writer's notebooks. Because she'd been so wrong about this assumption, she started to question all of the assumptions she'd brought to her research. She wrote about this change, using quotes from entries in her journal as she assembled her final project.

Student Work as a Data Source

- ☀ Formal assignments: writing, drawing, posters and projects, journals and logs, portfolios, tests, performances

- ☀ Informal work: doodles, notes, personal websites, student-generated publications (song lyrics, 'zines, poems, program notes)

Student work, whether it's formal or informal, provides insights into how students construct their worlds and interpret ours—in their own language and oftentimes in genres that are not school-sponsored. Student work helps us see development over time, strengths and weaknesses, ranges of genre, as well as how these things relate to our teaching, our curriculum, and the standards by which we work. It's not surprising that many teacher-research projects depend almost entirely on collections of student work. Remember to get students' permission (and, if they're under eighteen, their parent/guardians' permission) to duplicate or study any piece of student work.

> ⚙ Student work, whether it's formal or informal, provides insights into how students construct their worlds and interpret ours.

When Elizabeth collected data on seven university students' literacies, a two-year study that resulted in her 1991 book, *Academic Literacies*, she found important clues in their private writing, doodles, and drawings, as well as in the assigned writing they did in courses across the curriculum (political science, art history, Russian literature, outdoor education). The students also kept class-assigned journals on their collaborative process as they wrote together in an advanced composition class, and the class's assigned reading logs allowed Elizabeth to examine themes that connected to their later writing. In addition, she worked with her focal students as they prepared for essay tests, saving their drafts for later analysis.

Student Histories as Data Sources

- School anecdotal records (guidance counseling, cumulative personnel folders, former teachers' comments)

- Standardized test scores

- Demographic data (school, town, state)

- Community alliances (after-school jobs, clubs, scout troops, churches, formal or informal athletic organizations, volunteer activities, lessons and training)

Student records and histories provide clues to their interests, talents, and challenges, both in the school beyond our classroom and in the larger community; they help bridge the gaps between school, home, and community. Records, remember, are confidential and as closed as the folders in which they reside. Don't go snooping without a reason or without sharing your intentions with your source. If you think knowing a student's history will be helpful, then of course explore it. A student's academic performance shouldn't be the sole influence on our judgments. A scout leader, cleric, athletic coach, or employer may provide insights that are not available from an administrator or a former teacher.

Steve Vanderstaay, a former high school teacher turned college professor, conducted an in-depth case study of one "juvenile offender" in an attempt to understand how the social justice system interacts with the education system. His research highlighted how agencies and institutions can ignore the needs of the people they serve by not sharing records efficiently or not collaborating with one another by making case histories available. Steve had access to all this data by obtaining signed releases and appropriate permissions from the young man, his family, his school, his probation officers, and his social workers and was careful to use it only in the best interests of his subject.

Steve examined the tests the young man took during his twelve years of school and the anecdotal records his teachers kept. He interviewed the young man's mother and other relatives, who shared family photographs and offered oral histories about his growing up. He obtained permission to examine police records, court records, probation records, and demographic information about the local crime rate and he read newspaper accounts of local crimes. Steve's is a fairly dramatic example of a research project that uses confidential student information but a fine example of an imaginative search through one person's accumulated records to arrive at a total portrait of that person.

Surveys and Inventories as Data Sources

- ☀ Published "instruments" designed to identify particular features of student learning (writing and speaking apprehension surveys, personality inventories, interest inventories)

- ☀ Unpublished (and sometimes anonymous) teacher-generated surveys designed to reveal student, family, or community member opinions or experiences

The survey provides baseline data. You can use a survey to choose informants for closer study or to reveal larger themes. Even when your research focuses on a few students, a creatively designed survey sharpens your overall picture of the larger group, its environment, and its specific features. Although surveys provide good background information, such data are not entirely reliable. Many people are put off by surveys and if they fill them out at all do so perfunctorily. And the results can't always be trusted, especially when the respondents remain anonymous. Use these instruments sparingly and only in connection with additional data that will confirm or challenge the results.

North Carolina teacher Christina Adams taught a journalism course focused on producing the high school yearbook. She used surveys and inventories throughout her study to spotlight the many skills students develop as they create a yearbook. In three surveys over the semester-long course, she asked her students questions about editing, interviewing, photography, business, accounting, marketing, copyrighting, computer design, and production. The questions ranged from open-ended ones ("What obstacles or difficulties did you face in your position as editor?") to ones with specific answers ("What factors will influence the price of the yearbook, and how can we plan to adjust for them?""What business contacts can you identify in the community from whom to solicit advertising support?"). From the surveys she identified the various skills she wanted her yearbook curriculum to address, and she was able to align these skills with state language arts standards, thus proving the value of the course. Her final curriculum project also included the philosophical background of experiential learning, interviews with members of the yearbook staff, students' reflections on their experience creating the yearbook, and sample text from the yearbook itself.

Interviews as Data Sources

- ☀ Notes on informal conversations with students, colleagues, parents, administrators, mentors, community members

- ☀ Taped and transcribed formal interviews with students, colleagues, parents, administrators, mentors, community members

- ☀ Taped classroom talk (pairs, small groups, large discussions, teacher conferences, meetings)

- ☀ Family, school, and personal stories

As we are using the term, an *interview* is a conversation (documented either by notes or a recording) in which key figures in your study talk (or sometimes don't talk!) to one another or to you. The conversation should be as natural as possible, with questions planned but never forced. When you allow the conversation to take its natural course, it will hold far more value than if you stage it using predesigned questions whose answers you've already anticipated. Interviewing, like good conversation, is a highly developed skill that takes practice, flexibility, risk, and empathy. The best interviews are those in which your interviewees talk more than you do. People usually enjoy having someone's focused attention and interest, so don't be afraid to ask for interviews and set them up. Be polite and prepared, and remember that someone's long digression may offer you more data than your carefully planned questions.

> ☼ *Interviewing, like good conversation, is a highly developed skill that takes practice, flexibility, risk, and empathy.*

Jeff Righter wanted to explore the relationship between reading and writing for his Florida high school juniors, asking "Could I encourage my students to adapt an 'aesthetic reading stance' by guiding them to craft their own poems and stories?" (Jeff's reference to "an aesthetic reading stance" comes from his exploration of Louise Rosenblatt's reader response theories [1978].) He interviewed three students monthly throughout the school year about their writing (multigenre projects and original poems) and the books he'd assigned them to read in his class. In all his interviews, Jeff was interested in identifying the language the students used to discuss their reading in relationship to the writing they'd done in his class. For instance, Chris admitted to a sharper eye in her writing ("I chose the word *winnowed* in my poem, because I think it conveys a softer tone because of the way it sounds") after having paid attention to the verbs in Robert Creeley's poem "Oh No" ("I can more easily pick out techniques by employing them in my writing"). Without responding to his research question directly, in her conversation Chris gave Jeff the information he was after.

Archives as Data Sources

- ☀ Records from town, school, home
- ☀ Museum collections
- ☀ Historical society collections
- ☀ Libraries' special collections
- ☀ Newspaper records
- ☀ Brochures, pamphlets, posters, kiosks, and bulletin boards
- ☀ Websites and public chat rooms
- ☀ Family attics, basements, trunks and scrapbooks, boxes and files

The records in an archive are not always organized for our particular purpose. Nevertheless, we need them to provide the historical background or long-range view of the issues we're trying to understand. Archival data can enrich or explain by bringing your ideas—and those of your subjects—to life. Give yourself the treat of exploring your town's public records, just to get a sense of what they contain. Other sources of public information (newspapers, brochures, websites) can help you place your studies within larger social and cultural contexts. Private collections offer a window into one family's (or one person's) place within a community or subculture. Websites are great

> ☼ **The records in an archive are not always organized for our particular purpose.**

examples of contemporary archives, in which both public and private information is stored, organized, and displayed according to the perspectives of their creators.

Expand your definition of what an archive is. Don't limit your hunt. You want your study to offer appropriate local knowledge, include historical information, and be enhanced with "local color." But remember, too, that for school-based studies, a single box of report cards, newspaper clippings, and students' drawings and projects can be a critical and useful archive.

Lia Schultz is a college administrator who has been both a teacher and a curriculum director at a community college. Lia was taken by a complicated idea. Many students label themselves "first-generation college-goers" even though a longer view of their family histories would prove otherwise (immigrants, for example, whose parents and grandparents were educated professionals in their countries of origin). Lia began with her own family's archives in an effort to understand who among her ancestors were "educated," and in what ways. The project stemmed from an exhibit that she and her mother had assembled for her rural Iowa town's sesquicentennial celebration, which included photographs, letters, diaries, and journals from townspeople. Lia's collection of old family textbooks had fascinating handwritten notes throughout, showing that the books had been traded from one sibling to another. But her father and grandfather had been farmers and claimed they were not "educated."

When Lia began to trace her family's educational history using archives in Washington, D.C., as well as several New England and Middle Atlantic states, she was able to chart the complicated path of schooling that members of her family took from their earliest arrival in pre-Revolutionary New England to their westward journey toward Iowa, generations later. What Lia found is an American story we don't often tell, because we don't trace it far enough. For many Americans, at various times and for various political, social, and economic reasons, the markers of a person's formal schooling do not tell the whole story. People in Lia's family had been formally educated prior to their move westward to the prairie. At certain times in American history, an eighth-grade education was the mark of an "educated person." Lia's archival work, still in progress, challenges the terms we often use without regard for their historical context: "first-generation college-goer" or "educated family" is much more complicated when we look closely.

Artifacts as Data Sources

- ☀ Mementoes (dried corsages, matchboxes, event programs)

- ☀ Photos, video or audio recordings

- ☀ Personal possessions (collections, trophies, sports memorabilia, quilts, wall hangings, stuffed animals)

- ☀ Unique classroom objects (a reader's chair, a stuffed bear, a lab desk, a special rug, a puppet, a candy jar, a windowsill full of plants)

Anthropologists use the term *material culture* to describe the artifacts that particular people use to represent themselves or their group affiliations. Questions about unique or interesting artifacts are often an interview's springboard. People are more comfortable telling the details of their lives and work through stories related to objects, pictures, or other possessions.

Don't let your research subject's material culture pass you by. Look around and ask questions about interesting things within the settings you're studying. Especially in schools, it's easy to ignore the special and unique material contributions teachers and students make to their environment. When you do notice artifacts, you'll most always find stories.

Sue Gradual, an art teacher in a rural New Hampshire elementary school, was involved in a two-year state community heritage project. With the help of Sue and her colleagues, the students in her school interviewed senior citizens (anyone over fifty) in the surrounding communities. The students returned with piles of stories about the sixties, the Cold War, Vietnam, the Great Depression, World War II, the roaring twenties, and life in their own towns during those eras. What was particularly remarkable about Sue's project was the material culture involved. She had each student create a rag doll (a rural New Hampshire tradition) to represent the interviewee. Tiny crafted artifacts on the dolls (bread pans, farm implements, ledger books, aprons, military regalia), showed the students' depth of understanding of the historical eras that affected their community and their living friends and relatives. Those artifacts became evidence for Sue that her art students were, in fact, researchers themselves.

> ⚙ When you do notice artifacts, you'll most always find stories.

Experts as Data Sources

- ☀ Books

- ☀ Speeches

- ☀ Articles in professional journals

- ☀ Magazines

- ☀ Web or Internet resources

- ☀ Films, videotapes, TV and radio programs

Any study you do as a teacher is a contribution to a professional conversation about your topic, whether you publish it or not. For that reason, you need to ground your study in the available source material, both professional and popular. If you're working your way through this book in sequence, you've already gathered a lot of background information through the "bridgework" you did in Chapter 3. As you're collecting data, be on the lookout for two self-defeating attitudes. First, thoroughly checking bibliographic resources could convince you that you have nothing further to say. You need to remember that no one will do your study in quite the same way you will, and no one will see your data—or combine your data—the way you will. Second—the reverse side of the coin—if you *don't* do a thorough background search, you could be surprised or uncomfortable when your colleagues or administrators refer to a related study, article, book, or documentary of which you're unaware.

Cathy Greenwood conducted a study she called "Getting Real—And Studying It." She required her students in a private New York middle school to "go public" with two pieces of writing each trimester (in the class's own publication, magazines that publish young writers, contests, or letters to an author or a public official). As a foundation for her work, she consulted experts herself, reading broadly about student publication (reviews for kids by kids in *Voices in the Middle*, published books by other teachers about publishing student writing). She listed magazines that publish student work. She interviewed a few master teachers about techniques for encouraging student writing. In a paper she wrote for our research class, she listed thirteen books about publishing student work and ten books about the research process. Eventually, Cathy published her project as a book for colleagues.

SNAPSHOT: Charlotte Foth Questions a Gendered Curriculum

Charlotte Foth is really bothered by what she has come to see as a male-oriented sophomore English curriculum in her Wisconsin high school. A professional development course has introduced her to issues of gender, a topic she hasn't thought much about in her many years of teaching. "Questioning the literary canon isn't unique to me," she notes, "it is a philosophical and pedagogical battleground for many." Her case study of two female sophomores and one male sophomore is titled "Where Are the Girls: Why Balancing the Sophomore English Curriculum Matters." Her yearlong research project becomes a strong argument for curriculum change, which her high school puts into effect.

Charlotte's legwork generates data from many sources. First, she inventories the old literature curriculum (*All Quiet on the Western Front*, *A Separate Peace*, *Julius Caesar*, and a series of short stories with male protagonists). Jenny, one of Charlotte's focal females, remarks on how the reading in class turns her off, "Everything we read is about guys and war."

Charlotte also begins her study with some thorough bibliographic research. She reads books and articles in two categories: gender awareness in teaching and professional commission reports. She also searches out literature with female characters to replace her school's traditional choices, which seem to focus heavily on males. Eventually, she settles on *Antigone*, *The Pearl*, and *The Diary of Anne Frank*.

She interviews her three focal students many times as she gradually introduces the new curricular choices. Her transcripts offer interesting insights: "After reading *Antigone*, Molly shared that she began to have the courage to start talking more in class." Charlotte sees immediately that her female students better identify with female characters. But her finding is not limited to females. Adam, too, gives *A Separate Peace* an F and *The Pearl* an A, remarking, "You picture yourself in that person's shoes, think about what you would do if you were them, and then you read on."

Obviously, three students' evaluations of three standard texts as they're being replaced by three others doesn't provide enough data for making a curriculum change. That alone won't convince anyone. But Charlotte also collects broader student data. At the end of the year, she surveys her three sophomore classes (about a hundred students) to determine which literature has been their favorites and why, as well as how literature has made them rethink their own lives.

More data come from the student journals in Charlotte's three classes. The writing prompts they design indicate their interest in gender-related topics:"Describe the perfect guy or girl." "Who has it easier, guys or girls?" "What characteristics annoy you about the opposite sex?" Charlotte also gathers almost a hundred reader responses about their identification with heroes, heroines, protagonists. Charlotte herself notices that her class discussions have changed: "There was little dialogue or interaction when I was teaching male-only literature, but class discussions came alive again when I began to include gender-balanced reading."

Polling her students, analyzing their journal topics and reader responses, and documenting her own reaction to their class contributions leads Charlotte to design one more data source. Since she frequently asks her students to role-play in class, she has her students write about who plays what roles."I wondered, what do girls think when they see boys bargaining to get out of playing the role of a girl? Why is it that when asked if they had a choice of what sex they would want to be, most girls said they would like to be boys, but not one boy said he would like to be a girl?"

Charlotte looks closely at the writing of her three focal students from the viewpoint of gender-related themes and then interviews each one in connection with a finished piece of writing. Molly, for example, has written an essay about spousal abuse in *The Pearl*. In a follow-up interview, Molly suggests, "I think I would have a speaker come in and talk about abuse in relationships, maybe. Get all your classes together, maybe not the whole school, just while we're doing this book. Or, maybe do some research and get another teacher or somebody from guidance to talk."

Charlotte's data include seven sources: her own research journal, polls and surveys, student work (journal prompts, reader responses, formal essays), transcribed interviews with her focal students, her role-play field notes, student accounts of their reactions to role playing, and a wide range of bibliographic material in two categories. This combined data and her systematic study of it give Charlotte the expertise she needs to convince her English department colleagues to institute a change in the sophomore curriculum.

Eyework
Methods and Methodologies

The sense of discovery and excitement that pervades a classroom is not simply a set of words; it is a set of qualities, including a sense of energy that must somehow be made palpable through prose.... One does not—nor can one—tell it all ... the writer must be selective in both perception and disclosure. The making of a fine meal does not require the use of everything in the pantry.

—ELLIOTT W. EISNER, *The Enlightened Eye*

- Historical Approaches
- Quantitative Approaches
- Linguistic Approaches
- Ethnographic Approaches
- Approaches Featuring Cultural Critique

There she is, Stacy, sitting in the corner, staring out the window, yawning, a ring in her nose, an asymmetrical haircut, large-rimmed glasses, torn carpenter jeans, and a shrunken tee shirt. We're mystified by her mixture of anger, resistance, bewilderment, inattention, and her honesty about how bored she is. When we pass her desk, she smiles and says, as she always does, "What's up?" as though she wants us to know she's there but hasn't a clue that we expect her to be writing.

The anxiety we feel stimulates questions. Sometimes we answer the questions formally. Sometimes one set of questions leads to another. Sometimes we don't answer the questions with which we began. But always, we learn something about ourselves, our students, and their perspectives. Always, when we ask questions, our research teaches us something about our teaching.

Knowing our choices of methods and methodologies helps us articulate and follow our questions in an orderly way. *Methodology* and *method* are not interchangeable terms, although they are frequently used that way.

A methodology is the academic home sheltering a family of methods. Methodology is the philosophy and theory—in short, the fundamental ideas—that undergird our research. Methods are the activities we use (journal keeping, taping and transcribing, interviewing, running numbers and graphing statistics, looking through archives, searching the Web) to conduct research.

We've invented Stacy (a shortening of the metaphorical "Stasis") and her (slightly exaggerated) situation as a means to tour some of the formal methods and methodologies from which teacher-researchers draw. We'll introduce key methodologies and the research activities that accompany them, offer a mind-work exercise for each methodology, and accompany it with a short snapshot of a teacher who's tried the particular set of methods. The fundamental idea in this chapter is this: what you see depends on how you look. We think of it as "eyework."

> ⚙ *Methodology is philosophy and theory; methods are the activities we use to conduct research.*

Teacher research is a hybrid methodological approach; in teacher research we use whatever we need to answer a question and share our findings. We sometimes mix quantitative and qualitative research approaches. Teacher research draws on the academic disciplines that support us as educators: sociology, anthropology, psychology, history, linguistics, mathematics, the natural sciences, and much of the "liberal arts." Every research design needs to have a *dominant* methodology (as Eisner writes in the chapter epigraph, "The making of a fine meal does not require the use of everything in the pantry"). On the other hand, when we're engaged in school-based inquiry, we draw from whatever resources we can to determine where to look next.

> ⚙ *What you see depends on how you look.*

Stacy's Backstory

There are any number of possible explanations for Stacy's confusing behavior and her self-identified boredom. Her records include test scores, teacher comments over the years, grades, and occasional memos from guidance counselors. She's never been tested for anything "special," either giftedness or learning disabilities. Her mother left the family two years ago, and Stacy lives with her father and five brothers. Her larger extended family has lived in the town for four generations and owns a local hardware store where she works after school. We went to school with her two aunts, one of whom is now our colleague in the local middle school.

Looking at Stacy's daily journal, we find occasional entries about science fiction novels and video games: a total of eight pages about the plots and characters. One journal entry discusses her feelings about working in the hardware store and a fight she had with her older brother. Fourteen daily entries are missing, and three times during this report period she didn't turn in the formal writing assignments based on the journal. We had to give her a D for this quarter in English. As far as we know, she doesn't stay after school for any activities, and in general has no close friends, either male or female. We tried sketching a sociogram during class group work, an old tool we learned in graduate school. (A kind of flowchart of how seating affects class interactions. Draw arrows on a seating chart. Designate who interacts with whom—and when.) It showed that many students would be glad to work with Stacy, but no one ever selected her as a first choice, at least not while we were looking. Confirmed our hunch. Because of her low grade in English, we're wondering whether it's time to arrange a meeting with the guidance counselor or to call her father.

Our own research journal shows that she has placed one draft of her writing in the revision box for peer response. Her reading log lists six books, but her writing folder and portfolio are thinner than anyone else's. During one third-period class in October, in a ten-minute focused observation, our research notes reveal that she chewed her pencil vigorously six times (as if she were hungry), tugged on her nose ring (which we think must have hurt), stared out the window for three minutes straight, wrote in her journal for two minutes, and then opened her book bag, pulled out a box of colored pencils, and drew one picture in her journal for five minutes. At the end of our observation, she ripped out her drawing, scrunched it, and shot it into the wastebasket.

We're certainly—but unconsciously—engaged in many types of teacher research related to Stacy. Our thoughts and observations about this student are so deeply ingrained and automatic that we would not call what we're doing "teacher research." But in fact, it is. Our ten-minute focused observation of Stacy (noting chewing, tugging, and drawing) shows the skills of a seasoned researcher. We've learned the value of observation and note taking in inservice workshops on qualitative research, the sociogram years ago in a university sociology course. But we also use quantitative methods when we count the pieces of Stacy's writing, note what is there and what is missing. We record the number of books Stacy has read. We compare Stacy's portfolio to those of her peers. We translate all these numbers into a holistic evaluation and eventually a grade. Pursuing our hunches informally, we look at Stacy's history—her records, her life outside school, her family. We further investigate Stacy's uses of language—in her talk and in her writing. We begin to form a type of cultural critique based, perhaps, on Stacy's missing mother—or on Stacy's passion for science fiction.

Historical Approaches

Historical methodology answers a research question by looking at its past in an attempt to create a narrative to support the evidence. Historical researchers work with records, archives, maps, drawings, publications (newspapers, books, letters, journals, films, websites), oral histories, and interviews. They document visits to museums, historical houses, historical societies, exhibits, important field sites.

Using historical methodology in a teacher research project about Stacy, we investigate the genealogy of her family in this town, including the history of the hardware store. We interview her aunts, her brothers, her father, and other relatives who have known this girl as she's grown up. We look at old newspapers for accounts of her ancestors as well as articles about the family business.

> ⚙ *Historical methodology answers a research question by looking at its past in an attempt to create a narrative to support the evidence.*

More specific historic educational research includes her school records (transcripts, test scores, grades over the years); from them we arrive at a pattern of academic achievement. We conduct informal interviews with her previous teachers, administrators, and guidance counselors. We try to find out if there are other records available to us through her church, Girl Scout or camp leaders, or athletic directors. As her teachers, our major concern is to understand her educational history. (Some of the records are appropriately inaccessible for important ethical reasons.)

Worried about her ungainly glasses, we investigate school medical records for eye problems and discover that she hasn't had an eye examination since her mother left. Even though the hardware store's financial records are publicly available, we realize they'll shed little light on Stacy's situation. A journey through the town newspaper archives reveals information about Stacy's family's athletic achievements and civic contributions. We also discover that the hardware store has always prided itself on its corner lending library. Is this where Stacy gets her interest in science fiction?

On the other hand, we also know that too much historical information may get us off the track. We try to guard against gathering data that leads to inappropriate conclusions or recommendations.

SNAPSHOT: George McLaughlin Tracks Down Immigrant Town History

George McLaughlin, a high school history teacher in Rhode Island, is curious about how new immigrants adjust to the history of their communities. He and his ESL students, together, want to understand their immigrant neighborhood as it was a hundred years ago. George's students come from Vietnam, Brazil, and Eastern Europe, but they know that earlier inhabitants of their neighborhood have been Irish and Portuguese. In their archival research and their observations around town, they discover intriguing information about one man who came to the town from Ireland about a hundred years ago. They look through old newspapers, photographs in the historical society, library holdings about the wave of Irish immigration at the turn of the last century, and the original house where the man lived. As a result of their research, George and his students are able to reconstruct this man's influence, first as a shady criminal and later as a town leader. Eventually, their historical research becomes a museum exhibit and a local festival celebrating immigration in Rhode Island. For George, the project offers insights about active community involvement as immigrant students help construct the history of their new homeland.

Quantitative Approaches

Many funded research studies in education present the evidence in numbers, charts, and tables. We're accustomed to reading about "scientifically based" studies that count and predict as they evaluate our diets and bodies, our cars and vacuum cleaners, our favorite movies and TV programs, even our pumpkin-growing abilities. American culture lends high credibility to measurement and outcomes that offer a way to identify and reward the "bottom line." For example, it's more cost effective to teach over thirty students per class, but decades of research and thousands of teachers suggest that smaller class sizes yield better teaching and learning.

Quantitative methodology can help us understand many features of schooling (and of daily living): how many students, how many desks, how many books, how many minutes per class period or block, what weights and percentages to attach to what assignments within a grading period. We chart daily attendance. We fill out spreadsheets and graphs for student evaluations. We write annual reports that must include numbers and statistics about almost everything we've done and everything we want to request for the year to come. Numbers rule in our culture; we use them to organize and represent what otherwise seems chaotic.

> ⚙ *American culture lends high credibility to measurement and outcomes that offer a way to identify and reward the "bottom line."*

Quantitative methodology answers questions we can't answer any other way. Using numbers and statistics as methods, we're able to identify and visualize both inequity and fairness: per-pupil spending, tax dollars applied across school systems, reading and math scores as they relate to local socioeconomics. Creating a pie chart or a bar graph lets us better envision comparative data about very focused items: How many students answered question 3 correctly on a statewide reading test? How many twenty-minute tutoring sessions do I need to offer per week in order to accommodate the overall student body in my basic skills center? How many kids from downtown Chicago interpret the word "shucking" differently from Iowa farm

> ⚙ *Numbers rule in our culture; we use them to organize and represent what otherwise seems chaotic.*

kids on a standardized vocabulary test item? How many students who take advanced placement courses earn college credit for their work? Like any research methodology, a good quantitative study involves creative thinking, inventive design, and careful analysis.

The purely quantitative study, as a part of the traditional scientific method, is based on a researcher's hypothesis that the study will either prove or disprove. In order to investigate hypotheses and achieve statistical validity and reliability, researchers need to conduct their studies with large numbers of people ("N"). It's only from large numbers that a study can generalize from its sample to a population as a whole.

To include Stacy in a quantitative study, she would need to be one among many. We could study where her scores fit in relation to other ninth graders, girls, white middle-class students, children of business owners, students who prefer science fiction, families who have been in towns for four generations. A more focused study might look at factors influencing school achievement for ninth-grade girls and boys who work twenty hours a week after school at family businesses, come from single-parent households, or read science fiction and have above-average reading scores. These studies would place Stacy inside a larger population and answer important questions about very specific features of her life in and out of school.

Important information about Stacy comes from quantitative research into her own records. Hypothesizing that she is a strong reader with tastes that don't fit her school's literary values, we analyze her standardized reading test scores for the ten years from kindergarten through ninth grade. Finding she was always at least two grade levels ahead of her peers, we wonder about the reading choices in the traditional curriculum, which don't include Stacy's interest in science fiction. Hypothesizing that her mother's absence has affected her school achievement, we graph her grades over time, perhaps finding a huge dip during the year her mother left, perhaps not. Hypothesizing that her school attendance is influenced by her boredom, we chart her attendance over the years and look for patterns. Noticing sporadic attendance each year in early spring, we wonder whether she puts in extra hours at the hardware store when gardening season begins. To monitor her distractibility in class, we count how many times she shifts tasks during a ten-minute period in each of her classes for a week and then create a chart showing this information. Wanting to better understand her social contexts, we wonder whether she has some key friends we don't know about. We prepare additional sociograms for each of her other classes to see if she has peers who choose to work with her, and then design a comparative chart.

A quantitative focus on Stacy results in a package of statistical visuals that show her in relation to her classes, her school, her town, her state, her region, and country. But depending on the data, we can also see her in relation to race, class, gender, age, and her generation in contemporary history. These kinds of data put Stacy into larger contexts and give us information and clues to follow in our research. However, while useful, this information is not contextualized, nor is it particular to Stacy. It may not help us at all with the problem of why Stacy claims she's bored in school.

No one quantitative study can account for the large range of contextual factors that influence any particular person's learning. Quantitative researchers are often pressured to generalize beyond the scope of their findings. The ethical challenge of quantitative research is to design studies that matter, use the information they produce wisely, and account for their limitations. But to see quantitative research in opposition to other methodologies is not to understand the power that creatively chosen numbers and statistics and brilliantly conceived quantitative research designs can have in supporting other methodologies.

◈ Mindwork: Count, Measure, and Chart

Identify something related to your research project that you can measure or quantify. For example, an English teacher might count the number of pages and drafts that 150 students write when they have free choice and compared them with the number of pages and drafts written on an assigned topic. A math teacher could count the number of alternate ways 60 students use to solve one math problem, as demonstrated in their math portfolios. A biology professor might chart the midterm grades of 500 freshmen to see if they are an indicator of who will pass the first-year biology course. An art teacher could compare 100 students' use of perspective in their drawings prior to and after a formal unit on perspective in the Renaissance.

Next, gather your data and decide a few different ways you might represent it visually. Choose a standard form: a bar graph, a line graph, a table, a pie chart, a plot configuration (scatterplot, stem-and-leaf, box-and-whisker), or perhaps simply a list. As you're graphing or charting, you'll see patterns emerge that may be helpful to your research, no matter what methodology or methods you've chosen to dominate your study.

SNAPSHOT: Hayley Walton Checks Time-on-Test

Hayley Walton, a middle school language arts teacher in Ohio, wants to see how much time during an academic year is devoted to testing in her school, particularly in preparation for the statewide writing test. She gathers evidence: school notices about the tests, announcements via email and intercom, inservice preparation workshops required for teachers, practice time in her classroom, meetings with her interdisciplinary team devoted to test-taking strategies, conferences with students and parents anxious about the testing process, actual time devoted to the tests, and time spent discussing the tests with students afterward. She also gathers information about how various local schools publicize and disseminate the state scores. Hayley's school is neither labeled "at-risk" nor does it reward salary increments according to student scores, although both practices are common across the United States. However, Hayley feels the pressure for her students to excel, and she confirms her intuition that her school spends more time on testing than it does on curriculum or classwork. She's used quantitative tools creatively to prove her hypothesis. Backed up by data illustrated clearly in numerical and visual displays, she is able to prove to her colleagues and principal that testing time is swallowing up curriculum time.

Linguistic Approaches

Linguistic methodology focuses on language, both oral and written: the features of text and talk. Linguistic researchers might collect personal writing, published writing, transcripts of conversations or interviews, environmental print (graffiti, local signs), and certain kinds of verbal performance (slang, jargon, forms of word play), in order to analyze the features of oral and written discourse.

Applying a linguistic methodology to Stacy involves studying the written and oral language that surrounds her: her own, her school's, her peers', her family's. We gather evidence of her written language from her journal, her assignments, her folders, and her portfolios to try to determine patterns of interests and abilities. One formal assignment, for example, reveals that Stacy has mastered compound and complex sentences,

> ⚙ *Linguistic methodology focuses on language, both oral and written: the features of text and talk.*

understands the correct use of the semicolon, and shows sophisticated vocabulary and syntax for her age level. In her reading log, we see Stacy adopting jargon and scientific language from science fiction novels as she summarizes the plots and describes the characters. If we are lucky, we are able to look at the notes she passes to others in our class or retrieve her drawings from the wastebasket and check the captions or phrases she's written to accompany them. We begin to realize that she uses written language well within the scope of what's appropriate for her age.

If our linguistic approach considers oral rather than written language, we listen to Stacy's talk in a variety of contexts. We record her as she participates in a writing group, a whole-class discussion, and a conference with us. We tape her interactions with customers at the hardware store. We invite her and a few of her peers for a focused interview about the latest video games. We interview Stacy, her other teachers, her peers, her family, and others who know her in order to analyze linguistic features of her talk—for example, her use of the phrase "What's up?" Can she shift registers? Does she say "What's up?" to her other teachers? Does she use this phrase with her peers? Her customers? Her grandparents? Shifting registers, to a linguist, is often an indication of someone's awareness within particular social contexts. As we analyze, we wonder whether "What's up?" is simply a teenage affectation or an indication of her inability to understand what's appropriate in different situations.

Of course, language is only one dimension of a learner's toolkit. It would be unethical to draw limiting conclusions based on writing or talk, particularly when we take words out of context. On the other hand, language is the means by which we communicate. To exclude linguistic methods in our work in schools is irresponsible.

◈ Mindwork: Document Oral Language

The language used in our classrooms is often invisible unless we consciously make it part of our research. Record twenty minutes of class conversation—not a lecture or a minilesson, but a discussion between you and your students. Listen to the tape a few times, looking for moments of tension or complications or cross-purposes, and then transcribe such a five-minute segment: write it down word for word;

Continued on next page

Continued from previous page

identify who says what; include pauses, speech inflections, and tone; and be sure to note the time and date of the conversation.

Next, analyze this transcript for a single feature:

◈ Number of topic changes

◈ Conversational turns

◈ Interruptions

◈ Frequent uses of certain vocabulary

◈ Questioning techniques

◈ A linguistic element of your choice.

Write a description of this little slice of language, from your point of view, and then speculate on what the students' perspectives might have been during the same five minutes. How could this linguistic information be useful or relevant to your classroom-based research? What might the students say about it? In a fuller linguistic study, you'd want to share the tape and transcript with your students or colleagues and identify any differences between your analysis and theirs.

SNAPSHOT: Carol Center Hears Herself Talk

One semester Carole Center, an instructor at an urban university in Massachusetts, decides to study her classroom discussion techniques in her basic writing class. She tapes, transcribes, and analyzes moments of discussion and is surprised at what she finds: she dominates her class discussions. "I am involved too much. . . . I spoke about 30 percent of the time . . . which was forty-six times during a thirty-minute discussion. In comparison, the next two most frequent speakers spoke seventeen and sixteen times, respectively. I dominated the discussion by speaking frequently while the students were speaking, either interrupting to take back the conversational initiative or comment about their talk while they were talking." She notices, too, as she listens for language, that she asserts her authority when she "calls students on" their use of "questionable" language: terms such as "white trash," "gay," "retard," "sucks," "bullshit." Carole pays attention to linguistic features in her classroom to see how she is conducting discussions and how she can improve that process.

Ethnographic Approaches

Ethnographic methodology considers the entire culture in which people live and interact, answering the broad question, "What's going on here?" Ethnographic researchers notice, record, and interpret rituals, rules, behavior, materials, and language within specific, particular settings. Ethnographic methods include mapping space, listening for language, interviewing people, gathering materials, observing and documenting daily activities within a culture or subculture. While ethnographers enter a culture as outsiders, their goal is, over time, to understand the perspective of insiders in that culture and combine those perspectives. In other words, as we describe in Chapter 2, they become both participants and observers.

> ⚙ *Ethnographic methodology considers the entire culture in which people live and interact, answering the broad question, "What's going on here?"*

As ethnographic researchers studying Stacy, we quietly observe and take field notes, with permission, on her school day, her interactions at the hardware store, and over time, perhaps, her position within her family setting. We hang out with Stacy, accompanying her as often as possible in as many settings as possible, for as long as possible, attempting to understand Stacy's insider "worldview" without losing our own. Our eventual goal is to create a textured story of the culture and subcultures to which Stacy belongs. We may end up writing about Stacy as she behaves in several different classes at school, at home, and at the hardware store to construct a fuller story about the culture in which she lives.

To accomplish such a portrait, we spend many months gathering observational field notes about Stacy in context. We transcribe taped interviews, sketch and map the spaces she inhabits, collect materials from Stacy's many subcultures (her chewed pencil, her discarded drawing, her journal entries, her school records, her interactions with customers, job evaluations, and, with her and her father's permission, records of her participation in other organizations to which she belongs). Using multiple data sources, we attempt to create the narrative of Stacy's story as both she and we interpret it.

Any method that helps us see Stacy's perspective will be useful. To enrich (anthropologists use the term *thicken*) our collection of evidence, we draw from other methodologies. We might conduct historical research about Stacy's family and look linguistically at her writing, as linguistic and historical researchers do. We might collect statistics and demographics and other kinds of quantifiable information: her stanine scores, her salary raises at the hardware store, how many hours per week she babysits. We add this material to our ever-expanding stash of field notes and material evidence about what we've seen and heard as we've spent time with Stacy.

We might use this data to represent Stacy in terms of contemporary adolescent life, ninth grade in American schools, or one or another sub-culture to which she's attached. In fact, we go into our enthnographic re-search not exactly knowing what goes on in Stacy's culture, what her story is, or where within her culture she fits. The ethical dilemma we face is iden-tifying with Stacy so deeply that we are unable to offer any useful obser-vations or interpretations. Becoming too much of an insider (or too much of an outsider), we use the material Stacy has shared with us to tell a story that serves our interests but does not appropriately serve hers, her family's, or her school's.

While teacher research borrows much from ethnographic methods, we cannot presume to claim that we're "doing ethnography" or even conduct-ing "mini ethnographies," since as teachers we cannot ever fully adopt the outsider's or fieldworker's point of view in our own classrooms, nor can we spend large chunks of singularly dedicated time to creating a full-blown ethnographic study while we are teaching.

◈ Mindwork: Try Ethnographic Observation

Understanding what happens in cultural contexts requires a number of data-gathering techniques, all of which depend on close observations, recorded in thickly detailed field notes. Visit a colleague's class over a period of time (at least three visits, during your planning period, for example) and gather as much information as you can.

On one visit, try to map the use of space:

◈ Where are the bulletin boards and what's on them?

◈ Where does the teacher place her desk?

◈ How much time does your colleague spend at the desk? Elsewhere in the room?

◈ What's the configuration of the students' desks?

◈ Where are the books and supplies and how often do the students use them?

◈ What special items do you see that are unique to this classroom?

Continued on next page

Continued from previous page

◈ How do the teacher and the students interact? Create some kind of map or chart detailing at least five minutes of interaction.

On another day, observe the people:

◈ Watch one student for five minutes, recording her physical behavior as well as her language in great detail, including the times she's interrupted or distracted.

◈ Watch your colleague's language and behavior for five minutes.

◈ Record other details in the classroom, like signs, posters, PA announcements, audiovisual equipment, computers either in use or at rest.

◈ Count or assess something that interests you: slogans on tee-shirts, types of shoes, colors of book bags, hair styles, the classroom's architectural details (ceiling tiles, floorboards, blackboards, whiteboards, window arrangements, heating and ventilation systems).

By the third day, this mass of information should suggest a particular idea that will help answer "what's going on here?" Follow up on a theme or two that you see in your first two days of field notes. Say you've noticed a cluster of students passing notes while they were supposed to be reading silently. This observation generates more questions:

◈ Are these note passers otherwise active in classroom discussions?

◈ Is this activity taking up all their time?

◈ How much reading are they doing in class?

Write a memo to yourself about what other data you'd collect to confirm or contradict what you think you've discovered in these three days of observation. Interview the teacher, the cluster of students, the students who sit around them. Look at their reading journals, scores, or grades. Most important, watch again to see if this is a continual habit or pattern.

SNAPSHOT: Wendy Caszatt-Allen's Eighth Graders Meet College Writers

Wendy Caszatt-Allen, a language arts teacher in a middle school in rural Iowa, conducts a study with her students and a class of preservice teachers. Eighth grader–university student pairs keep "conversation journals" over a semester, acting as full collaborative writing partners. Each pair shares a single journal. Each week there is a specific writing task for both the eighth grader and the college student, and each week they respond to each other.

In her notes, Wendy describes her eighth graders' enthusiasm when they read the new entries from their university partners. "I hauled the journals back and forth between my classroom and the university, finally purchasing a cart because back strain became a real issue. When I rolled my cart into my eighth-grade classroom, their curiosity razored in on the crate of spiral-bound notebooks. Nothing until they had been passed out. An intense silence followed. Concentration. Then readings punctuated by giggles: "Look at this!""What did she write this time?""Oh, wow, look at this!"

Wendy describes an encounter she has with Justin and Jordan, who both are partnered with university student Laura:

> Laura has decorated the inside front cover with drawings in fine marker. Trees, a little red bicycle, water, music notes, a cross-stitch hoop cloth, pictures of books (*To Kill a Mockingbird*, *World Atlas*), images of water, fish, clouds, rain and sun, moon and stars, all as indications of "self." Justin and Jordan smother the back of the notebook with pictures of K.I.S.S. in full, uncensored glory. They work hard and diligently all period, borrowing a glue stick and markers from me. Just before the end of class, the two boys approach me.
>
> "Should we cover it up?" Justin asks, showing me the close-up of one of the band members with his tongue extended.
>
> "We could rip it out," Jordan answers. "The glue isn't really dried yet."
>
> "We don't want to scare her, Ms. Allen," Justin explains. What I really think is that for these two boys and their college partner, collaboration was born at that moment.

Wendy combines description, dialogue, and details from the setting to re-create a focal scene that illustrates two of her students better understanding their university partner within the cultural space that is her own classroom.

Approaches Featuring Cultural Critique

Researchers who approach a study with a particular ideological or political agenda are engaged in cultural critique. The research will be influenced by contemporary theory: feminist, Marxist, postcolonialist, psychoanalytic, traditionalist, fundamentalist, localized, regionalized. No matter what methods they use, cultural critics are sensitive to clues of power, race, ethnicity, gender, and class as they gather and interpret their data. They announce their theoretical agenda at the outset, and it influences how they conduct the entire study, analyze the data, and design the final product.

> ⚙ Researchers who approach a study with a particular ideological or political agenda are engaged in cultural critique.

Here are some simplified examples.

Studying Stacy within a psychoanalytic framework, we examine all of Stacy's writing and talk for evidence of how she feels about her absent mother, her disconnection from her feelings, her overidentification with her brothers and father, and her inability to bond with other girls.

Within a postcolonial framework, we see Stacy's writing and classroom behavior as it's been shaped by the power and language of a school system that dominates her, leaving her with neither choices nor personal agency. Her boredom illustrates her resistance to the colonizing power the teacher represents. We are interested in the drawing in her journal—and how she throws it out—and note her reluctance to conform to the requirements of her assignments.

A Marxist critique of Stacy's situation focuses on class and power differences among the students in the school and within the context of the town overall. Stacy's family has lived here for four generations and as owners of a business have a higher-than-average income; their work in the hardware store and their loyalty to their customers suggests working-class values. A class-based analysis of Stacy emphasizes that she's surrounded by males, chooses to wear carpenter pants, hangs out at the video arcade, works in the hardware store, and has few peers as friends. We observe her school behavior and examine her reading choices and writing themes for indications that she's marginalized by her class identity and by the school system.

Like any other research lens, cultural critique has limitations. It can only tell part of the story. For instance, we can be so involved in looking at issues of class that we ignore features of Stacy's life that may lead to different interpretations. By collecting statistics about the family's finances and their leadership in the town, we would discover how solidly middle class the family is. Conducting interviews with Stacy and her family, we might discover how proud the family is of their business success and their financial comfort. Looking at Stacy in school, we might not notice that her sporadic achievement doesn't match her high scores on tests or that her pencil chewing and elaborate drawings suggest she's a visual learner. The danger of any theoretical lens is that it drives us to look only according to a pre-established agenda. Yet to ignore issues of power, gender, race, or class in a school or a community is equally dangerous.

> ⚙ *The danger of any theoretical lens is that it drives us to look only according to a pre-established agenda. Yet to ignore issues of power, gender, race, or class in a school or a community is equally dangerous.*

Critical theory offers important research possibilities. Understanding cultural critique enriches our ability to see the social and political forces that surround our schools and communities. But no one intellectual theory or category is ever sufficient to account for the complexity of the lives of teachers and learners in their real-world contexts.

◈ Mindwork: Try Critiquing Culture

As a teacher who prides yourself on thinking about equity, it's sometimes counterintuitive to critique your own classroom. But it's important to discern the subtle cultural tensions within any group. Whether we admit it or not, these tensions are there.

If you are reading this book for a university course, have one person bring to class an assortment of food items from which to assemble a snack for the whole group. Be sure these items are not obviously compatible or easily divisible (cheese and crackers, or ten apples for ten people, for example). Put them in a large grocery bag so the class doesn't see them in advance. Ask two volunteers to leave the room, identifying some difference between them (male and female, old and young, shy and assertive, etc.). After the volunteers leave, assign pairs or groups of participants to take different kinds of field notes from different methodological perspectives: power, gender, use of space, use of time, use of language (turn taking or topic changes, the actual words each snack maker uses). After the note takers understand their tasks, invite the two snack makers into the room to use the contents of the bag to make a snack for all members of the group. The only conversation can be between the two snack makers, and the note takers must concentrate only on their assigned topic.

This exercise reveals two very powerful ideas. First, observation from a particular point of view (linguistic, spatial, temporal, cultural, power orientation) yields very focused data. Second, the more pairs of eyes and

Continued on next page

Continued from previous page

ears recording one simple human interaction in a single setting, the richer and more detailed the data, however ordinary the situation. Whether you plan to conduct studies alone or with co-investigators, this exercise makes you aware of how much there is to see in any human cultural setting or exchange and how much data can emerge from even ten minutes of observation. It invariably illustrates the complexity of studying human action within a limited period of time in a particular context, since many people watching the same event will have a variety of interpretations, even within their assigned focus. Any study, whatever the methodologies or methods, needs to capture many slices of data informed by different perspectives.

(If you're interested, here are some examples of how this exercise has played out. An older woman and a younger man reverted to maternal dominance and childlike obedience. Two young women, drawing on their pasts as waitresses, produced an assembly line for spreading peanut butter on apple slices, serving everyone from a common tray they made from a notebook. A snack maker with a theater background took on the role of the host of a TV cooking show, relegating her partner to carrying out the tasks as she narrated them.)

SNAPSHOT: Mary McCullough Studies Ethnicity in Sixth-Grade Friendships

Mary McCullough coordinates the longest-running voluntary busing program in the country, the METCO program between Boston and its suburbs. METCO began in the late 1960s as an attempt to provide "quality education for urban students of color and lessen the racial isolation of white suburban students." Mary has worked for this program since it began, and she has seen the demographics change with the generations. Black families have moved comfortably to the suburbs, and immigrant populations of various racial backgrounds are now bused into the suburbs.

Her research focuses on how sixth-grade girls of different racial and class backgrounds maintain their school friendships. Her experience as a middle-class suburban black adult who has worked for METCO for so many years determines her political agenda. She indeed discovers that class trumps race and that even in a program in which a "host" family is assigned to each student, the friendships students form at school only infrequently cross over into the home. With this information, she sets out to discover ways to implement more "authentic" activities that would promote friendships across class and racial boundaries.

Homework
Preparing the Working Proposal

> A plan is a net for catching days.
>
> —ANNIE DILLARD, *The Writing Life*

Teachers plan. We plan our daily lessons. We plan long term for curricular units (sometimes ones we don't yet know much about) and for large-scale projects. We plan for interruptions like testing and field trips. We plan for emergencies like snow days, surgeries, funerals. We plan around holiday restlessness, town festivals, and prom fever. We plan around our family and seasonal obligations and our attendance at professional workshops.

Since planning is not new to us, drafting a proposal for conducting an inquiry makes sense. A plan can be what Annie Dillard refers to in the epigraph above as "catching days" so that neither the days nor the plan floats by with nothing accomplished. But planning a complicated research proposal may seem daunting: "C'mon, how can I propose a project I'm going to do when I haven't done it yet?"

Of course we don't know all the details of a project until we complete it, but we can lay out a working plan. And, as most of us learned early on when our lesson plan for a day took a week, a plan can be unrealistic. Your proposal for a classroom research project needs to anticipate all the real demands of both your home life and your school life. It needs to allow time for library research and classroom note taking. It should include time for getting permissions and funding (if you need them). And your plan should give you ample time in which to draft and revise. How do overly committed and all-too-busy teachers make time—and take time—to do the work

> *Your proposal for a classroom research project needs to anticipate all the real demands of both your home life and your school life.*

we need for our project? Like everything else in life, it's neither easy nor without sacrifices. But a solid, detailed, realistic, focused working proposal can help.

The "homework" for a research project is to write a sturdy but flexible proposal that pulls together a research question and corresponding research methods, anticipates data sources, identifies related bibliographic and archival material, and projects your possible findings. This forces you to envision a future that you haven't yet experienced, so you'll need to build in some buffers: everything inevitably takes longer than you think it will.

As you plan your project, you may want to consult your prepwork from Chapter 1 again, review the mindwork exercises you've done so far, scan all the chapters of this book in succession, or read back through the table of contents to build a general sense of how you want your research process to proceed.

> *Research planning works best when you apply the same rigor and realism you apply to curriculum unit and lesson planning—even when you have to allow yourself time to change your mind.*

The proposal you create will serve many purposes. Like a good research question (the subject of Chapter 2), it will establish the parameters of your inquiry and set out how you intend to share the results. You'll also need to estimate a time line. One thing you can be sure of: you'll revise your proposal many times during the course of your work. Research planning works best when you apply the same rigor and realism you apply to curriculum unit and lesson planning—even when you have to allow yourself time to change your mind.

Why a Research Proposal?

Besides being an outline or plan, the research proposal documents your commitment to your goals; you are building a plan that will scaffold your work and allow it to be completed successfully. Begin with you. The first thing you need to do, whether you are working alone or with other teacher-researchers, is take inventory of your own personal and professional needs. Once you do, you'll be able to accommodate your wider audience's needs.

It's easiest to move backward from the end of your project:

1. Check a calendar that corresponds to the months, semesters, or report periods within which you hope to accomplish this project.

2. Write in any unchangeable commitments.

3. Decide what type of product you want to share. How best will you disseminate your work?
   - A website?
   - A CD or video?
   - A schoolwide show or exhibition?
   - A new curriculum?
   - An article?
   - A series of professional development workshops?
   - A talk at a regional or national conference?
   - A project in support of national or regional board certification?
   - A combination of the above?
   - Something different?

   Designing the outcome of your inquiry helps you begin to organize what you'll need to do to conduct it.

4. Set an appropriate target date for completing your project. Think about:
   - Things that might interrupt, stall, or sabotage your data gathering, analysis, and writing up of findings
   - Sports seasons, yearbook or school newspaper deadlines
   - Parent-teacher conferences and grading periods
   - Teacher inservice days and holidays
   - All the special events you participate in or sponsor, from food and clothing drives to school plays and clubs
   - Your family or social commitments.

5. Once you have blocked out these commitments, ask:
   - What seem to be the best available working periods?
   - What might I give up to free the time this project will take?
   - Can I allow myself regular research rhythms, chunks of time for the project? An hour or two of quiet time per day? A half-day each week, with some long chunks during school vacation periods?

6. Mark time on your calendar for observing, interviewing, gathering materials, reading, writing, analyzing, and revising. Ask:
   - When will I begin to gather data (observe, interview, record discussions, collect artifacts, read available published material)?
   - When will I end my data collection? Will it be all at once, or will I slow down the data collecting as I crank up the writing?
   - When will I do my search for professional material related to my topic?
   - When will I have time to analyze my data, determine my findings?

SNAPSHOT: Beth Rosen Cope Arranges a Time Line for "Classic Literature in a Classic Girls' School"

English teacher Beth Rosen Cope is switching from a coed school to an all-girl school. She will be teaching some of the same literature she has taught before, and she wonders how all-girl classes will affect student discussions. Faculty members at her new school have assured her that classroom talk is, in fact, very different. (The school prides itself on it.) Beth builds an inquiry project around her curiosity. She begins planning her project the summer before she begins teaching in her new school. Her goal is to present her final results the following summer, first delivering some preliminary observations in a talk at a professional conference in April. The time line on pages 106 and 107 includes only Beth's research process, but it accommodates things in her personal life: planning her wedding, moving to a new city, and adjusting to a new school, faculty, and student body.

◈ Mindwork: Create a Time Line

This is your project. For it to work, you need to adjust your personal and academic calendar to meet the deadlines you set. Teaching and research require different rhythms, and you need to synchronize them as best you can. Based on your inventory of your personal and professional obligations, make a realistic time line for your research project. Schedule regular blocks of time for:

◈ Observing

◈ Interviewing

◈ Gathering materials

◈ Reading

◈ Writing

◈ Analyzing and interpreting

◈ Revising

Outline your research process in an order that best fits your schedule: month by month, week by week, even day by day. Use transparent overlays, hash marks, or color codes (red zones for extra busy times, for example) to indicate the different phases of the process. Identify the most challenging parts, and allow additional time for those.

Continued on next page

Continued from previous page

When you look at your completed calendar, see what story it tells about your life. Are there:

◈ Temporary adjustments you'll need to make in your personal life to accomplish this research?

◈ Changes at school you might make in order to make this research proceed smoothly?

Hang your completed, annotated, color-coded calendar next to your research question. You have a proposal, the key instrument of your research. You have a plan.

Who's Your Audience?

So far, we've been using *plan* and *proposal* interchangeably. Until now, your plan has been your own, a calendar just for you. But a proposal has an audience other than you, whether you're seeking permission to carry out a project that will enhance the curriculum or the community; whether your research will lead you to graduate school credits, a degree, or some other certification; or whether you want to compete for funding to carry out your work. The purpose of writing a proposal is to convince a reader that your idea for doing classroom inquiry has enough merit to be worth doing or worth funding—or both—and that you are capable and qualified to carry it out. Once you have a handle on your own personal time line, your job is to persuade your audience that you need to conduct this study.

> ⚙ The purpose of writing a proposal is to convince a reader that your idea for doing classroom inquiry has enough merit to be worth doing or worth funding—or both—and that you are capable and qualified to carry it out.

The audience for your working proposal may be as familiar as your principal, colleagues, and the parents and students in your own school, or as unfamiliar as a national grant funding agency. In addition, you may have more than one audience for the proposal and therefore may need to prepare it in several formats. In all cases, however, research proposals include similar features and require similar types of information. If you are applying for a grant to receive outside funding, you'll also need to follow the required guidelines very carefully.

The most difficult part of writing grant or research proposals is using language that is direct, clear, and free of jargon. For example, although almost every teacher in the United States knows what SSR or DEAR

August

Draft research proposal
Check out grant possibilities
Gather bibliographic materials I already have

September

Begin my teacher journal
Become familiar with my new school environment
Begin to collect artifacts—student writing, response
    journals
Take classroom field notes
Email teacher partner for moral support
Meet with English department chair and principal to
    get permission
Obtain and file student and parent permissions
Read research articles and books from bibliography

October

Begin teaching unit on the novel *Their Eyes Were Watching
    God*
Assign analytic essays on *Their Eyes Were Watching God*
Choose students to interview
Confer with public school colleagues who also teach *Their
    Eyes Were Watching God*
Continue classroom field notes
Tape small-group conversations
Continue teacher journal
Read articles and books from bibliography, take notes on
    relevant ideas

November

Have students keep dialogue journals about their reading
Interview two key informants about their journals
Transcribe taped small-group conversations
Interview English department chair about teaching in an
    all-girl school
Interview parents about their choice of an all-girl school
    for their daughters
Gather artifacts related to the school, particularly
    brochures, historical accounts, and recruitment
    publications
Continue teacher journal
Continue reading and taking notes on bibliographic
    materials

December

Interview case study students again
Continue teacher journal
Continue classroom observations
Introduce new unit on the novel *The Great Gatsby*
Take notes or tape classroom conversations on the novel
Analyze essays on *The Great Gatsby*
Interview colleagues about teaching at an all-girl school

Beth Rosen Cope's time line

January

Finish data collection—fill in data gaps
Begin to analyze data
Re-interview two case study students
Outline research study based on themes suggested by the data
Comb teacher journal for themes

February

Begin drafting talk for National Council of Teachers of English
Consult with teacher partner about her NCTE talk
Organize findings, check against themes
Revisit materials, analyze, analyze, analyze!!
Gather relevant artifacts for talk—maybe take some photographs

March

Write talk, practice talk, make overheads and visuals
Continue revising, analyzing, filling in gaps

April

Give talk at conference (exactly twenty minutes)
Revise talk into longer presentation and possible publishable paper

May, June

Continue revising
Choose two readers for revised draft, ask for response
Check written study with informants

July

Present finished study at summer institute
Send essay out to a journal: *English Journal*??

means, you need to spell out this contemporary reading practice in plain descriptive terms: "a designated quiet period of time when everyone is expected to read without interruptions." In addition to descriptions of teaching practices, your proposal should identify any published teaching programs or packaged materials, so that an outsider coming into your classroom would understand the difference between such programs and ones you've devised yourself or with local colleagues.

Our daily teaching lives are so familiar that we often forget that we belong to the subculture of schooling and share language, behavior, habits, rituals, and beliefs specific to that culture. Writing a proposal requires abandoning "educationese" for plain, simple prose. As we translate, we come to understand better what we are proposing. We need to ask whether what we are writing makes sense to an audience. When you write a research proposal, it's wise to get a reading from a friend or relative who can give it a cool eye and an objective ear. Choose someone who does not share your academic or professional background. You'll be surprised at the questions this person will ask; it's a fine way to see what you can't see and learn what you need to clarify.

> ⚙ When you write a research proposal, it's wise to get a reading from someone who does not share your academic or professional background. You'll be surprised at the questions this person will ask.

Writing for Grant Agencies

If you are seeking outside funding, you'll need to follow the agency's specific proposal guidelines, posted on their websites or in their brochures, when you submit the grant application forms. The most common mistake you'll make as a new grant writer is not thoroughly reading, understanding, and acknowledging the goals and priorities of the agency from which you are seeking funds. Do your homework. Think about who they are and why they are offering funding. Many teachers procure funds from local service clubs, businesses, or civic organizations who want very much to support the work of local schools. Learn what their mandates are, what kinds of projects they want to help, what kind of assistance they're willing to offer. Look at your own plan and see where you envision—and can describe—a match.

> ⚙ If you are seeking outside funding, you'll need to follow the agency's specific proposal guidelines, posted on their websites or in their brochures, when you submit the grant application forms.

For larger regional or national grants, the guidelines can seem stern and foreboding. We envision points being lopped off for not having our name in the proper place. We hear stories from colleagues about humiliating rejections. Is it even worth the trouble to apply? But think about it from the position of the grant givers. When a funding agency receives thousands of applications, and among them is one that describes its project sloppily, does not have letters of support attached, uses staples when they've requested paper clips, leaves important questions blank, or submits an unrealistic budget, the reviewers are hard pressed to consider this application professionally prepared, let alone assess its merits. Enough said. Just be sure to read the forms and rules for submission as carefully as you would if you were entering a contest or applying to graduate school. The stakes are similar, and so is the acceptance process.

The National Council of Teachers of English provides a great list of grant primers (www.ncte.org/about/grants/resources), including links to free tutorials. Since NCTE offers several annual grants specific to teacher-researcher projects, this is a good source of funding for English teachers. Bonnie was privileged to have an elected term on NCTE's Trustees of the Research Foundation, the grant-giving board that reviews these proposals. She learned that although the competition can seem daunting, a solid proposal that describes a project and realistic budget does receive respect and attention, and often money as well.

Once you know the grant agency's purpose and have practiced writing a grant proposal, pay attention to the exact wording and try to make your language match that of the granting agency. This is not a devious trick; it is an important strategy to assure the grant-givers that your project meets their criteria. Study the organization's language and purpose in their published materials, in print and online, and challenge yourself to use some of that language in your writing. If, for example, the grant says that the "proposed learning should improve the applicant's teaching practices and student achievement," feed some of these focus words back into your application to signal the grant givers that your purpose is in line with theirs. For example: "My teaching practice of collaboration will improve as I work with a seventh-grade art teacher on creating puppets for this environmental recycling project. Our combined students' achievement will not only be enhanced by greater awareness of the problems contemporary garbage poses, but our students will become better future citizens who are more likely to recycle." Perhaps even more important, employing the language of the grant will help you better understand whether or not your project really does fit a grant agency's stated goals.

> ⚙ *Employing the language of the grant will help you better understand whether or not your project really does fit a grant agency's stated goals.*

Once you begin to look for grant announcements, you will find them everywhere: local newspapers, state or regional education fliers, the bulletin boards in your teacher's lounge or principal's office, professional and regional journals, *Education Week, The Chronicle of Higher Education*. Some school districts have grant officers or offices devoted to grant information. Don't overlook small corporations, churches, clubs, or agencies in your area that may have an interest in funding projects that support your community.

Many national and international organizations offer grants and awards for innovation or devote grants to particular ideas like social justice, environmental sustainability, or new media. The National Education Association Foundation, for example, awards learning/leadership and innovation grants in all disciplines to K–16 teachers across the country and gives short summaries on their website, by state, of the kinds of research they have most recently funded. Over the years, the Spencer Foundation, the Annenberg Foundation, and the Woodrow Wilson Foundation, among many others, have been advocates for teacher-research studies, both large and small. Some granting agencies give modest amounts of funding to individuals ($500–$2,000) and groups of teacher researchers (up to $5,000). Others offer more substantial sums for more substantial projects. When you begin looking at funding sources, you'll see more possibilities than you ever imagined. And once you've written a successful grant proposal, it is much easier to write the next one.

◈ Mindwork: Find a Grant Source

Go online and find at least one funding agency you think might offer a grant for a classroom research project like yours. Read the website information, download the application form, and analyze what kinds of information they require:

◈ Who or what is the agency?

◈ What are its goals and purposes?

◈ With whom does the agency—or its members—associate?

◈ What other kinds of projects have they funded?

◈ What criteria do you meet?

◈ What criteria, if any, are you missing?

◈ What assumptions does this grant (or this agency) have about education?

◈ Does the description fit into your own philosophy of teaching? Why or why not?

Continued on next page

◈ Analyze the language of the grant, noting key words and phrases. What words are focal in writing an application?

Make a short note to yourself about this grant website, or bookmark it on your computer. If your answers to these questions seem to be a good fit with the project you want to do, try writing a proposal. If not, file the application form and your analysis of it; you may be able to use it later.

Outlining a Working Proposal

After establishing your audience and developing a time line for your project, you're ready to develop a full-fledged working proposal. We've used the generic proposal outline on page 112 with many teacher-researchers across the country. It probably asks for more information about you and your relationship to your project than more formal proposal forms do (reflecting our bias toward reflective research and writing); otherwise it covers the same territory.

◈ Mindwork: Write a Working Proposal

Write a working proposal based on what you're thinking so far about your project. Use the following headings, or fill out an application provided by a funding agency. One way or another, you'll want to include these features, in approximately this order:

Working title for the project

Your name, affiliation, and position

Background (position, purpose, significance, rationale)

Research question and subquestions

Related research

List of permissions required

Data sources

Methods and analysis

Time line

Plans for dissemination

Possible findings

Projected budget

Generic Format for a Working Proposal

Background (or Position Statement): Why are you drawn to this topic? How does your personal, educational, and professional history relate to your topic? What is the purpose of your study? Why is it significant? Discuss what difference your research will make to you and your students.

Research Question and Subquestions: Include the primary question and/or set of related questions you intend to ask about your topic. Define any special terms that might be confusing or might need refining after you begin your research. Discuss the overall purpose and significance of your question and why it is important.

Related Research: Position your research topic within similar studies that have already been done (for example, published teacher accounts of classroom work, books or articles you've already read on the topic, books on theory you might want to read or use while you're conducting your research). The list you make in this section will be the start of your working bibliography.

Permissions: List the permissions you will need for this project. (When you receive them, file them in a safe place.) You may have received oral permission from your principal or supervisor to carry out the project, but we advise you to get this in writing as well. As we discussed in Chapters 2 and 4, you'll need written permission from your students, as well as their parents, in order to use any of their written or spoken words. If you have any doubts about whose permissions you will need, remember that it is better to have more than you might use; you never know who will move or become ill and drop out of your pool of informants.

Data Sources: Identify the data sources you'll want to consult in answering your research question: class records, student writing, school or community archives, the work of experts, other useful print and nonprint sources, your journal, your field notes, conversations with other researchers. Decide how you'll collect the data: interviews, observations, taped discussions, Web citations.

Methods and Analysis: Discuss how you will gather your data to ensure that you will answer your question. What methods do you expect to use—with your whole class, with your chosen informants, with the other supporting informants you'll need to interview. What sites will you need to visit? What demographic information will you need, and how will you obtain it? How long do you expect to take

field notes? Gather your data? A good look at the methods you use will help you as you move forward with your study.

Time Line: When and how will you carry out your research plan? Chart a realistic time line, or use the one you prepared in the mindwork exercise on page 111. Give yourself flexible but realistic deadlines. Remember to allow plenty of time for analyzing your data, revisiting data sources to "fill in the gaps," and drafting and polishing the written documents that underlie your presentation, whether it be an essay, a talk, a website, an exhibition, or another kind of public forum. Any form of dissemination requires sharp, concise, descriptive, well-revised writing.

Possible Findings: What do you think will happen? What are your hunches about what you'll find? How do you hope this work will change your teaching practices and your students' learning? The surprises you find when you return to these early assessment may be the most important knowledge you acquire. By anticipating your outcomes—and being aware that your study will both confirm and refute your ideas—you organize your own thinking. (We discuss findings in detail in Chapters 8 and 9.)

Dissemination: How are you going to share the results of your study? Decide on the way you'd like to broadcast your results and who would benefit from learning about what you've learned. Dissemination can take many forms; you don't need to pick just one. Beth Cope, for example, knew from the beginning that she would give a talk at a conference and present her work later as a professional article for other teachers. Holly Richardson undertook her study of the students' storytelling heritage in Aniak knowing she'd create an anthology of their written versions of the oral stories and give it to the community. (We'll discuss dissemination in detail in Chapter 10.)

Budget: If you are applying to a funding agency, you will also need a detailed budget. But even if you are not requesting money from an agency, you might make yourself a personal budget for things such as tapes, postage, photocopying costs, file folders, books, Internet charges, perhaps even travel to a professional conference where other teacher-researchers are presenting their studies. Many teachers also incur costs for gatherings, festivals, and presentations associated with disseminating the results of their research. These special events often have no one to support them but us.

SNAPSHOT: Jennifer Gorzelany Monitors Email Writers

Jennifer Gorzelany has been a high school English teacher in several independent schools in New England. She forges close mentoring relationships with her students: "With an average class size of eleven or twelve, independent-school students have come to expect a certain amount of one-on-one attention." She feels that her students' ongoing email relationships have made them more comfortable as writers: "They've grown up with this form of communication, which is immediate and casual. Maybe email could be a way to enhance the writer's workshop experience in my tenth-grade class." Jennifer identifies several factors that support her idea: students have access to computers, the writer's workshop format works well in small classes, independent-school parents and students expect more personal access to teachers than their counterparts in public schools, and home phone numbers have begun to be superseded by email addresses and voice mailboxes.

Some excerpts from her proposal are shown on page 114. Notice the precise language Jennifer uses. It's not clever or entertaining or literary; it's meant to guide her and keep her focus sharp.

Jennifer's study doesn't evolve exactly as she has planned; studies never do. But the basic focus remains the same as her proposal guides her throughout the semester. Her case study students surprise her with some new insights. They test her assumptions. She finds no indication of students' insecurity about writing, but she does find that email is an important outlet for quiet students. After she conducts this study, she makes a more firm and formal commitment to incorporating emails between herself and her students, as well as between students and their chosen writing partners, in her writer's workshops. Her plan remains a flexible guide, always present to remind her of her intentions and document her research journey.

Making Ongoing Adjustments: The Best-Laid Plans

As a teacher you often have to change your well-made plans. You get the flu and are absent for a week. Too many students fail their end-of-the-quarter exams. Your school's basketball team goes to the state finals and many students take off from school to attend the game. The drama department is going to present *A Raisin in the Sun*, there are enough copies in the book closet, and you decide to teach it.

Jennifer's Proposal

Research Question: In what ways does personal one-to-one email correspondence affect the writer's workshop experience for one teacher and her students in a tenth-grade classroom in an independent school?

Data Sources: Emails, student interviews (first everyone, and then focal students), student writing samples, recorded writing conferences in class, my journal tracking kids' experiences in writer's workshop.

Related Research: *Teachers at Work*, by Susan Moore Johnson; *Writing Relationships*, by Lad Tobin; *Writing and Sense of Self*, by Robert Edward Brooke; writing conference work by Tom Romano and Donald Graves; research on student-teacher relationships in the writing classroom, on email discourse in schools, and on independent school teaching.

Methods and Analysis: During the first week of school, I plan to survey all my tenth graders about their writing history and which kinds of writing support they have sought out or made use of in the past. I will also give the students my school email address on the first day of school so that if they have questions, they can contact me that way. My early assignments will include a couple of email conversations in response to their reading of the Bible, in hopes that a few students will latch on to the email conversation as a way to clarify their reading of assigned text or to share an opinion they might have been afraid to disclose in class discussion.

After the first few weeks of school, I hope to identify four students who have been particularly engaged in email conversation about classwork. I will then monitor these students' emails and interview them twice monthly about their experience in writer's workshop. I'll try to ask the survey questions repeatedly throughout the year, both of my consultant students and their peers, to determine whether or not email conversations increase their reports of support during writer's workshop. I am also interested in communicating with other teachers using writer's workshops and understanding their experiences with email. If I can find a colleague who is also willing to monitor the use of email and its impact on writer's workshop, even if it is just anecdotal, I would like to include this information in my study.

Time Line:
September: collect surveys about writing history, identify four students as possible case studies, begin keeping teacher journal.

October: complete first and second set of student interviews, keep teacher journal, have conferences with focal students about writer's workshop experience.

November: continue student interviews, teacher journal, conferences with students. Begin organizing data and findings, submit informal report by the 29th.

December: organize, code, analyze, and interpret data, continue teacher journal, submit portfolio representing data sources and midproject findings, continue to monitor student progress in writer's workshop experience.

Possible Findings: Like all researchers, I have some big assumptions about the results of this study before I conduct it:

1. I assume the kids who choose to be active, voluntary emailers will be either insecure academically or socially or "Type A" personalities who like to be reassured at every juncture that they haven't gone off track.

2. I assume that those students who initiate email relationships will report feeling more supported in their writing than those who do not, and that the students who email will be more confident about their writing.

3. I assume it will be natural for these students to enter into an email relationship with me, their teacher, because I'm familiar with independent schools and the close student-teacher relationships they foster.

You write a proposal in order to have a research plan, but you are realistic enough to know you may need to make adjustments and accommodations, from minor to major, in your research questions, the data or artifacts you collect, the informants you consult, even in how you decide to disseminate your findings. Things change, especially in schools, and you change with them. But creating a plan and having it at your side gives you a "net" (Annie Dillard's lovely metaphor) for catching the days of your research life.

Footwork
Covering Your Tracks

> Three most important skills for the qualitative researcher are tolerance for ambiguity, sensitivity to context and data, and good communication skills.
>
> —MAX VAN MANEN, *Researching Lived Experience*

It's not much of a leap to adapt our teaching to our research studies; teaching and researching include similar "footwork," organizing and producing evidence from sources. As teachers, we already have systematic ways to observe and interpret our students' interaction and behavior; research questions and field notes are simply more formalized versions of what we already do. We listen to our students and chat with their friends, parents, and other teachers. Recording and transcribing interviews takes us one step further toward documenting language. We redesign our spaces, reorganize chairs and tables, move desks and shelves, so the task of mapping space comes easily. We outline and re-outline our lessons, our assignments, our curriculum, our books and supplies. Typically, when we are busy doing familiar footwork, we don't give ourselves the time to be analytical or reflective.

But research projects need analysis and reflection, require that we choreograph our footwork—that we keep a record of it so we can see the whole dance, not just the individual steps. Combining multiple data sources to validate, check, confirm, or challenge our assumptions is the process of triangulation. Accumulating and analyzing multiple sources and employing varieties of research methods makes a study more persuasive, "thick" with detail, texture, and information.

In this chapter, we follow the footwork of Karen Wohlwend, a researcher and first-grade teacher, as she pursues her project, "Worst Best Friends." (One of its published forms, "Chasing Friendship: Acceptance, Rejection, and Recess Play," is reproduced in Appendix C.) Over the eight months of her research, Karen

> ⚙ *Accumulating and analyzing multiple sources and employing varieties of research methods makes a study more persuasive, "thick" with detail, texture, and information.*

uses many of the strategies that teacher-researchers depend on for gathering, triangulating, and interpreting data and then writing about what they have learned.

Keeping a Research Journal

You are the most important research instrument you have. Your research journal is a way to track yourself as you carry out your study, reflect on your hunches and insights as they build into verifiable information. You'll use it to record your opinions, feelings, digressions, annoyances, and the surprises you encounter. It becomes a record of your history in relation to the topic and the research process—the assumptions and beliefs you hold, and how they change as your knowledge and experience accumulate. When you keep a research journal consistently throughout a project and then return to it as a source of data, you'll be able to cite yourself and your shifting perceptions in your final project.

SNAPSHOT I: Karen Wohlwend's Research Journal Records Her Thinking

Teacher Karen Wohlwend has always wondered how young children learn about forming friendships, and she decides to watch children on her school's playground. It takes a lot of observations and jottings in her research journal for Karen to come to her research question, "In the world of children's culture, who gets to be a friend, and who decides?" Before her first formal observation of the children at her school, she writes about her own history of childhood play. In a section of her research journal headed "Activating My Prior Knowledge" she recalls:

> Our unfenced backyards merged into a giant playground of grass, vegetable gardens, and raspberry cane forts, bounded on two sides by twenty pastel-painted wood-sided bungalows. Each yard held its own treasures. Ours was the mountain ash tree, prized for its orange berries

that we ground into juicy pulp, sprinkled into oozing mud pies, or picked just to pelt each other. The house next door boasted an abandoned chicken coop, alternately employed as a playhouse or a jail depending on the day's play theme. Left to our own devices, we connected our days together with sagas of play, each day a new episode. One summer, we staged a neighborhood circus where cats, encircled by chicken wire mesh, paced in their "lion cages," acrobats twirled on the top rung of a rusted swing set, and dueling ringmasters shouted conflicting directions to everyone. So many of us were in the circus, we had to import an audience of kids from the next block.

Our rules were simple: "No telling!" and "No throwing berries at the cats." . . . When we got frustrated with each other, we would break off into splinter groups and retreat to our hideouts in the bushes behind the raspberry canes. At other times, the play theme would absorb the conflict. Once, infuriated by overzealous bombardment in the berry and crabapple wars, my friends and I announced we were quitting. The next day, we were back in—as medics—converting our garage into a hospital.

Later, as she begins to take notes while she observes more formally on the playground at school, Karen's journal becomes more analytical:

On the playground, most teachers step back into more of an outsider role. The large number of children teachers must supervise during recess precludes teachers on "recess duty" from focusing on a particular child or event. There can be 70–150 children on the playground, and adults usually intervene only to stop unsafe conduct or to enforce school rules. As a result of this "hands-off" stance by adults, the playground offers the best chance to see what play looks like outside the classroom when independently crafted by children.

Still later in her study, fortified with observations from her researcher's journal, Karen challenges the common assumption that play is good. She wonders whether attempting to create democratic behavior in her classroom works among these children. She asks herself a series of questions:

I am caught in the middle of conflicting roles: as a playground supervisor who must provide a safe environment, as a nurturer who wishes to comfort all those in conflict, as a school authority who seeks a fair and equitable resolution to conflict, and as a leader of a democratic classroom who tries to empower learners. Is the friendship meeting structure that I've created any more empowering to children than existing school practices such as tattling to invoke adult authority? If negotiation can be appropriated by children to legitimize group harassment of an individual child, is it any less painful than an adult-imposed punishment? Are the friendship meetings actually authentic negotiations leading to a joint agreement or are they merely another form of suppressing children's emotions or intentions with words borrowed from adults? Is this just another way of pressuring children to conform and "get along" with the larger group?

Karen's journal becomes a record of her teaching beliefs and assumptions; her conflicted observations about children's behavior on the playground and in her classroom; and her questions about her own role as a teacher, supervisor, nurturer, and former child who played in less institutional circumstances. Reviewing and rereading her researcher's journal allows Karen to begin to position herself in relation to her study of children's friendship and play behavior and to track her own attitudes about children's friendships. Later these journal entries help her analyze her data.

Taking Field Notes

The research journal provides an interior view, a close-up of your thoughts and feelings as you conduct your study. Your field notes provide an exterior view, focus a wide-angle lens on the people, language, places, and material in your study. To take good field notes, you need to observe closely and participate interactively, returning to your subjects with your questions again and again. And still again. As you record field notes, you become better at appreciating what is at first invisible. You'll start to gather a collection of notes that will serve as a source of data. You'll take far more field notes than you'll use in your final descriptions.

No matter how you decide to record and collect your field notes, it's important to find a system that works for you in connection with the project you've chosen. Like a lesson plan, there is no one single accepted format for taking field notes. Each study demands a different design for note taking; each researcher needs to adapt note-taking strategies to suit

> *The essence of teacher research is not to duplicate what someone else saw and thought but to describe and interpret data in its particulars. Every researcher's field notes are unique.*

schedules, students' activities, the rhythms of the school day, and his or her responsibilities in the sites being studied. The essence of teacher research is not to duplicate what someone else saw and thought but to describe and interpret data in its particulars. Every researcher's field notes are unique.

Taking field notes is not an end in itself. You will need to return to them to locate themes, recheck assumptions, cross-check dates and times, categorize and code your observations. To be able to accomplish this easily, follow these standard procedures:

- Number and date each page similarly, including time and place of observation ("Friday, April 5, 10:05: third period, writing group").

- Record sensory details (sights, sounds, smells, textures, tastes) rather than summary details ("Three freshmen, clustered near the door, listen to headphones, popping gum, tapping pencils, one student listens to cell phone messages, another crunches pretzels and drinks diet coke, no textbooks" rather than "Three annoying and impolite students by the door not paying attention to me").

- Distinguish between verifiable information and your own value judgments ("A pair of orange Nikes," not "An ugly, garish-colored pair of new sneakers").

- Note words, phrases, summaries, actual conversations, and insider language ("Tricia asks, 'When will this section of the homework be due?' Chad says, 'It sucks that we have three reports due on the same friggin day.' Melanie whispers, 'Give it a rest'").

- Jot down notes to yourself about other sources you might want to check later and questions about people or behavior to follow up on ("Wonder if Brenda's playing volleyball again this season; she seems tired; check with Coach Pat").

- Make the notes readable, if only to yourself.

There are many systems for taking field notes, in many academic disciplines. There are whole books devoted to field notes, and we mention some in our bibliography. Two of our favorite methods are *double-entry notes* and *social science coding*:

1. Double-entry notes let your mind spy on itself, generating further thinking. Divide a page vertically, using the left-hand side for direct observations and concrete, verifiable details: "A pair of orange Nikes, men's size 12, laces open." On the right-hand side capture your personal reactions, opinions, feelings, and questions about the data on the left: "Ugly color, garish orange, dirty. How does he run with the laces so loose?" It's a good idea to number each observation (the left side) and response (the right side), thus clearly matching your data and your corresponding thoughts.

2. Social science coding, drawn from sociology and anthropology, helps you sort your data as you gather it, separating your observational notes (ON) from your personal notes (PN) from your theoretical notes (TN). Coding your notes after you've taken them forces you to reread and sort your field notes by categories. Whether you use ON, PN, and TN or create your own set of notations, these categorizing codes help you move toward analysis and see the data you've gathered in a different way.

You can treat your field notes as you would any kind of source material. Your field notes are an original source, a primary source that no one else has recorded in the same way you have, at the site you've chosen, about the question you've investigating.

> ✿ *Your field notes are an original source, a primary source that no one else has recorded in the same way you have.*

SNAPSHOT II: Karen Re-creates a Vignette Based on Her Field Notes

Here is an excerpt from Karen's original double-entry field notes, recording an incident involving her key informants, Jeff, Kevin, and Paul.

Later, in her "Worst Best Friends" essay, she uses the incident to illustrate a point about friendship while at the same time interpreting the data:

Jeff sat sobbing, his tousled head sunk into crossed arms. Lightly touching his shoulder, I quietly asked, "What's wrong?"

A watery "They hate me" precipitated a fresh torrent of sobs. I sat down on the hard metal bench next to him. As Jeff looked up, I repeated, "What's wrong?"

"Kevin hates me!" Fresh tears welled up and slid down his freckled cheeks.

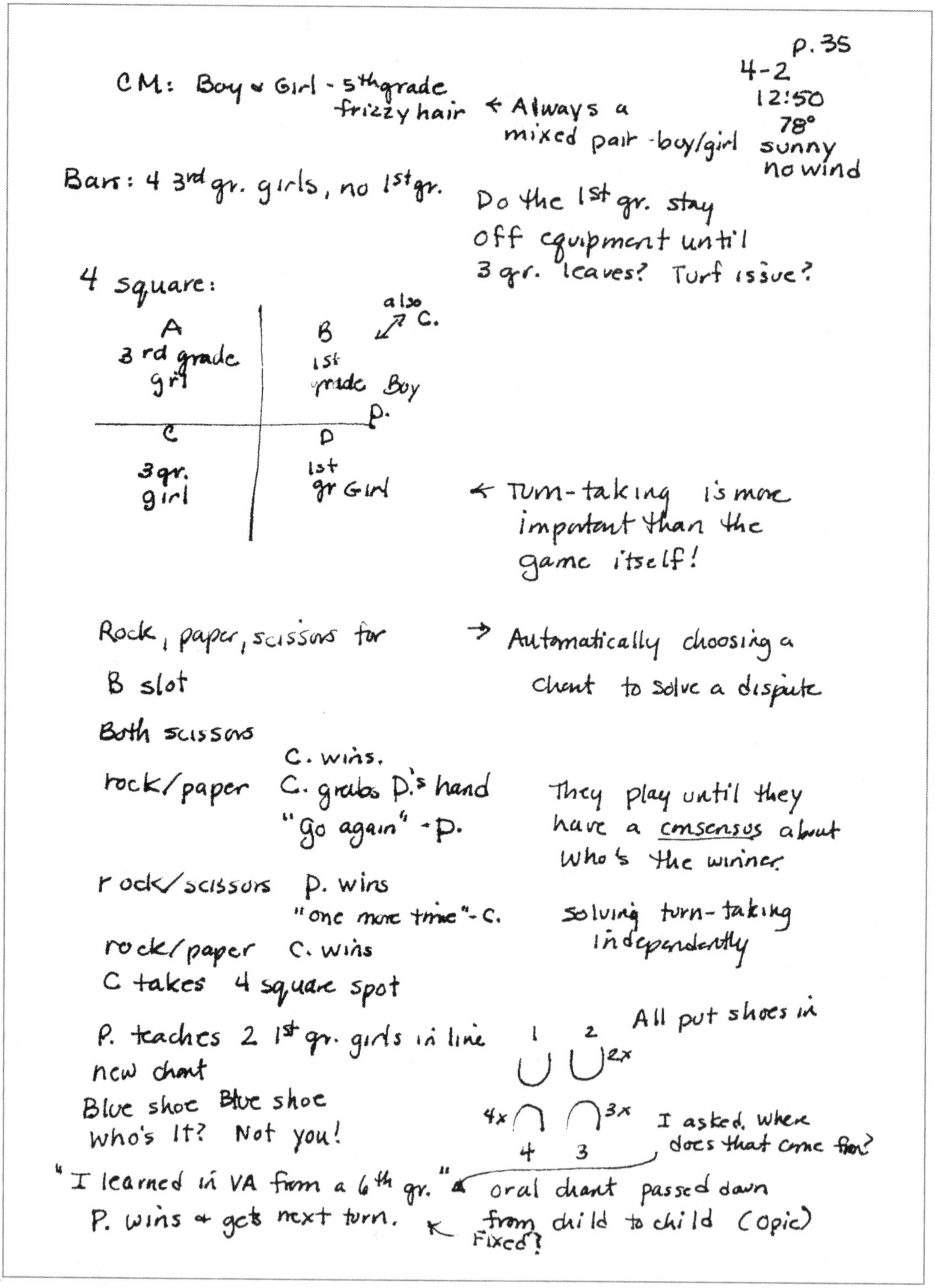

p. 35

4-2
12:50
78°
sunny
no wind

CM: Boy & Girl - 5thgrade
frizzy hair ← Always a mixed pair - boy/girl

Bars: 4 3rd gr. girls, no 1st gr.

Do the 1st gr. stay off equipment until 3 gr. leaves? Turf issue?

4 square:

A 3 rd grade girl	B 1st grade Boy P. (also C.)
C 3 gr. girl	D 1st gr Girl

← Turn-taking is more important than the game itself!

Rock, paper, scissors for B slot → Automatically choosing a chant to solve a dispute

Both scissors

rock/paper C. wins. C. grabs P.'s hand "go again" - P.

They play until they have a consensus about who's the winner.

rock/scissors P. wins "one more time" - C.

solving turn-taking independently

rock/paper C. wins

C takes 4 square spot

P. teaches 2 1st gr. girls in line new chant

Blue shoe Blue shoe
Who's It? Not you!

All put shoes in

1 2
∪ ∪2x
4x∩ ∩3x
4 3

I asked, where does that come from?

"I learned in VA from a 6th gr." ← oral chant passed down from child to child (Opie)

P. wins & gets next turn. ← Fixed?

Fig. 8–1 *Karen's field notes*

"What happened?"

"I asked Kevin, 'Who's your worst best friend?'" sobbed Jeff.

Puzzled, I prompted, "What's that? Your next-best friend?"

Jeff shook his head. "No, *not* your best friend. Somebody you don't like the most." The sentence ended with a stifled sob. A fat tear dropped off his chin, leaving a small maroon blot on his red sweatshirt.

A "worst best friend," the opposite of a best friend. In first grade, a best friend can turn into an enemy and back again in the space of a day. "*He's* my new best friend so *you* can't be my best friend." Children create and test social connections by exploring degrees of friendship. Often when "best friends" pair up, they exclude all others from their play: "If I play with you, you can't play with her." The tension between exclusion and inclusion permeates peer relationships on the playground. Although singed by rejection from yesterday's best friend, children flutter back to establish an exclusive relationship with that same friend on the following day. This exploration of what it means to be a friend seems to compel some first graders to form and dissolve bonds daily, causing many injured feelings.

Jeff blurted out the rest of the story. Jeff had asked Kevin to name his worst best friend, and Kevin had obliged by naming Paul, another boy in the class.

Jeff continued, "Then we found Paul. Then Paul said, 'Hmmm?' And then I told Paul that Kevin doesn't like him. Paul got really mad and left us. And Kevin said, 'I hate you' to me!"

◈ Mindwork: Examine a Slice of Your Field Notes

Having a huge folder of observational and personal field notes may make you feel really secure, but unless you understand what those notes are telling you about your project, they are only raw data. Here's where analysis begins.

Early in your project, look back at a section of your field notes and locate a little segment that you think may find its way into your final presentation. Select field notes that are concrete, verifiable observations or contain your personal thoughts and feelings—or both, if they relate to the same theme or incident. Underline or highlight the material or

Continued on next page

Continued from previous page

pull it out and transfer it to a new page. Expand it into a fuller memo to yourself, drawing on as much detail as possible from your original:

◈ What details might you add?

◈ What details have you left out?

◈ What other data have you already collected that are relevant to this segment?

◈ What further data might you get to strengthen these notes?

◈ How do your notes connect to a growing hunch or theory you have about your research question?

It's important to do this all the way through your project, even when you think you don't have enough data. As you reflect and expand, you'll see connections as well as gaps that will lead you to further data collection and triangulation.

Choosing and Interviewing Informants

Interviews are the bones of any fieldwork. You need your informants' words to support your findings. Without informants' voices, you have no perspective to share except your own. You bring to life the language of the culture you study as you record the people in it. But, especially in school, how do you choose the people to interview? As teachers, we want to treat students in all of our classes equally, but at the same time we know we can't collect detailed data from everyone. Our advice is to treat everyone as a co-investigator but single out specific students who

> ⚙ *Interviews are the bones of any fieldwork.*

you think will illustrate interesting features of your question. Qualitative research doesn't require "representative," "sample," or "control" groups. You don't want informants who will tie your research story neatly in a bow. Rather, you need articulate informants, willing to cooperate with you, who illustrate the tensions involved in the research question you're asking. It's okay to choose them for those reasons.

Allowing people to speak for themselves seems an easy-enough principle to follow. But there are some important strategies for both asking questions and listening to responses. In interviewing, you must be structured and flexible at the same time. While it's important to prepare for an interview with planned questions to guide your conversation, it is equally important to follow your interviewee's lead. Like teaching, asking interview questions involves collaborative listening.

Questions run along a spectrum from open to closed. Closed questions are those with a single specific answer: *How old are you? How many brothers and sisters do you have? What's your favorite subject? How many failing grades did you give last term? What textbook did you order for next year?* Closed questions are sometimes necessary to obtain crucial information, but they're not good for encouraging conversation. Open questions, as the term implies, require you to listen, respond, and follow your informant's lead, because you're not looking for a single answer or a preplanned response. It is easier to be more conversational, diverge from your established questions, share experiences in common, try to get inside another person's perspective.

> ☼ *Closed questions are those with a single specific answer. Open questions require you to listen, respond, and follow your informant's lead.*

Here are some sample questions that encourage people to share and describe their experiences:

- ☀ Tell me more about the time when . . .

- ☀ What stands out for you when you remember . . .

- ☀ How do you describe yourself to yourself?

- ☀ What's a typical day like for you?

- ☀ Tell me about the person who taught you how to . . .

- ☀ Describe the story behind that artifact (picture, booklet, bulletin board).

You don't want to be like the bumbling journalist at the scene of the fire, asking a victim how he feels about having lost his home. Rather, a good combination of closed and open questions will make you more like media interviewers Oprah Winfrey, Charlie Rose, Geraldo Rivera, and Terry Gross, who seem so at ease as they allow people to talk about themselves and us to listen.

Many people think that the key to an interview is a set of good questions. But most times the key to a successful interview is being a good listener. Good listeners guide a conversation without interrupting or directing it back to themselves. Good listeners use their body language to let informants understand that their words are important. They encourage response with verbal acknowledgment and follow-up questions. In the best interviews, you need only ask a few questions to elicit a flood of information.

Whether you're interviewing a group of students about one incident (as Karen does in the snapshot below), or one person in depth, the interview should be comfortable. Just as we try to make our classrooms respectful communities of learners who can safely talk and interact with one another, our job as interviewers begins with establishing rapport. Most people, including students, like to talk about themselves. At its best an interview should be like an everyday conversation, neither forced nor inauthentic.

SNAPSHOT III: Karen Interviews Four Children

One day, Karen witnesses an ugly incident just outside the borders of the playground that leads to a series of interviews she hasn't planned:

> I recognized Kevin, taller than the rest, his back braced against the rough brick wall of the school, bare fists clenched at his sides, ringed by girls who were taking turns screaming at him. As I got closer, I could see Janelle jabbing her finger into his puffy nylon parka, teeth bared, her contorted face bright red. When she stopped to breathe, another girl started in. The rest of the eight or nine girls stood shoulder to shoulder, forming a half-circle around Kevin. Shocked by the harsh confrontation, I wondered what could have happened to warrant this reaction. As I pushed open the heavy outside door, the girls scattered and Kevin fled too.

Her earlier classroom survey about friendship choices has identified several students as social isolates, Kevin among them, and Karen realizes she needs to investigate this bullying incident to help her understand the complexity of first graders' friendships.

In the following excerpt from Karen's final course essay, she reports on the four interviews she conducted. To create a readable text, she reports the dialogue as a first-person narrator:

> I interviewed the children separately, starting with the child whom I assumed would be the most reliable source. I thought Janelle, an obe-

dient, verbal child, would give an honest complete account. Another surprise. Her version, although partially accurate, was full of omissions and turned out to be the most misleading.

I began by asking Janelle to join me at the round picnic table; Kevin was nowhere in sight.

"Tell me what happened with Kevin."

Janelle stood to deliver her report, arms crossed. "Kevin said, 'Come and'—something like—'Come and fight me!'"

"Then what happened?" I prompted.

"People came and got help from other people. And I said, 'You're not being very nice' and 'I don't like how you're acting.' Then everyone took off [at the point that I came out the door] and he started to push us."

Kim's account offered the first contradiction: the girls were pushing Kevin down after they ran from the blocking circle. However, Kim had no idea why she was joining in the verbal and even physical attack on him. Determined to get to the root cause, I asked her, "But what happened before that?"

"He wasn't even listening to us. . . . He wasn't even saying anything. He was 'noring us and wouldn't listen."

I had seen Jill on the outer end of the semicircle and had noticed that she did not run away as the circle broke up. According to Jill, the other girls then "were rolling Kevin around and pushing him around. I was by the basketball hoops," she was quick to point out.

"What happened at the beginning?"

"Before?" Jill wrinkled her nose. "Oh. One person said, 'Let's go make a plan. Let's start a blocking circle.'"

"What's that?"

"Getting in a big circle and getting lots of people and blocking people."

"Is that something people do a lot?" I asked, momentarily lapsing into my researcher role.

"That was the first time."

"Okay. Did Kevin do something? Why was everyone mad?"

"He hurt their feelings. I think he said something that hurt their feelings."

I began to see that I was not the only one who didn't have a clear picture of what was going on.

As Karen tries to gather more data about her friendship questions and the punishments children devise for excluding and rejecting other children, she doesn't have to step very far from her role as teacher: she would have talked to these girls anyway in her capacity as a supervising adult. But she uses the opportunity to add to her data. Her research journal shows how she listened to students' multiple perspectives, along with her own, to triangulate the data:

> The other interviews revealed vague motives and multiple contradictions. The girls' confusion about the actual reason for the confrontation suggested that the focus was on excluding Kevin and on recruiting friends to include in the girls' group rather than on resolution of the original conflict.

Recording, Transcribing, and Logging

Teachers, more than most, know how much happens in the "underlife" of our classrooms (or in any busy cultural context). Audio and video recordings are real-time records of the complicated classroom interactions that are relevant to our question. As we gather data from multiple sources, we depend on these recordings for triangulation and to add texture to our studies. For example, an audio transcript can be transformed into dialogue on the page, as we saw in Karen's account of the bullying incident. A videotape helps us describe a scene in much greater detail than our field notes could provide. Field notes alone are often not enough evidence of what happens in an interview or a class.

These days, we have sophisticated equipment and lots of choices for capturing voices and interactions in real time. Sometimes our students can even help us use these tools, because they've grown up with them. Even media usually reserved for presentation (websites, slide software, video streaming), in the hands and minds of creative thinkers, can become important research aids. (One teacher-researcher we know created a website to manage a complicated set of data that she could not visualize any other way.) On the other hand, despite the enormous options we have, we need not be seduced by them. The media must fit the message. If you want to focus on one informant's words, a small inexpensive tape recorder is just fine. If you need to record a whole group talking in a larger noisy classroom, you'll need a more sophisticated recording system with a directional microphone. If all you want is words, a video representation will only intrude and distract.

Like all other aspects of the research process, recording and transcribing requires a tidy system that is up to us to design. Computer programs, CD burners, video streaming, and Web technology are great friends to researchers. They support our needs and offer us organizational patterns that we might not otherwise know. But the footwork depends on us. Like a simple graphite pencil in the hands of a writer or an artist, any contemporary media tool is only as good as the mind behind it.

Our own research projects have depended on transcriptions from simple audiotapes, not because (or not just because) we're old-fashioned, but because we're language teachers and it's language we're after. The counter on the tape recorder lets us keep track of slices of conversations. Once we finish recording, we listen to it soon afterward (often in the car while commuting or doing errands), noting themes or categories and identifying sections we want to transcribe. Then we create a log that includes topic, numerical sequence, date, and time (4/24/2005, Amy talks about Metallica's group therapy documentary, Tape 2, 037–162; 4/28/05, Amy's mother discusses her dislike of heavy metal and how it's ruined her daughter's social interactions, Tape 2, 364–422). The more time we spend logging and describing what's on our tapes, the less time we need to spend transcribing them.

> ⚙ *Any contemporary media tool is only as good as the mind behind it.*

You know a good interview when you hear or watch it. As a transcriber, you must then bring your informant's speech to life as accurately and appropriately as you can. Find ways to note pauses and hesitations, to describe intonations and unusual speech rhythms. Most researchers agree that a person's grammar should remain as spoken. If an informant says "he done," for example, it's not appropriate to alter it to "he did" unless the informant chooses to change it when you later offer the transcript to him to read for accuracy. Scholars in anthropology, folklore studies, sociology, and education recognize that there's always interpretation involved when one person translates another person's speech into writing. Always check with your informants when you've transcribed their words. This is part of the ethics of research.

> ⚙ *There's always interpretation involved when one person translates another person's speech into writing. Always check with your informants when you've transcribed their words.*

◈ Mindwork: Interview, Record, and Transcribe

1. Transcribe one five-minute segment from a taped interview you've conducted. (Typing out five minutes of transcript takes more time than most people realize, so select something you'll want to use in your study.) Provide some background information about your study and the purpose for which you've chosen this particular material.

2. After sharing the background information, play the tape for a colleague and ask for a response. Look at the transcript together while you're playing the tape. Then ask your colleague about what was read and heard:

   ◈ Does the transcript seem accurate?

   ◈ What was the best question you asked?

   ◈ Are there any speech patterns that stand out?

   ◈ How would your colleague describe the feel of the interview?

   ◈ How does your speaking time compare with your informant's? Do you lead the informant or listen?

   ◈ Are there interruptions? Do you cut off a train of thought or enhance it?

   ◈ What are the different ways you could use this interview data, and what ways could you interpret it?

3. Write a reflective account of what you've learned from this exercise. Most new researchers are very surprised by what they find out and are able to sharpen their interviewing skills.

Listening for Language

If you've been teaching for a while, you've heard slang and jargon come and go, overheard each year's special phrases in the halls, the cafeteria, and the gym. If you've taught in more than one region of the country, you've become sensitive to regionalisms in everyone's speech. You've heard years of education-speak as it's shaped by politics and sharpened by trends. You've seen "No Child Left Behind" turn into "Let No Child Go Untested," "No Child Left Unscathed," and "No Child Left Learning." You've been admonished to do "research-based teaching," "teacher walkabouts," and "kid watching" and to fortify your classrooms with the "question of the day," "sustained silent reading," and "daily oral language."

Listening to language helps you move further into a culture or a subculture and become more intimate with it. Asking a student to explain her special language, jargon, and slang moves you away from your outsider status to analyze words and their uses from an insider's perspective.

> ☼ *Asking a student to explain her special language, jargon, and slang moves you away from your outsider status to analyze words and their uses from an insider's perspective.*

SNAPSHOT IV: Karen's Glossary Assists Analysis

First graders can explain their language as well as anyone else. During her research Karen Wohlwend constructs a glossary of insider terms used by the children on the playground. This glossary helps her with her analysis, helps her locate signs of inclusion and exclusion:

> Looking over this glossary of terms, my first impression was surprise at the number of terms that emerged from a review of my field notes. As I wrote definitions, I began to see that the children had a specific use for each term. I first grouped the words by the types of things they described: rules, equipment, roles, tactics, and general play. Then I looked to see how the rule or play or tactic was being used. Often an activity would have multiple uses, but I chose what seemed to be the most socially prominent use for the purposes of locating patterns among the words. Finally, I identified what the purpose might be for using a tactic, role, or play activity in the larger context of the playground culture. For example, the "spider" is a piece of playground equipment that has many social uses in the children's play.

Here are two terms from Karen's glossary:

Spider: Geodesic dome; a large domed play structure made of hexagons of metal pipes and joints.
   Purpose: Exclusion—permission is sometimes needed to join play inside the dome or to be freed from the dome when it is used as a cage.
   Use: Solo play, group play.

Lookout Tower: Equipment
   Purpose: Group permission is sometimes required for access.
   Use: For physical challenges such as climbing to the top, hanging upside down; as a jail; as a base of safety.

The data from her glossary and her researcher journal sharpen Karen's analysis. The commonly used words help her see the tensions related to her research question:

After sorting and regrouping the terms, I saw an underlying tension between exclusion and inclusion on the playground. It appeared to me that many of these words cluster around the tension between including friends and rejecting others on the playground; a scramble for dominance and access. Even the play activities can be seen as attempts to explore conflict through mock fighting and tests of toughness. Other tensions that I considered but did not find evidence of in the playground glossary: overt/covert behavior, compliance/defiance of school rules, seeking/resisting adult involvement, and freedom from/restraint through rules.

◈ Mindwork: Build a Glossary

Every classroom study has insider terms or special language that would be impenetrable to an outsider without explanation.

1. For your own study, write an alphabetized list or glossary of the insider language related to your study. Consider:

   ◈ Special language in your curriculum

   ◈ Contents of bulletin boards and displays around your room

   ◈ Special terms students use with you about rituals particular to your classroom.

   What does your list reveal about your study?

2. Alternatively, analyze your informants' use of language by interviewing them or looking carefully at transcripts of their talk. Read or listen specifically for the purpose of making a glossary or list of insider terms.

   ◈ Ask several students to define some of the key words you've heard. Check them against their peers' and your own definitions.

   ◈ Invite a research partner (a student, colleague, or friend) to look at your data or spend time in your classroom, and ask that person to note all the words that seem unfamiliar.

Mapping and Documenting Spaces

We carry our sense of place into any research project, whether we're studying a familiar or an unfamiliar space. But, particularly when we're teaching and researching in our own space (classroom, school, familiar town), we need to step outside and make that space explicit. Mapping space involves more than just listing details or inventorying our room. Drawing maps or diagrams gives us information that would be difficult to get merely through observation; it helps us understand our classrooms and field sites—not just what they look like, but how our informants inhabit them. By tracking who goes in and out at different times of the day and how they use different areas, for instance, we may discover something to improve our teaching.

Bonnie remembers when she was student teaching well over thirty years ago, her cooperating teacher sat in the back of the room and mapped her movements one day. His notes revealed that she stood stiffly behind the desk, gripped the teacher's chair, made little eye contact with her students, and spent most of the time feverishly writing on the board, her back toward the students. As a researcher, you'll be able to lean on your already developed observation skills and learn how to "read" the activity and interaction within a space.

SNAPSHOT V: Karen Maps Spatial Patterns

Karen's research project takes her away from the familiar space of her classroom to a less familiar space—the playground. At first, like any teacher on recess duty, Karen sees the playground as chaotic, a mass of movement. But when she begins to map the activity of "the social isolates," a pattern of play emerges. Her map in the following table contrasts Paul, who was excluded from play, and Todd, Casey, and Kyle, who were in constant motion throughout the twenty minutes she observed them.

In her research journal, Karen writes about how she constructed this chart: "My map of the adventures of Paul, Todd, Casey and Kyle on one snowy day resembled a 'Family Circus' cartoon, with the boys' trails weaving and looping back upon each other. Mapping the physical space helped me track the interaction of the four boys as they played."

Play Activity Patterns of Three Boys on a Snowy Day

Paul	Todd, Casey, and Kyle
1. walked east on sidewalk, stopped and watched boy swinging tetherball	1. climbing/sliding on equipment
2. walked west on sidewalk, stopped and told me others were throwing snow on the ground	2. snow diving face first
3. walked east on sidewalk	3. air karate (kicks etc. without partner)
4. walked west on sidewalk, watched children building in snow, stopped and talked to me about the whiteness of the snow	4. lying in snow
5. walked east on sidewalk	5. rolling in snow
6. walked west on sidewalk, returning with basketball, stopped and dribbled in place; two girls walk past on sidewalk without talking to Paul	6. sitting at picnic table, talking
7. walked east on sidewalk, dribbling	7. sitting at picnic table, talking
8. walked west on sidewalk, dribbling soccer style with foot, then began kicking the ball continuing for the first time past me finally losing control of the ball and kicking it into the snow	8. packing snow on snow mound (chair); sitting briefly on snow chair
9. asked Mrs. Gordon, the other teacher, to go out and retrieve the ball from the snow	9. rolling in snow
10. talked to Mrs. Gordon	10. falling in the snow
11. returned, walked past me, continuing east on sidewalk, dribbling basketball with hand	11. throwing snow chunks on the ground
12. walked west on sidewalk without ball, continuing past me	12. mock fighting (kicks etc. w/ partner)
13. walked back and forth through puddle on sidewalk	13. jumping and air karate moves on waist-high balance bars

◈ Mindwork: Map Space and Reflect

Map either your classroom or your research site twice, first without people in it, then with people in it. In the second map, design your own system for illustrating how people use the space within a twenty-minute period. Focus on the following:

◈ What do you see?

◈ Are there places where people don't go? Places that are off limits?

◈ Do people take turns as they use the materials available in the space?

◈ Do people try to rearrange the space to accommodate their own needs?

◈ Do any power differences emerge as you look at the space with your researcher eyes that you'd miss with your teacher eyes?

◈ Are there leaders and followers?

◈ Who dominates the space? How do they do it?

Keeping Track of Data

In her study, Karen has used a particularly rich set of data sources and a wide range of research methods to triangulate the data:

Data Sources	Method
Research journal	Analyzing and reflecting on entries
Field notes	Categorizing and coding observations
	Locating assumptions
	Locating of themes
	Beginning analysis
	Creating a glossary of terms
Informant interviews	Analyzing transcripts
	Coding
	Reflecting
Mapping space	Charting, mapping, drawing
	Analyzing power issues

Her footwork, while impressive, is really just a systematic extension of the skills all good teachers already know and use.

Careful and reflective analysis helps us evaluate the range of data we have collected in order to fill in any gaps. It is the key skill of being a "reflective practitioner" (Schon 1983). Taking time to reflect on what we do as teachers strengthens our teaching and our understanding of students. Karen might have remained on the fringes of her school's playground, acting as an uninvolved guard and doing her duty. She might not have investigated the presence of or reasons for social isolates in her classroom. But her curiosity as a teacher and desire to help understand and integrate children who seem unable to play with others drives her to do systematic teacher inquiry.

Because she is taking a research course, Karen first writes about her research in an ethnographic essay, "Worst Best Friends: Struggling with Friendship on a First-Grade Playground." It is her first study as a teacher-researcher, and while she is fearful of doing research, she brings to it all the skills teachers develop over their years of experience. At the end of the essay, she meditates on what her research reflects about her teaching:

> Throughout this study, I've reflected on the writings of Vivian Paley. In *You Can't Say You Can't Play*, Paley creates a kindergarten rule that prohibits children from excluding any child from their play. She describes the tension between preserving children's freedom and protecting children from continual rejection: "But can this kind of morality be legislated? And what about that other moral imperative; the right to choose one's companions, unpressured and unopposed. Well, you can still choose your own companions. No one is telling you *not* to play with someone" (1992, 73).
>
> While teachers can mandate conditions of respect within the classroom, we cannot ensure inclusive groups at recess. If the children have not internalized these small habits of kindness and made them their own, they do not translate to the playground. Ultimately, they need to make this transfer on their own terms, although we can give them opportunities and encouragement.
>
> Children's lived experiences are messy, filled with conflicts with other children and adults, and continually negotiated within the context of the identity expectations that bound their play. The playground is one of the few spaces in schools where children have the time and autonomy necessary for working through peer social issues. More research is needed that investigates children's friendships within their local context and that takes into account children's shared social history and peer culture. Teachers can intervene to enhance this process if we understand and

appreciate children's friendship as a struggle with group membership and cultural expectations so that we can effectively respond to the social reality that children experience on the playground.

The dissemination of Karen's extensive research does not stop with one course essay. Incorporating the photos she took during her research, she creates a PowerPoint presentation for her colleagues at two professional development conferences. She also revises her essay for publication in a professional journal, *Childhood Education*, and thus is able to share her work with a national audience of interested readers. In order to make the appropriate revisions, she is careful to read other issues of the journal and notice the language, the average length of its articles, and the style the journal uses. In short, she conforms to the rhetorical conventions that characterize the journal's "conversation." Since we've had the privilege of sharing her field notes, her very personal journal entries, and some quotes from her course paper, we also provide the full published article as it appears in the winter 2004–2005 issue of the journal (see Appendix C).

When we invited her to be the central "snapshot" for this chapter, we asked Karen to describe the changes she'd made. Here is the email she sent, accepting our invitation to share her work with you—and discussing how she revised her original essay for the journal:

Hi Bonnie and Elizabeth,

You're thrilled? I'm ecstatic! I am so honored to be included in your book! Any way you'd like to use the research study essay or the published article would of course be great—but it's really wonderful that you're thinking of using both pieces! (Okay, I know there are lots of exclamation points here but I am really excited about this!)

Just a few things that I want you to know about the article. One of the things that amazed me was the transformations that happened in writing up the study for the journal article. The manuscript was, of course, sent to anonymous reviewers. One reviewer insisted that the article be written in [the] third person so in places I write with this disembodied voice and refer to "the author's study" which is a little surreal. Writing in third person made it almost impossible to write about examining my own stance. I couldn't write, for instance, "The author experienced considerable angst when she uncovered her assumptions about. . . ." Very strange.

On the other hand, one of the really useful things that happened was that because this journal required practical applications for teachers, I had to ask myself, "So what?" and "What does this mean for other teachers on the playground?" And out of those questions came this tidy little chart for observing and analyzing playground interactions that is a distillation of everything that I did during the entire study.

Anyway, I'm delighted to be included in your book. Count me in!

An extensive research project, with all its data and insights, can lead in many directions. This chapter illustrates the course of Karen Wohlwend's research project from her earliest ideas to the ways in which she decides to disseminate her work. Holly Richardson's research with high school students, which we summarize in Chapter 1, became a book for her students' local community, several conference presentations for Holly's colleagues, and an illustration of the research process for our book. Although we offer only snapshots of their work, the other colleagues we mention in this book follow entire research trails with similar footwork. By "covering our tracks," documenting our process in multiple ways while we're on the journey, we end up with lots of choices for the final outcomes of our studies. There are no boundaries for ways to share our work other than our own creative design. But like any long journey we take for the first time, the most important reward of such footwork is the set of personal insights we gain from having followed the trail to an end, one that meets our expectations and exceeds them with surprises, offering views we haven't seen before.

> ⚙ By "covering our tracks," documenting our process in multiple ways while we're on the journey, we end up with lots of choices for the final outcomes of our studies. There are no boundaries for ways to share our work other than our own creative design.

Deskwork
Interpretation and Analysis

> To pull meaning from the cascade of data you have generated
> . . . you will be working to organize, categorize, thematize, and
> textualize yet again in order to make meaning of your developing
> understanding. . . . Let the data talk to you.
>
> —WENDY BISHOP, *Ethnographic Writing Research*

You've covered your office floor and your dining room table and maybe even the hallway in between with neatly organized data. In one corner a canvas tote bag slumps with student papers, organized alphabetically. In another corner sits a plastic hanging file with transcripts of all the interviews you've conducted. Tucked next to it is the box of eight cassette tapes of the interviews, with a list of log numbers, just in case you need to review them. At one end of your grandmother's maple dining room table, arranged by date, are all the field notes from your classroom observations. Lined up at the other end is your teacher-research journal, its three-hole-punched pages batched by month. Brochures, fliers, and copies of reports are stacked high in the middle of the table. The professional books and journal articles you've read, dog-eared and riddled with pink sticky notes, line the radiator cover. Taped to your walls are maps and diagrams of your students' comings and goings; flowcharts of their conversations; and photos of your key informants, the classroom, and the school property. Hanging over your computer is the mantra that has driven your research—your research question—printed in a 22-point Old English font.

You survey all the work you've done, feeling proud but a bit lost, wondering if all these data mean anything to anyone, certainly whether they will mean anything to you. Your footwork is cooling down, and your deskwork—hard thinking, imaginative reflection, and focused concentration—is about to heat up. Sorting through data, interpreting, analyzing, and making meaning, is your reward for all that has gone before. No one can do this work for you, because no one has lived through the research experience you have. No one understands the order and significance of these materials you've arranged so carefully. You know the questions you're trying to answer. You know the data you've collected to answer them. But answering the questions involves more than simply assembling a report of the information in the piles.

We both know the feeling. We're always overwhelmed at the beginning of this phase of deskwork, no matter how many research studies we've done.

Elizabeth tells this story. After gathering over a hundred pages of interview transcripts from her two key student informants, as well as transcripts of classes she's observed over the course of a year, she seeks out her mentor. She flies into his office with her three large notebooks of transcripts. "Look, Tom! Here's my study! See all the transcripts I have? All the data I've gathered about these students and their classes? I'm practically finished. Would you like to read them?" Tom ignores the notebooks she thrusts at him. "No way. You have to *show* me how to read them. That's your job. Come back and see me when you've interpreted this data. Then I'll know how to read it."

Bonnie tells a somewhat different story. She has piles of data—sixteen tapes, hundreds of transcripts of interviews, two boxes of files of her informants' work, three notebooks full of her own research journal, a cardboard carton of brochures and artifacts from the program she's been studying. She has to tiptoe through the spaces around her desk in her tiny basement office. One evening, a scientist friend comes over for dinner, a man who has done much research in metallurgical engineering. He pops his head into her basement office, not able to step in farther than the doorway. "Hey, Bon. Congratulations! Now that you've collected all your data, all you have to do is write it up!" She smiles politely through clenched teeth. "That's what *you* think," she mutters to herself.

Elizabeth's story illustrates a researcher too close to her data, almost in love with it. She wants to believe anyone and everyone will be interested in her transcripts, field notes, and student work. It's easy to forget that the job of a researcher is to reinterpret the data through close analysis for a larger, interested audience who has not experienced what she has, seen what she has, or thought about it in the ways she has. Elizabeth's mentor knows she needs to return to her transcripts and make sense of it all. At this point, all pieces of the carefully arranged data seem equally important. She needs to step back and realize that it isn't the data that are important, it's what the data say to her. She must let the data speak: first *to* her and then, *through* her, to an audience.

In Bonnie's story, an engineering scientist's perspective misinterprets this kind of research. For him, the most laborious part of the research is the gathering and sorting of data. From his perspective, Bonnie is almost finished. From her perspective, she has barely begun. What lies ahead is harder than gathering what is spread out over her floor and the other horizontal surfaces of her office. Her job now is to decide which data belong to her question, which papers in which piles have thematic connections to papers in other piles, how one data source relates to another, things she hasn't yet begun to think about. She hasn't noticed that one piece of a student's writing connects to something he jotted in his journal the same day, and in turn corresponds with a comment he made in an interview the day before, which fits with something his writing partner had told him a week earlier. Bonnie's job is to triangulate all data items related to one potential theme—or, in Wendy Bishop's words in the epigraph, to "pull meaning from the cascade of data."

> ☼ Researchers must let the data speak: first to them and then, through *them, to an* audience.

Sorting: Now What?

In qualitative research, no single piece of data stands alone by itself as evidence. Sorting data involves making connections among several related sources. When you consider your piles of data, you may find yourself sighing heavily and asking, "Now what?" If you're like most researchers, your piles are probably arranged by type (sometimes we call it *genre*): transcripts, field notes, research journal, artifacts, student work, photographs, professional books and articles, perhaps additional categories specific to your study. To begin the process of sorting your evidence, dig into each pile, thoroughly reread what you have, listen for the specifics that speak to your question, mark each one with a highlighter or sticky note, and shift it to a new stack marked with a possible theme, recurrent topic, or repeated idea. You can always remove the sticky notes (or delete the category) if your thoughts about categories change.

> ☼ In qualitative research, no single piece of data stands alone by itself as evidence. Sorting data involves making connections among several related sources.

SNAPSHOT: Michele Navone Sifts Data

Michele Navone, a teacher in Hawaii's Honaunau School, is researching the reading strategies of fourth graders who tested below grade level. At first, Michele phrases her research question this way: "What reading strategies do fourth-grade students use to become more effective as readers and writers (as shown through two focal students)?" These are her subquestions:

a. Will the daily routine of minilessons modeling the use of specific strategies in reading workshop change their choice of strategies?

b. What reading strategies will students choose most frequently?

c. What writing strategies will students choose most frequently?

Her school uses a developmental reading assessment kit that includes a survey of the strategies students use while reading. Michele has collected data that confirm her students' abilities to identify a range of reading strategies promoted by the program: "sound out words," "chunk words," "skip words," "ask questions," "reread," "preview/predict," "reflect," "look at pictures," "synthesize." Michele has charted students' responses to three reading surveys, which she's administered over three months. She's gathered many spreadsheets of students' survey responses and turned them into useful graphs. The two case study students show an improved ability to identify (according to the program's categories) strategies they use in their reading. Should she want to prove that the school's experimental reading program is successful, she has data to do it.

But Michele is interested in more. She wants to know how students' knowledge of these strategies will affect their reading outside school, whether it will inspire their writing, and whether they can talk about these strategies spontaneously, without prompts from the program. She has become more interested in the relationship between reading and writing. "The more intensive or daily these teaching strategies are," she writes, "the more confident students seem to feel in trying out the language describing them and, I hope, using them in their independent reading and writing."

By looking for connections between the school's new program and her interests in students' other literacies, Michele has identified a possible hole, questions that involve independent reading and writing strategies. Then, by sorting through her data, she sees that she needs different data to support her study. She needs to make lists of what her students are reading, interview them to find out about their out-of-school reading habits, perhaps observe her particular case study students as they read, talk to parents or other teachers, and investigate existing reports of their past reading performances both in and out of school. With charts and spreadsheets, Michele can create a visual picture of the school's new program as it's being implemented. But in order to answer her own research question and its subquestions, she'll need to connect her existing evidence with more genres of data.

Her revised question becomes more specific: "What reading strategies (of the ones the program teaches) do two fourth graders use routinely in a classroom reading workshop? Which strategies will the students *say* they choose for reading? for writing?" With her question revised, Michele is able to direct her sort through the data she's collected and also begin to answer her question about how the students use the program's goals to further their own reading and writing.

◈ Mindwork: Sort First

1. Make a list of all your data sources, categorizing them by genre and checking to see that you've dated everything you've gathered.

2. Label your piles. What genre do you have most of? least of? none of at all?

3. Check your labels against the list of data sources you made in your proposal. Are there any surprises? What bothers you at this point?

4. Look back at your research question. Your first sort should be for the evidence that you regard as most important for answering your question. Can you begin to make connections between different genres of evidence? For example, do you see a rubric you've designed with your class that a student has used to describe a piece of her writing? A snippet of a transcript in which a student discusses the reason for behavior you've recorded in your field notes?

5. Develop a strategy for connecting pieces of data you may have lurking in separate piles. Colored markers, hanging folders, large pieces of newsprint, sticky notes, and new computer files are the researcher's best friends because they are malleable and can be rearranged as the need arises.

Triangulating: So What?

Triangulation is the process of verification using multiple sources of information. Researchers use the term to discuss ways that evidence is validated, cross-checked, or challenged. Despite the prefix *tri*, the word does not necessarily mean three. Rather, it means *multiple* sources—more than two. Triangulation gives stability to a study. Just as four wheels balance a car, a tripod supports a camera, or a five-pronged trivet holds up a hot dish, a data source must be stabilized by more than two pieces of related evidence.

Triangulation offers texture, depth, and credibility to a study. You wouldn't necessarily believe one person's snip of gossip, but when you begin to hear the same story from several disparate perspectives—and see evidence for yourself in several different places—the story becomes richer and more believable. As you're adding color and texture to construct a possible narrative, you're also challenging evidence that does not fit well with the snip of gossip you heard in the first place.

> ✹ Triangulation is the process of verification using multiple sources of information.

When your data accumulate and you start to sort through it, you begin to answer the most difficult question of all: so what? Interpretation and analysis come naturally, since triangulation requires that you scrutinize, match, and connect your data closely within the frame of your research question. Like putting a puzzle together, you will triangulate continually as you make more and more connections among the data sources. But unlike a puzzle, the final outcome is based on your design, your discoveries. No one will put it together exactly as you do, and that is entirely appropriate to qualitative research. As you become more expert at understanding the intricacies of your topic and question, you develop an almost magnetic attraction to the data that fit. And you learn to discard (at least for your current project) the data that don't fit. This process, of course, takes time, independence, and concentration.

> ✹ Interpretation and analysis come naturally, since triangulation requires that you scrutinize, match, and connect your data closely within the frame of your research question.

SNAPSHOT: Kelly Richards Sets the Stage for Triangulation

Kelly teaches English in Rhode Island at a private high school that is very concerned with assessment. Her research question is self-reflective: in what ways can she engage her ninth graders with their writing so that the process of assessment becomes more explicit and instructional—for them as well as her? From the first day of class, Kelly has asked her students what she should consider when she reads their writing.

Her students have complied by helping her construct assessment rubrics for their writing assignments: in-class writing, expository essays, an essay on *The Odyssey*, a lengthy biography, and their ongoing portfolios. She has also accumulated a few copies of emails from a research partner in another state, who suggested some professional reading about assessment. Her data collection also contains all student comments on which the rubrics were based.

Kelly speculates on a few ideas that might lead her toward more data with which she will be able to triangulate, perhaps shift the direction of her study. "By conferencing with students individually, I am involving them in the assessment process without their even knowing it. . . . They also have a way of talking about [assessment] because they have been involved with the criteria from the beginning and talked about it specifically in terms of their own papers."

Kelly knows that her work is incomplete and that in order to stabilize her study, she'll need to gather more data: transcripts of student conferences, student papers and commentaries on their revisions, her teacher-research journal or field notes documenting how she and her students have developed the five rubrics. In doing her research, Kelly discovers her own interest in portfolios as an assessment tool. She recognizes that she prefers portfolios over individual rubrics as a way for students to evaluate their own writing. So she may want to shift the focus of her research project—or even revise her research question—as a result of attempting to triangulate her data.

◈ Mindwork: Triangulate Your Data

Find three or more snippets of data from different piles that focus on the same moment in time, idea, topic, or theme. You might find three people's comments about one event, person, idea, or item. You could find one person's thoughts as they play out over a period of time. Lay out your array of artifacts—put them on a table or the floor—and try to see relationships among them. Write about the connections you see. Try to answer some of the following "so what?" questions.

Continued on next page

Continued from previous page

1. What moment, idea, topic, or theme do all these data sources support? How do you know?

2. How many perspectives have these data sources captured? What others might there be?

3. How do these data sources answer your research question? What other sources might you need to gather?

4. What difference do these data sources make in terms of teaching and learning? What might a colleague learn from looking at this?

5. Are there other questions that these data support? If so, what are they? Might you revise your research question as a result of this set of data?

6. What do you need to do next?

Getting Stuck and Unstuck

You've organized your data, sorted through them, and found some instances in which items match one another enough to triangulate. You've done some writing about these instances of triangulation, finding them emerging as potential themes in your study. But you don't know what these themes actually mean, and how they fit together.

You feel stuck. You have project paralysis. Research revulsion. Inquiryitis. Writer's block. Everyone's work seems smarter than yours. You know your teaching is just fine. You love your students and they love you. You're just about ready to pitch all the data into a dumpster and forget all about teacher inquiry. "It's a lot of hooey," you think. "Forget it," you mumble, slam the door on all your piles of data, and watch old movies during your free time for a week. And one of the movies gives you an idea you hadn't thought about before.

Sometimes it's necessary to take a break from your research. You need to get a fresh perspective, let the question simmer in the corners of your mind, let the flavors and textures of the data blend together. You'd be surprised how often ideas come forward while you're taking a vacation from them. Your engagement with the question and the data will eventually reward you. Just as our students become discouraged when they're learning something new or pushing themselves at the edge of a difficult task, a researcher's energy ebbs and flows over time. Teachers in all disciplines know that the hard work of interpretation and analysis is the hard work of critical thinking. And sometimes it feels lonely and bleak. Here are some ways to get unstuck:

Read. Pick up a study you admire, and think about how the researcher put it together. In any given paragraph, try to identify the data sources; you might even list them. Look for the researcher's themes and compare them with what you'd like to be doing.

Make contact. Call or email an empathetic and interested friend. Describe your study, show her the proposal, share data, or give her a sample section you've written. Ask about what your friend sees and hears and imagines.

Review. Reread your proposal and all the short mindwork exercises you've done in this book. We designed them to help you document your thinking processes as you go—to see where you've been and what thoughts you might have forgotten.

Take professional action. Visit a colleague in another school, or observe a colleague teaching in your own school during your planning period. Go to a relevant professional meeting, a lecture, a reading, a seminar, and listen to others talk about teaching. Find a good video or CD presentation related to your topic. Sometimes seeing others' work will remind you why you do (and don't do) what you do.

Seeing Patterns Emerge

Interpretation and analysis, as all teachers know, are important and sophisticated acts of critical thinking. Working with triangulated data will lead you to see those initial patterns that will become the themes within your finished study. The themes may be modest ones. Your goal is not to change the world or even to change the school but to help you understand yourself, your own teaching, and your classroom. Try not to ignore what may seem obvious or trivial. But recognize that without

> ⚙ *Your goal is not to change the world or even to change the school but to help you understand yourself, your own teaching, and your classroom.*

interpretation, we don't know what our data mean. Like the unanalyzed data loading up Elizabeth's tote bag and the disconnected but well-collected data Bonnie still had to write about, they simply sit there.

As in music, a theme is a phrase that recurs strongly enough to be memorable—and, in itself, invites creative variations. A theme in a school-based inquiry project can be small: the importance of reading aloud to students for a half hour every day, the value of inviting students into curriculum planning, the significance of listening to students describe how they explain their writing processes, how three students connect one culture's historical period to its literature.

The smaller the theme and the more specific, the more strongly it can influence your classroom and your teaching. Large themes often produce vague or clichéd generalities: "workshops enable everyone," "out-of-school reading enhances in-school reading," "keeping journals helps students understand the material better," "recognizing sustainability efforts in environmental science will make my students better citizens." But each of these broad, vague ideas, unconfirmable as stated here, could evolve into a huge variety of clear, focused, interesting, and innovative roads to seek more evidence to confirm and challenge your hunches. Like a healthy but vague first draft of a story or a new arrangement of musical notes that almost forms a melody, a large theme, along with specific evidence within your data, can suggest how you'll revise and sharpen your ideas. Identifying specific themes in your research will spark your own creative energy and produce variations, harmonies, and counterpoints you would not otherwise be able to access.

> ☼ *The smaller the theme and the more specific, the more strongly it can influence your classroom and your teaching.*

SNAPSHOT: Polly Lepic Discovers Themes in a High School Art Class

Polly Lepic has been a high school art teacher for twenty-five years. Over the years, she's developed a particular interest in the artwork of special-needs students, especially those labeled BD (behavior-disordered). Here's Polly's description of herself in a positioning statement she writes about learning to do research:

> I started to understand the nuts and bolts of fieldwork as an artistic craft. I also started, in my own mind, to understand the difference between being a teacher who pays attention and being a researcher involved in a research project. . . . [A researcher] must be warm and caring, a good communicator and listener, empathetic and authentic, sensitive to a continually changing scene, the reasons for the changes, and the significance of it all. . . . At first everything is important as [a researcher] searches for clues. A researcher must be able to handle ambiguity. I feel I have been in training for qualitative research my

entire life, whether it was my experiences as a child, my graduate work, my teaching, or my life as an artist.

Polly begins her project with a "working theory," her own personal and passionate commitment to something she thought she already knew:

> Although many BD students have difficulties in traditional public school, they often thrive in their art classes. Why? Because of my experiences in the classroom as an art teacher, this was a topic in which I was very interested. If only I could define the experiences these students might be having in the art room community with the art teacher and with their art making that was leading to their success, then I could share it with others. At the very least, I would understand it enough to improve my own teaching.

She has often observed that "despite the mysterious label," BD students typically succeed in art classes, and as they continue to do well, the BD teachers send more of their students to her art room. She knows she isn't alone. Other art teachers have observed similar successes with special-needs students, and she is curious about how and from whom they acquired these labels in the first place and what strategies helped their success.

During one school year, Polly leaves her own classroom, obtains the appropriate permissions, and spends time in four other art classes as a participant-observer during the classes' twelve-week trimesters. She collects data and focuses her attention on the BD-labeled students. She visits BD teachers in their environments: "I had never set foot inside the BD classroom, a temporary unit behind the school, and knew nothing of what took place inside. Some of these students would come to my class with teacher associates and some wouldn't." Her art classes are elective, as are most art classes in secondary schools. She wants to see what the art room's environment allows students to do that their other classes don't. The students, in Polly's words, are "a little calloused about having helpers/ researchers/extra teachers in their classrooms. . . . Their interactions ranged from ignoring me, to asking me for help with a project, to wanting to talk about the latest social dilemma in their lives." But she watches them create art and talks with them, their teachers, their special-needs teachers, and their paraeducator "associates." "In the end," she writes, "my formal participants were four BD students at three different schools, three art teachers, two student teachers, four BD teachers, and two associates."

She spends the following school year back in her own art classroom teaching, analyzing the data she has collected, and writing about what she has learned. "I reread my notes, reflected on meaning, and looked for the universal by sorting through the particular. This year of distance from the project, while I was working with BD students in my own art classroom, was important to the final way I presented my experience." She quotes educational researcher Sharon Merriam, "Data analysis is a complex process that requires moving back and forth between bits of data and abstract concepts . . . between description and interpretation" (1998, 78). She persists in asking herself questions: What have I not observed? What did I expect? What data collecting am I not using that could shed light on the research?

Polly's research sets out to see the art class from other perspectives as well as her own, and her scheduling plan allows her to do it. During the course of her initial year of observation, her "working theory" turns more formal and systematic, into one research question and three subquestions:

Main Question: What is the nature of successful/meaningful art experiences for this special population in the regular education art classroom?

Subquestions
1. How do these special students find success in their art class experience?

2. How do environmental factors/labels/attitudes play a role in the students' educational experiences?

3. What is happening in the art room that provides positive, meaningful experiences for these students?

For many years, Polly has been bothered by the school's constant scrutiny of BD students, and, at the outset, she wants to seek "what is good," remembering reading Sarah Lawrence-Lightfoot's *The Good High School* (1985). She writes, "Since BD students have already been labeled as imperfect, I found it only appropriate to seek out the good in their experience." Her research demonstrates that these students, like most students, "are influenced by a multitude of forces: their own cultural histories, their disabilities, their self-images, and their environments, just to name a few." Polly's data lead her to interpretation, triangulation, analysis, findings, and ideas for further projects.

Like many professionals, Polly has taken courses throughout her teaching career, and read on her own the work of many educational and artistic philosophers and theorists who speak about the value of the arts. Her background reading, coupled with her field notes, her interviews, and the students' artwork, constitute her data for this project, and her case study students add their own artifacts to her data collection. She photographs their artwork and shares the photos with them during interviews, as well as later with her readers. "As it turns out," Polly writes, "students shared other items with me: role-playing game books, writings, and favorite pieces of jewelry" (see Figures 9–1 and 9–2). The more data she gathers, of course, the richer the study and the firmer the findings. Polly's data allow her to interpret and analyze what she sees and what her informants say about what they experienced. Collecting it and making sense of it, she assures us, happened simultaneously.

Her four focal students, Martha, Tony, Damien, and Lucas (all pseudonyms), help to illustrate the importance of art in any curriculum:

> Each of the four students participated in the cognitive challenges inherent in art work. Tony used art to give form to his imagination and humor, and through his experience [in a museum] with a Jackson Pollock painting, he made connections with the movement in ceramic glazing and graffiti on the Berlin Wall. . . . Damien's knowledge and interest in role-playing symbols was enlarged through his work of making new art. And Lucas engaged in serious problem-solving, manipulating tools and materials to achieve desired effects. But it was Martha who reminded me of one of the most basic reasons that we have art in the curriculum: "art has a unique potential to enrich our lives simply because it has the power to delight us" (Kindler 2000, 4).

Along with the very broad idea that art classes are good for the school curriculum, Polly is also able to identify and name six themes that seem most relevant for these BD students in their art class:

1. *Tools for life.* In art classes, Polly's data show her, students make decisions and have control over what happens next. "With art tools and materials," she writes, "this control is immediate and visible. Playing around with boundaries and adjusting to what happens next is an important lesson in improvisation.

Fig. 9–1 *Tony's wire sculpture of a man posing, lying down with head on hand*

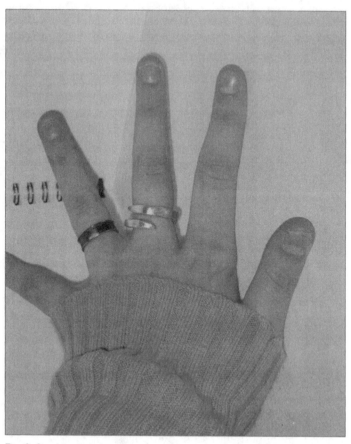

Fig. 9–2 *Martha's hand displays her cast sterling silver ring*

2. *Origination.* Polly uses a term from Martin Buber ([1947] 1970) to identify what she calls "the originator instinct" and the ideas of John Dewey ([1938] 1963) that connect experience and education. She finds this instinct evident in all the work of all four students in her study. Tony, she notes, "used it to release his humor and make complex connections between his experiences and the art he saw." Damien "wanted to bring form and substance to the many images from his role-playing books; one project was so important that he carried the drawing around with him in his pocket for days." Lucas, competent with equipment, saw art class as an opportunity to work with his hands, which he claimed was why he liked art, and he made gifts for his girlfriend. Martha "proudly wore the art she made." Both Martha and Lucas "enjoyed the tactile and sensory experiences that come simply from making, working with tools and materials, and watching their efforts transform simple metal into beautiful objects."

3. *Success.* Another theme Polly extracts from all her data is about the intricacies of success. "The notion of success is complicated. When something does not work the first time, that does not mean it is a failure and all work stops. Various solutions need to be explored; sometimes the third right answer is the most successful." Polly identifies the theme of artistic success in all four of her case study students as she describes them in her written study. "In the art room, the successful learning experience might involve helping others or working through a fear."

4. *The art room as workshop.* An art room's environment differs from most academic classrooms. Polly observes that it "comes with its own set of rules which make sense and the need for students to interact and help each other. . . . They can move around, ask questions, get help, and give help to others. . . . Even though there were many silly antics," Polly writes of Tony, "he used the art class to the fullest extent as an outlet for his creative energy." In the workshop of the art room, students, teachers, and associates all trade services as learners and mentors.

5. *The art teacher as a facilitator of success.* During her time in others' art rooms, Polly was certainly better able to confirm this theme than she would have on her own. "I saw art teachers act as coaches, inspirational leaders, mentors, skilled craftsmen, problem solvers, and

counselors, among other roles." She identifies "kindness and structure" from short interviews with thirty-three BD students, the four focal case studies, her observations, and the teachers' comments to her. Polly notes, too, that art teachers often characterize themselves as "a little bit different" and speculates that in order to tolerate difference, anyone must accept the notion of difference.

6. *Teachers' wishes for students' closure, decision making, and control.* According to one of Polly's colleagues, "I think it's about closure. How many times in their life did they have closure? . . . They're not particularly successful at anything. . . . When they go into the art room, I don't care whether it's good or not good, they can take it home. They touch it, it's tangible." This colleague describes making books in her class, remarking that although the assignment was the same, each book was different. "An environment providing decision-making opportunities is one laced with choices," adds Polly. "Kids in art are in control," said another colleague in an interview. "If you push the crayon this way, it moves. If you take a brush and they want purple and it goes this way, golly, they get purple. This is very cool." Polly concludes her discussion of this theme: "The art teachers in my study all gave up some of their own control to provide choices and guidance. All were aware of the possibilities and importance of students making decisions, good and bad."

Grieving for Dead Data

Polly sees lots of other themes in her data: what she calls the "home-base influence" of special-needs teachers, who have a particularly intimate knowledge of each student, and the important support role of paraeducators, the "associates" who, although they feel unprepared and inflexible after only a day's "training," are an important part of the two classes in which Polly found them. She sees these themes as ideas for further study, along with many others that her data raise. But she can't use them all.

You can't use every piece of data or every theme you find. Determining what you'll use is a matter of focus and relevance to the question you've worked so hard to refine and develop. Polly says, "Because I understand that everything influences everything else, my data sometimes touch on topics that this research does not directly address." Along with the interesting issues for BD students about associates and placements in classes, Polly wants to study the outside influences on the school lives of BD students "including family, friends, and sig-

> ⚙ *You can't use every piece of data or every theme you find.*

nificant others. . . . Except for Tony's friend Mark and Lucas' mention of a girlfriend, I saw no indication that my participants had friends. . . . There were continual hints of outside negative influences on my participants' successes in school: a mother's health problems, trouble with the law, switching schools every year, to name a few. Further research, though not important to my original topic, could only help the understanding of the complexities of BD-labeled students and the influences on their school lives."

Bonnie likes to joke about unused data as "dead," saying that a researcher, like a writer revising, is constantly "killing off" good stuff. Sometimes it feels that way. But like large chunks a writer removes from a text because they're irrelevant or a good metaphor that is simply over the top or unworkable in connection with the subject you're writing about, if we take care with what we excise, we do have the power to bring it back to life. Unused data is not really dead; it's just interred in a file box or on a peripheral drive, in the temporary resting place you've assigned it to. We never know when we might be able to use it in our future work.

Finding Findings

Sorting, triangulating, interpreting, and analyzing data for themes is what leads us to conclusions or helps us project ideas for more study. A "finding" in research *is exactly that*. Your evidence, data, and interpreted themes lead to your assertions that you've "found" something, no matter how small, no matter how temporary. Polly is able to assert findings about herself in relationship to her research:

> My entire life, in any given situation, I have been both teacher and student. Even now, in this situation, I am both the instructor and the learner. . . . With each of these individuals, I am reminded how important it is to hear their stories, to maintain dialogue. . . . Art class played an important role in the lives of each of these students. . . . They had to problem-solve, elaborate, be flexible, use their imaginations, be patient, and interact with others. They were accepted in the art room as regular students and pushed to do the work according to their abilities.

Polly notes that the schools in which she conducted her research are "good schools," that the results of her study are not necessarily to explain or control but rather to offer insights. She concludes her study with what we can call findings:

Throughout this research, I found that an art class offers positive opportunities for the BD student. It has many things built in:

1. Art teachers are already focused on instructing the individual and tolerant of differences.

2. Rewards are built in, in the form of an art piece, which can be touched, given away, or shown to others.

3. Rules are a natural part of the process.

4. There exists a wide range of acceptance for ability.

5. There exists a wide range of acceptance for personal choices based on personal interests, a control-giving situation.

6. There are reasonable opportunities for social interaction.

Her study may not change anything other than her own teaching. But it will enrich the insights of the readers with whom she shares her written work. It has already offered opportunities for her informants—the students, the teachers, and the associates she's worked with—to reflect on their work in the art room and what it has meant for their learning and growth. On the other hand, like all research, the themes, interpretations, findings, and clear description exist now in a way they've not existed before—for anyone who wants a clear, focused picture of "behavior-disordered" high school students in art classes. Her two years' worth of careful observing, collecting, sorting, interpreting, and analyzing offer new and deeper knowledge to whoever seeks to find it.

A Final Word About Deskwork

Polly's findings lead us back to an idea we've discussed throughout this book: you are the most important instrument of your research. The purpose of your "deskwork" is to make your data speak to someone who wants to listen. In order to share your research, you make meaning of your understandings as they develop, of "who you were, where you went, what you saw, what you think you thought you understood, and what meaning you think your reader might make with you from these experiences. . . . Let the data talk to you" (Bishop 1999, 92).

☼ *The purpose of your "deskwork" is to make your data speak to someone who wants to listen.*

With any qualitative study, but particularly one that involves teacher research, we talk the story with the voice of an informed researcher who chooses, selects, constructs, and interprets the voices and perspectives of others. What finally emerges from our piles of data is not a contrived story but rather one that is verifiable and confirmable because it is always based on the vast amount of sharply focused material we've collected, sorted, interpreted, analyzed, and rendered accessible to a reader.

Handwork
The Craft of Dissemination

> You can approach the act of writing with nervousness, excitement, hopefulness, or even despair—the sense that you can never completely put on the page what's in your mind and heart. You can come to the act with your fists clenched and your eyes narrowed, ready to kick ass and take down names. . . . Come to it any way but lightly. Let me say it again: you must not come lightly to the blank page.
>
> —STEPHEN KING, *On Writing*

Shaping piles of material for an audience is never easy. It is a challenge not only of analysis and interpretation but also of rhetoric and craft. Our colleague Tom Newkirk likes to say, "The scholarship is in the rendering." In other words, your research findings become your scholarship as you shape them for someone else to understand. In the same way a sculptor renders a human head from a hunk of clay, your writing renders your abstract concepts into concrete words that lead others to experience what you've experienced and learn what you've learned. Decisions about how to shape your material in the form you choose to work for the audience you are trying to reach are part of what we call "handwork" because it involves intricate craft: shaping, weaving, smoothing, polishing, tending to the raw material with your informed knowledge to prepare it for presentation to an audience. No matter what form you choose in which to share your work, it will involve writing.

Approaching the act of writing, as Stephen King tells us in the epigram above, is something we do with our intellect and our emotions, not to mention our hands, no matter what we're writing about. It's always much easier to think about writing and talk about writing than it is to write. Whether we face a blank page, a blank screen, or an empty auditorium, we remember that our work is neither light nor finished. Writers love to write about writing and to own up to their own quirky, sometimes wicked writing habits and rituals. Researchers face common issues when it's time to turn a project into something to share with an audience: we choose the form (or forms) it will take, determine how and with whom we'll share it, and then shape it using the tools of language, rendering the piles of voices, writings, artifacts, and experience into smooth text. It's both exciting and exhausting, and always, we think, worth the effort.

Whether your goal is to create a computer-generated media presentation for the school board, a museum exhibit for your community, a Web page for your class or a class across the globe, a workshop or a poster for a professional conference, a journal article or a book chapter, each product requires similar writing processes, with attention to invention, drafting, and revision. And each requires a similar awareness of the rhetorical situation: of yourself as writer/crafter, of your audience, and of content (in this case, the findings and the evidence from your study). What we know about composing supports us as we approach dissemination.

> ☼ *What we know about composing supports us as we approach dissemination.*

In this final chapter, we'd like to consider how we can choose an appropriate form for dissemination and then apply what we know about the craft of composing to inquiry work. Seriously. King cautions us to approach writing and publication with seriousness: "This isn't a popularity contest, it's not the moral Olympics, and it's not church. But it's writing, damn it, not washing the car or putting on eyeliner. If you can take it seriously, we can do business. If you can't or won't, it's time for you to close the book and do something else" (2000, 107–108). You have invested too much thought and energy in the research process to walk away and do something else. It's now time to lean on what you already know about writing and rhetoric as you craft your project for others.

The Rhetorical Situation

Recently, parents in an elementary school in Connecticut took issue with the way teachers were returning their children's papers covered with red ink markings. Parents complained to the school principal that such comments were "stressful" to their children. The school decided to ban teachers' use of red ink in favor of other colors. This incident raises questions, not about lack of teachers' knowledge about red ink affecting students' confidence, but about allowing teachers, not principals or parents, to make pedagogical choices and trusting them to do so. The story ran in the national media: newspapers, radio, and television. The coverage was huge. One teacher we know in another state, upon removing his sweater at a doctor's appointment, had to explain to his doctor why he had a red pen in his pocket and how he marked his students' math papers. The doctor recounted his own children's reactions to teachers' red marks. But the situation goes further than a controversy over red ink in Connecticut. It sends a message far deeper: Why do teachers get such negative press? How much publicity comes from our own efforts to attract the confidence of parents and the public? Understanding rhetoric and its value gives us a stronger public voice.

Rhetoric is most often defined as the art of persuasion. Greek philosopher Aristotle described the rhetorical event (in our example above, the plea to banish the red pen) as having three important interacting elements: *ethos* (the self or the speaker/writer), *logos* (the information), and *pathos* (the speaker/writer's sensitivity to the audience). This triadic idea, sometimes called the *rhetorical triangle,* crosses historical periods and academic disciplines, always with similar basic manifestations. In communication studies it appears as the model of *sender, message,* and *receiver.* In composition and writing scholarship it emerges as *voice, purpose,* and *audience.*

In our sample situation, the parents and principal (speakers/senders) sided together to construct an argument (purpose/message) about the damaging effects of red ink on students (the audience/receivers) to persuade teachers to stop wielding the red pen. The media (another speaker/sender) picked up on this message and broadcast it to an even larger audience beyond the school, making teachers look like the main producers of school stress. Teachers we know replied to one another with their own message based on experience and research, as did our colleague to his doctor: the content of what the red markings have to say to students outweighs the color of ink. It's too bad these teachers were too busy teaching to mount a rhetorical reply to an audience as large as those who read about the situation in the first place. Information based on experience and research (logos), mixed with teachers' knowledge and background (ethos) and teachers' understanding of a public audience (pathos) might have moved the situation in a different direction. Teachers' authority might have clarified (or even overturned) the public complaints.

We know what we're doing in the classroom and why we do it. At times, though, we put our rhetorical power on hold because of local, state, and national mandates as well as public pressures. But good data, well analyzed, intelligently interpreted, and creatively disseminated, allow us to both create and improve the conditions for teaching. When we conduct research we allow ourselves stronger positions, clearer evidence, and proof of what works best and why. When we disseminate the findings of our studies creatively, we gain rhetorical agency and put ourselves in a position to persuade others—teachers, principals, parents, the media, and of course, our students. As teachers, we have a responsibility to share our findings in the best ways we can imagine. We need to open our classroom doors and, through our rhetorical choices, allow the public to see what we've seen and learn what we've learned by virtue of our own personal insights and analyses.

> ⚙ *Good data, well analyzed, intelligently interpreted, and creatively disseminated, allow us to both create and improve the conditions for teaching. When we conduct research we allow ourselves stronger positions, clearer evidence, and proof of what works best and why.*

Questions of Pathos

When we begin a study, we need to understand ourselves and our positions, assumptions, personal biases—in Aristotle's terms, the *ethos* of the rhetorical situation. But as we progress, one of the most important decisions we need to make is about audience—sharing the information with others and who these others might be. We need to know the audience, need to exercise the *pathos* element of the rhetorical situation.

As we think about audiences, we want to ask questions like these:

- ☀ Who needs to know this information?

- ☀ What do they already think about it?

- ☀ How do I best broadcast the information (my data)?

- ☀ Where and when should I disseminate my findings? how and why?

- ☀ Who will most benefit from what I've learned? parents, other teachers, administrators, students, publishers, townspeople?

- ☀ What types of arguments will appeal to this audience?

☀ What is the most effective way to convince these people about my findings?

☀ What do I want to persuade this audience to do?

Not all teacher inquiry needs to end up in an academic journal or as a conference presentation. Karen Wohlwend's *Childhood Education* article on first graders' friendships (see Chapter 8) is both significant and powerful for the journal's readership (audience) of elementary school administrators, but Karen could present her findings in a variety of other ways: at a parent-teacher meeting at the school, in an advice sheet for pediatricians or child psychologists, as a public radio segment about preparing young children for school conflicts, or in a newspaper column on parenting issues.

The teachers you've met in this book have disseminated their research studies in ways that, depending on their circumstances, reached the audiences they wanted to persuade. Most of these teachers were interested in improving their own teaching. Many wanted to disseminate research findings among the parents and taxpayers in their schools' towns. Many chose to share their studies with audiences of other teachers. Many chose several different forms. Many are still choosing. Let's take a closer look at some possible audiences.

1. The self as audience:

   As we meet an audience with a message, we need to think "ethos" again, to consider our position, situation, and background in relationship to the audience. As speakers/writers/teachers who have conducted research in our own classroom, we can build real credibility and authority into a rhetorical occasion:

   • Who am I to be sharing this information?

   • What do I know about it that others don't know?

   • How did I come to know it?

   • What do I think about what I've learned?

   But sometimes the audience for doing teacher inquiry is only ourselves and our desire to present a better lesson or discussion or just to understand or reexamine ourselves as teachers and the assumptions, stereotypes, and overall baggage we bring into our classroom. This is an admirable goal and we've seen some courageous teachers take it on:

Beth Campbell, a "lateral entry" high school teacher, learned how to connect the literary term *irony* with her students' rap poems and songs.

Carole Center, a college instructor, studied her own classroom discourse in an effort to improve her group discussions.

Collyn Rybarczk, a high school teacher, investigated her own assumptions about having her brother in her class as a student and extended that to investigate more of her assumptions.

2. Students as audience:

In many studies, the focal audience is our students. Three teachers whose inquiries are used as examples in this book helped their students be more comfortable and capable writers:

Michelle Gioseffi, through the use of writer's notebooks.

Jennifer Gorzelany, through corresponding with her students via email.

Luke Flynn, through lessening the writing anxieties his students brought into his classes.

3. Curriculum and institutional policies as audience:

Many of our example teachers developed new curricula, policies, or institutional connections that went beyond the students in their particular classroom:

Christina Adams created a yearbook curriculum for a high school course that previously had none.

Charlotte Foth argued against the male-oriented sophomore curriculum in her high school and was able to include more works by women.

Keith Dodge invited his students to suggest reading and writing assignments for the school's AP courses.

Some teachers were interested in changing school policy. All of these studies demanded that the teacher-researcher consider a more extended audience of colleagues and principals in order to argue for the changes they desired. Projects that involved families and agencies demanded arguments that were grounded in an understanding of these particular groups' agendas.

Hayley Walton's study of the time spent on testing allowed her to convince her principal and her colleagues that their school curriculum was being skewed toward testing, not content.

Polly Lepic's study of behaviorally disordered students within art classes helped paraeducators work with those students in more thoughtful ways.

Marianne Richardson convinced her colleagues that spending time reading books aloud to elementary school students resulted in better reading comprehension as well as ideas about how books are made.

Steve Vanderstaay's investigation into the relationship between the social justice and educational systems allowed him to make informed suggestions to agencies on both sides that deal with troubled youth.

4. Local community as audience:

A number of our example teacher-inquiry projects were directed outward to the community. When projects are directed at community members, the insider language of school must be shed in favor of communicating with a more general population who need to understand the overall reasons behind the research.

George McLaughlin's high school students' research on the immigrant population of their neighborhood became both a museum exhibit and part of a community festival, celebrating immigrant populations in the state.

Wendy Caszatt-Allen reached out to work with the university to create a collaborative partnership between her eighth graders and college writers to get both groups to understand one another better as writers.

Sue Gradual's doll-making study was part of a statewide community heritage project.

5. Professional community as audience:

Still other teachers in this book presented their research more formally as talks or posters for local or national teacher organizations, an audience that shares the more academic language often found in professional journals.

Gail Russell shared her work on writing and reflection both with state educators and with local teachers in a writing-across-the-curriculum conference.

Beth Rosen Cope gave a talk at the National Council of Teachers of English annual convention in which she discussed the differences between teaching the same literature in a coed public school and in an all-girl private school.

Karen Wohlwend's project on first graders' friendships became a published journal article as well as two talks at national conferences, one on writing and one on research.

Disseminating our work to a variety of different audiences gives us professional agency and the power to bring about educational reform. It is also a mark of our personal courage, our credibility, and our confidence in the hard work we've done. When we think of ourselves as thoughtful, systematic inquirers, it is easier to resist the pressure to adopt programs, policies, and pedagogies that don't seem to fit our teaching contexts. Sharing ideas from our research matters, however small our audience may be.

◈ Mindwork: "Try On" a Few Audiences

Choose several different audiences who might want to learn about your particular teacher research project. First consider your in-school audiences: yourself, your students, your colleagues, school departments, the whole school, parent-teacher organizations. Next consider district, county, regional, state, national, and international educators and others interested in school policies. Finally, think about nonschool audiences such as community organizations, historical societies, local libraries, newspapers, newsletters, magazines, journals, and popular media.

Write a short letter to a representative of a particular audience stating the reason you have selected that group as an audience for the project you have completed:

◈ Give the title of your project and describe the form it will take.

◈ Summarize it and present your arguments for disseminating your research findings to your target audience:
  • What are the advantages of sharing your research project with this particular audience?
  • What difference do you hope it will make for their interests?
  • What changes might it bring about?

Continued on next page

Continued from previous page

Write another short letter, to someone who represents a different group. Write a third letter, to someone from yet another group. Examine all three letters. Think about the similarities and differences in audience and dissemination. Could a single dissemination design reach all three audiences? Would that be appropriate?

Choosing a Genre

Closely related to the idea of targeting an audience for your research is that of selecting a genre for disseminating it. This is another choice you'll need to make as you think about broadcasting your research beyond your-self and your classroom. With the options provided by computers, teachers currently have many more available genres for presenting their research than they used to. Certainly, the most familiar and accepted genres include student assignments, lesson and curriculum plans, and scope and sequence units, but there may be others that are more suitable for the audience you have selected. The teacher-researchers featured in this book shaped their studies into a variety of different genres:

> ☼ With the options provided by computers, teachers currently have many more available genres for presenting their research than they used to.

- ☀ Media presentations (computer presentations, videos, local television and radio shows). Gail Russell developed several PowerPoint presentations, which she used in inservice workshops for her colleagues at her high school. Karen Wohlwend offered PowerPoint presentations at conferences. Polly Lepic used slides, photographs, and an exhibit.

- ☀ Dramatic and artistic exhibitions (museum displays, library displays, performance art, community events). Holly Richardson invited the community in Aniak, Alaska, to hear the local stories her students had collected in an anthology. Sue Gradual exhibited her dolls in a special booth at a two-week state cultural heritage festival. George McLaughlin's studies of immigrant students became an exhibit at a local library as well as a series of news articles.

- ☀ Websites, brochures, bulletin boards, kiosks, anthologies (a combination of verbal and visual representation shared publicly with anyone who might be interested and wants to "visit" at their convenience). Lia Schultz's study of fifteen generations of her family's literacy became a photographic exhibit for her small community, as well as a website for anyone to find. Tara Lynn and Holly Richardson both produced anthologies of student work.

- ☀ Professional development courses (curriculum or pedagogical ideas shared with colleagues or students). Deanna Stoube used her study of how home literacy affected school literacy to develop curriculum and assignments for her preservice teachers. Keith Dodge, as department chair, uses his student panels each time he and his colleagues consider curriculum change.

- ☀ Academic conferences (poster presentations, workshops, panels). Many teachers we've worked with have presented alone and on panels at state, regional, and national professional conferences.

- ☀ Academic degree requirements. Many teachers we've worked with have presented their work as master's theses and doctoral dissertations, as well as National Board Certification portfolios.

Composing as a Process

No matter how you choose to disseminate your research to an audience, it will always involve acts of composing: brainstorming, drafting, redrafting, revising, revising again, and editing. Before you compose with pictures or music or pixels or electronics, you'll need to compose with words. Language gets your message across. Certainly, every medium has its own language, but each also needs to be planned and executed using written language. The writing process is similar whether you arrange a museum display or assemble a PowerPoint presentation. Our end products may look different, but each one involves language, and therefore each one involves writing.

Whether you've taught a writing course or only taken one, you already know a lot about your own writing process. Let's review the basics, focusing on what makes writing different when it's about the research you've done. As with much else in life, it begins with you and what you already know. Think about what and how you write, and expand your definition to include all the paperwork you do in your professional life: anecdotal reports, memos, lesson plans, handouts for students, recommendations, notes to parents and administrators, emails to colleagues. It's important to include personal writing as well: formal and informal notes to your family; newsletters; toasts and eulogies; birthday poems; holiday letters to friends; log or daybook or journal writing; and computer blogs, emails, and chat rooms. How do you get ideas on paper? interest the audience you're addressing? revise for meaning? edit and polish your work? Try not to treat your inquiry project any differently than you would any of these writing tasks. Lean on what you already know about how, when, and why you compose for an audience.

Incubation and Invention

Writers and researchers have taught us that we write even when we are not writing. Often, we do it away from our desks. Ideas incubate when we're in the car or the shower, while we're cooking or walking the dog. Our minds make the important connections that they can't make when we're stuck inside a developing text. It's not a matter of the visit from the magical muse, but more simply it's a matter of receiving the ideas that lurk in the corners of our minds. Invention, another term we've inherited from ancient rhetoric, is where it begins.

Of course, all writers and researchers procrastinate. We move furniture around, eat candy, take long naps, and pace in circles. But this, in a way, is writing, too. It's the incubation or percolation process when ideas grow and simmer. Behaviors that involve catching initial ideas and writing them down are actually part of the invention process, what teachers call "prewriting." When you are still imagining the shape of your final product, you may do some freewriting, listing, mapping, cubing, or countless other terms used to identify ways of getting ideas on the page. We hope you've done them already throughout the research process. Bonnie likes to call them "brain dumps." These are just starter ideas, thrown together in a pile for recycling later. Don't get too attached to your early writing, but don't throw it away either.

Still another way to get yourself started on your project is to develop a *lead* (spelled *lede* in the newspaper business), or a compelling opening. A staff presentation might begin with an informal story or relevant visual, but a lead for a teacher newsletter would perhaps involve an interest-grabbing review of a current problem. In either case, the lead helps the writer or speaker set the tone and establish voice and authority; most important, it invites an audience to meet the rest of the work. Spending time constructing a compelling lead can be a very good investment. On the other hand, a good lead might not come until after you've done the bulk of your drafting—and then it will help you shape a final product.

You have brainstormed about both your audience and a possible genre in which to share your teacher inquiry. You can imagine how your final product will look. Now try an exercise in invention. Think hard and further about your own composing process:

◈ What parts of writing are usually easiest for you?

◈ What parts are most difficult?

◈ Where do you usually get stuck?

◈ What resources do you have for getting unstuck?

◈ Who is your best response partner?

◈ To which writing texts do you find yourself returning again and again?

◈ What environment helps you work best?

We know you know the answers to all these questions, but before launching a new project, it's often helpful to reassure yourself that you have the information, sources, and support you'll need to complete it. Gather them all together in your mind and make two lists: what you have and what you need. Keep this posted near your computer and near your research questions to guide you through the composing process.

SNAPSHOT: Tara Lynn Finds a Controlling Metaphor

Tara Lynn, who teaches eighth grade in an inner-city alternative school in Newark, New Jersey, has developed a poetry unit in the hopes of providing her students with both the academic and life skills they need and now wants to study their reactions. In the positioning section of her research project Tara writes about how important poetry has been in her own life:

As a reader and writer of poetry, I have experienced over and over again how poetry can be a life compass. Poetry has helped me navigate my life and feel connected to myself and others. It has healed me in turbulent times and helped me celebrate in joyous times. When I set out to design my case study, I knew I wanted to give my students the gift of the poetry compass. I knew poetry could make them more human. To do so, I would have to steer clear of teaching poetry from a traditional standpoint.

Tara knows she has a responsibility to teach academic skills to her students. Their past experience has turned them off to poetry. She vows not to have them tear poetry apart but to see it as a way to lead their lives with what she calls "an illuminated compass." Using the compass as a guiding metaphor helps Tara design assignments that encourage her students to be "reflective, self-aware, and expressive," to learn to navigate their lives with the help of others' poetry as well as their own. The compass metaphor influences her project so much that she uses it to craft a formal course paper and create a presentation for her colleagues.

As she follows her three very different case study students, Tara's assignments encourage them to read poetry closely and then make an anthology of their favorite poems as well as to write poems in response to the books they are reading: S. E. Hinton's *The Outsiders* and Elie Wiesel's *Night*. And yes, she also has them write a poetry analysis paper, since that is required by her school's standard course of study.

Tara's students create self-portrait anthologies that they share with one another: after perusing many poems, each student settles on four poems and writes responses about each. They are fascinated by one another's choices and their comments, and they love trading anthologies to autograph and read. Each student becomes an expert on the particular "compass" he or she has designed.

Cassandra, for example, writes about a poem by Melissa Collette from *Chicken Soup for the Teenage Soul*: "The poem 'Inside' is really a poem about me. There are some things that I won't ever say to anyone. I will just hide things until it makes me sick as a moose." In another response, to "Anonymous," by Christopher Viner, Cassandra writes: "I can relate to this poem because it is about someone that is not really known. I think that is me because right now I am not known to anyone. I am really invisible to mostly everything and everyone around me. One part of the poem I really liked is 'My insides don't know my outsides.' I really think that is right because I don't really know who I am." As her teacher, Tara feels this reflection accurately describes Cassandra's attitude in that on the outside she is "caustic and volatile" but on the inside she is "vulnerable." The poetry portraits help Tara get to know her students more intimately as they are getting to know themselves.

Things do not go perfectly with Cassandra. After an argument one day, Tara has to ask her to leave class. After school, they meet and Tara points out that Cassandra has choices about the way she behaves, that her presence in school can be either positive or negative. Two weeks later when Cassandra hands in her poetry portfolio she includes a poem she has written called "Choices": "So many choices / For any and everything / Choices about colors: / Brown or Beige / Red, Green or even Tangerine." Cassandra's poem takes a more serious turn toward the end: "It is you / Who has the power / to choose / whatever you desire."

Tara makes sure that her students' toolbox of skills contains more than disparate lessons, that they also include human skills. She writes at the end of her study, "Focusing on human skills makes teaching and learning academic skills more organic." Tara's use of the metaphorical compass also helps readers of her study understand what she is setting out to accomplish. But far more important, Tara's students' unique poetry anthologies offer them insights into the universality of poetry's value as a "human compass" and the specificity of each person's poetic and life-involving choices. The dissemination of this project encompassed a course paper, a professional presentation, and a classful of student anthologies, but Tara's research will enrich her teaching for years to come, as well as one alternative school's attitude toward poetry.

Drafting and Revising

With research writing, a first or second draft usually yields only one of the multiple layers of data and information we have to share. But as in all writing, we draft, seek response, and revise as we shift our text away from our private understanding and closer and closer toward offering it to our chosen audience. Research writing by teachers is a unique genre; as we've said, it is a blended form. It draws on experience, like the personal essay. It has alliances with journalistic or scientific reporting because its main sources are researched data. Its relatives are anecdotal records and school reports because we use a range of student voices to bring our classroom research to life. Teacher inquiry often includes images, so it requires the conciseness of poetry. Recapturing classroom talk demands the dialogue of a drama or a novel. And since teacher-research writing describes people in the context of their classroom culture, it often seems like good anthropology or compelling documentary film.

Since research writing is its own form, the work requires its own techniques and tools. Combining disparate data into a draft is like baking a meringue and trying to add nuts or chocolate chips. The goal is to fold the ingredients into the stiffly beaten eggwhite mixture, not to stir it, not to

> ⚙ *Since research writing is its own form, the work requires its own techniques and tools. . . . It finds its shape and texture from the data.*

have it collapse. The meringue must remain strong and fluffy enough to hold the nuggets you drop into it. In research writing, you drop the multitextured data into your personal account of your classroom research so that it will blend with the narrative and not collapse either the story or the evidence. Similarly, by "folding in" your data nugget by nugget, piece by piece, you create a thick and strong mixture of data sources: descriptions, quotations, field notes, reflections, readings, personal experience, charts, maps, visuals, and more. Your research finds its shape and texture from the data.

While gathering your data, you've probably composed many useful pieces of text that you can use directly in your research writing. For example, you may be able to quote from your own journal notes or show maps and visual displays, as Karen Wohlwend did in her playground study. You may want to quote directly from your students' talk, as Holly Richardson did with her students' accounts of their ancestors' stories. You will want to excerpt transcripts, as Charlotte Foth did in her study of the male-dominated literature curriculum. If you want to share with your reader how your thinking changed over time, you may return to your research question and reconsider it, as Gail Russell did while she developed her tenth-grade writing curriculum. Another way to integrate the different types of data as you draft your final project is to use the mindwork exercises you've completed in this book.

These ready-to-use chunks of writing by themselves will not make a smooth ready-for-audience draft, but they may suggest a framework as you look at them, analyze them, recombine them, and organize them into the story you want to tell.

Working with chunks of text might suggest a lack of focus in other forms of writing, but in research writing your project has already found

> ⚙ *Working with chunks of text might suggest a lack of focus in other forms of writing, but in research writing your project has already found its shape in your guiding question.*

its shape in your guiding question, which functions as a "thesis statement." That's the good news. The bad news is that once you begin to write, you'll see that you can't use all of the data you've collected. Although you have a focus and analytical themes, once you begin combining data to re-create a picture or confirm a point, you'll need to decide what's worth using and what you must give up. One solution is to present a "slice," a cross-section of your data, in order to create an image or support an idea. Sometimes a well-written slice, like a good image, can illustrate a much larger context.

SNAPSHOT: Andy Clinton's Revision Renaissance

Andy Clinton is an accomplished teacher. But, like many of us, he has resisted revision for much of his life as a writer. "I've never really enjoyed revision," he admits. "In fact, I've always dreaded it." To him, revision seems like "just another excuse for people to criticize me and tell me why I should write the way *they would*, or make the points *they would* make. . . . The idea of writing a true draft, taking it apart, and doing something fundamentally new with it has always been foreign to me." After all his years in grade school, high school, college, and graduate school (as an English major), and now as a teacher of college composition and tutor in a high school writing center, he finds himself "still indignant at classes in which drafts are mandatory, stubbornly reluctant to do anything more with a paper that is 'just fine the way it is.'"

In a course called Approaches to Teaching Writing, he is required to revise and read about revision. Andy recognizes himself in Donald Murray's book, *The Craft of Revision*: "As luck would have it, I am not alone in this feeling. . . . Having never met me, Murray put his finger precisely (and uncomfortably) on the resentment I've always felt. If there were a defensive stink-gland against revision, I would clear the room."

As he works on a memoir with an in-class writing group over a six-week period, Andy watches his need for revision unfold: "I chose to write on a very personal matter of adolescent infatuation that still, more than a decade later, stings a little. As we moved from prewriting to a first draft, I unconsciously hid the details from my reader. . . . Why on earth would I need to expand on the geeky details of the setting, the interactions between my friends, my starry-eyed obsession with one of them in particular?" But Andy's writing group wants exactly those details: "They weren't just the context of my story; they *were* the story." Andy's group asks sincere questions, they push him for elaboration, they find potential buried in his words, and their enthusiasm for his voice and humor give him energy to revise further. He recalls:

> I remember hearing one of the art directors for the modern *Star Wars* films discussing his process for getting the most out of his drawings. In designing costumes, spaceships, alien creatures, and

other assorted bric-a-brac of the *Star Wars* universe, he would keep drawing, adding more and more detail, until finally he ruined the design by going a step too far. Then, miraculously, he would erase his last addition to find the perfect design staring at him. Without pushing it over the edge, he would never know how far he could take his ideas. With my group's encouragement, I began to allow for experimentation in my own writing. . . . The energy that took over was much less a drive to get the work done and much more a spirit of extended play.

Andy finds confirmation in another book he reads for this course, Ralph Fletcher's *What a Writer Needs* (1992). Fletcher asserts, "The writer's fascination with words has roots in the child's natural play with language" (33). "I play a lot," Andy admits, "I talk to myself, try out jokes, puns, skits, rhymes, voices, songs, harmonies. I do this at home, in the car, in the classroom, in public at restaurants, and in my poetry. Where I've never really done it before, though, is in revision."

By being given an assignment that expects many revisions and requires reflective writing about revision, Andy, with the support of his class writing group, is able "to free myself from my *in-stink-tual* defense against criticism or judgment in the revision process. . . . Where it had always hit me like a phaser set on 'stun,' revision now became an insistent child who wouldn't let me read the bedtime story without doing all the voices. The child gains satisfaction from this, but so does the adult. It's simply more fun to tell a story the right way."

Andy's writing, reading, and course experience influence his work—and consequently his research—as an intern in a high school writing center. He sees a lot of papers from one particular AP writing class, and they drive him crazy: "Check marks in the margins indicating an error in the corresponding line. The more check marks, the more errors to find. These errors are not circled, not corrected, not acknowledged as anything other than hidden evildoers needing to be destroyed . . . like a demonic Easter egg hunt."

He tries to analyze the perceived problems, as do the writing center students: "Inevitably, they want to spend time finding these errors and eliminating them, so the writing center staffer and the student end up playing an extended round of 'guess what I'm thinking' with a teacher who isn't even there. . . . It may be a method of teaching students to be better proofreaders of their own work, but it teaches them to see revision as making their papers 'correct' rather than making them more interesting or more expressive. . . . This is important editing, but not revising. The shrugging and eye-rolling of the writing center students leads me to believe that this strategy doesn't encourage them to value revision at all. Believe me, I can relate."

Andy focuses his attention on Alex, a young woman who is writing a series of vignettes for her English 10 honors class. As Alex revises with Andy and asks her friends to read her drafts, Andy sees that her definition of revision changes—as does his understanding of helping a student revise. "Writing teachers must enjoy a sense of play," he suggests, "if they want their students to be enthusiastic revisers. The joy of experimentation is far more important in revision than the crushing doldrums of error hunting. . . . With playful energy, the curiosity and guidance of multiple readers, and frequent opportunities for self-reflection, we can teach our students to approach revision the way we would like them to—as an opportunity rather than a punishment."

Practicing what he preaches, Andy adds a "Director's Commentary" to his final essay about his project. In this section he details the process of constructing the study and writing the essay. Here are some excerpts:

> I progressed from a two-page topic proposal, to a five-page draft/outline (with annotated place holders describing what I wanted to say that I hadn't gotten around to yet), to a revised draft with my own marginal comments on thematic issues I still wanted to develop and books and articles I wanted to incorporate. In the past, I've written papers mostly in one (very long) sitting. For this paper, though, despite my deeply ingrained instincts, I worked slowly, sometimes in fragments, but more or less consistently over several weeks. I didn't want to write a paper about encouraging revision without actually drafting and revising it several times. . . . This paper defied my expectations, and I had to put my money where my mouth is in revising it, but it taught me that the progress I've made in learning to embrace revision is something that will continue to serve me well, and can only help my writing.

◈ Mindwork: Respond for Revision

Good responses prompt effective revision. But in order to get them, the writer needs to know what to ask. You have a response partner, or a writing group of several colleagues you trust. No one is particularly confident about writing, asking, or responding, and you're all working on the kinds of research projects that require the new kinds of writing described in this book. Meet with your partner or group, each of you bringing a copy of your draft. Choose the section—or sections—on which you'd like response. As the author of an unfinished draft, you should be able to decide what you need. As a responder, it's your job to listen to what the author wants of you, offer your reaction, and not make value judgments ("it's sooooo good" or "oh, this really bothers me" or "I disagree"). Use some of these questions (or adaptations of them) to guide your session:

Questions of Summary

◈ Tell me about your project in one or two sentences. Perhaps a version of the research question would be a start.

◈ What surprised you while you were writing this draft, this time?

◈ What's the most important thing you want to say?

◈ What is your favorite part? What section is problematic?

◈ What section do you like?

Questions of Organization

◈ Can you tell me how this example connects with your main idea?

◈ I'm confused about . . .

◈ Tell me more about . . .

◈ At what stage do you think this project is? Second or third? Almost finished?

Questions of Revision

◈ What are you working on now? What may I help you with?

◈ How many separate projects could you write from this one draft? What would each one be about?

◈ What part of the paper do you want to work on?

Continued on next page

Continued from previous page

❖ How do you want to bring the reader into the paper? What kind of lead will you use? How will the lead connect with the main idea?

❖ How do you want to end the paper? What do you want the reader to think about after finishing? What kind of end are you planning?

Anyone should leave a writing conference, whether it's with peers or an instructor or even an editor, wanting to write more, so end it with the most important question of all: *what will you do next?*

Editing

Until our drafts and revisions have yielded something that says what we want it to say, we don't want to abort a growing piece of writing. Sometimes, especially in research writing, it takes as many drafts as we have data sources. But eventually we know when we've covered the territory, illustrated and documented what we have to say enough for a reader to make sense of what we've learned. At that point, we can begin the tinkering and smoothing that will polish our final product.

> ⚙ *Anyone should leave a writing conference, whether it's with peers or an instructor or even an editor, wanting to write more.*

Grammar and syntactical clarity, of course, make the ultimate difference to a reader. Strong nouns hold cultural meanings and create concise images. Verbs bring action to the page and free sentences of clutter. Adjectives and adverbs can be dangerous when we use them too frequently: they mask assumptions. "The perky dog greeted me with a loving lick" might be one person's view of a situation, but someone else might say, "The frantic, yappy dog attacked me with his wet and probing tongue." Two sets of adjectives and adverbs, two sets of assumptions, two attitudes, two perspectives. As researchers, we have a special responsibility to use language precisely. In bringing our observations to the page, we must translate our informants' voices and perspectives and yet acknowledge our own presence in our text. It is an exciting and creative challenge.

◈ Mindwork: Edit to Polish

Once your draft says what you want it to mean, try a few of these "precise language" strategies:

1. Clean up "word dust." Scan through your writing for words that don't need to be there: long strings of prepositional phrases, for example, hide weak verbs. ("He came in, sat in his seat, in the back of the room next to the window" might be more effective as, "He sauntered toward the seat closest to the back window.")

2. Find places in which a few lines of dialogue might replace your own description about what happened when there were people involved in a scene. "Yeah, what about it?" is much more interesting and alive than "She snapped out an impolite answer."

3. Try a "verb pass." Comb through your text for the sole purpose of identifying the verbs. Circle each one and try to find alternatives that might bring more action to your sentences and hence to your research. *Walk*, for instance, can become *saunter*, *toddle*, *dart*, *lumber*, *clomp*, *traipse*, *dawdle*, *slither*, or *pace*. Forcing yourself to find the right verb makes you look more closely at the action in your notes and at your field site. Finding the right verb may not happen, though, until you've drafted and redrafted, until you have the time to look only for verbs.

There are many other ways to check on your clarity of grammar and syntax: length of sentences, complexity of sentences, awkward punctuation, use of jargon, and so on. We recommend keeping a good grammar handbook close as you draft and revise.

Our Writing Research Heritage

This book is as much about writing as it is about research. The processes involved in composing for dissemination are inseparable from the processes of writing. And we have learned about them from a number of sources. First, we have inherited much of our understanding about writing from writers themselves. Second, the large and ever-growing body of formal empirical research by composition theorists and linguists regularly produces new findings and insights. But there is a third category: courageous practicing teachers whose work is based on their own classroom inquiry, often in partnership with their students. These writers have allowed us to peek into their classrooms and sit behind their writing desks, form research questions with them, and watch what happens. Here are the names of just a few: Deborah Appleman, Nancie Atwell, Maureen Barbieri, Glenda Bissex, Randy Bomer, Lucy Calkins, Todd DeStigter, Russell Durst, Lisa Ede, Karen Ernst, Ralph Fletcher, Danling Fu, John Gaughan, Shelley Harwayne, Doug Kaufman, Andrea Lunsford, James Marshall, Tom Newkirk, JoAnn Portalupi, Linda Rief, Marjorie Roemer, Tom Romano, Donna Qualley, Mina Shaughnessey, Susan Stires, Patricia Stock, Lad Tobin, Jeff Wilhelm, Ruth Vinz. We are in distinguished company.

We're lucky to have such an accessible heritage, such a rich archive of our work as teachers, researchers, and writers. These are people who engage in praxis every day, who have chosen to disseminate their classroom studies in books, articles, and other genres. Your research and writing, not to mention your teaching, will draw from and inform this heritage.

Being asked to generalize a list of ten "greatest hit" ideas about research on writing over the years is intimidating. Bonnie was given that challenge about ten years ago. "Okay," said a grant administrator, who admitted he knew nothing about writing, "I didn't even know it was a *field*. You know, writing. Like *themes*. You know?" And then he dropped the bombshell. "Name ten things writing research has taught you in the last four decades. And present them to my board of directors. You'll have twelve minutes."

It's a provocative question, and we've been working on it ever since. Since we think it will make a good summary, here goes:

1. *Writing is a social act.* Writers write for an audience, choose their genres accordingly, and appreciate response. It's important to find a tolerant, knowledgeable audience for every stage of the project, including invention. Teach your audience what you as a writer need at the time you share your writing.

2. *Writing is an interconnected act.* Writing and reading are inseparable. As writers, we incorporate the texts we've read; as readers, we read our own texts—section to section, sentence to sentence, idea to idea.

3. *Writing is a tool for working out thinking.* We use writing privately to record our ideas and growth, publicly to articulate for others what we'd like them to know about us. Writing is a link between "inner speech" (the thoughts that swim through our minds) and public articulation.

4. *Writing is recursive.* There are no distinct "stages," there is no one specific "process," but we can describe certain features of writing:

prewriting techniques, habits of first-draft writing, strategies for responding to others' drafts for purposes of revision, conferencing models, inventories of grammatical conventions and mechanics, publishing opportunities.

5. *Writing and grammar are different.* "Grammars" are the agreed-on conventions for how language is used within a particular genre or context. Errors of grammar are easier to correct than errors of thinking or documentation. Most often, writers commit one error or a cluster of errors rather than making multiple ones. These are issues of editing rather than meaning. But that's no excuse. If a writer is to articulate what she or he means, the final product must be error free.

6. *Revising and editing are different.* "Revision" means reseeing. It is opportunity, not punishment. It is not "correction." To revise means to try on another perspective, shift to another genre or point of view, speak in another voice, organize in an alternate way, insert data or more explanation, change tone, expand and elaborate, add someone else's ideas or words, locate and delete irrelevancies. Revision can be as radical as reframing a whole piece of writing or as precise as smoothing out bumpy piles of words into polished text.

7. *Writing is a responsibility in all disciplines.* Whether a writer creates a personal journal, an engineering memo, a scientific report, a clinical study, a script for a documentary, anecdotal patient records, a business marketing profile, expertise in writing means understanding both the demands of the discipline and the procedures involved in the task of writing for the appropriate reader.

8. *Writing about writing encourages writing development.* The act of writing is different with each piece we write. Describing our writing "freezes the action" and "captures the context" so we can see the conditions under which writing takes place, discern the differences from piece to piece. Reflective writing includes habits like maintaining a journal or daybook about what we're thinking, keeping a portfolio, tracking experiments in a log notebook. Such writings are notebooks of our minds at work and illustrate our metacognitive processes—to us.

9. *All writing involves collaboration.* Whether we write alone, within a visible community, online with invisible respondents, with a partner

(as we, Bonnie and Elizabeth, are doing this very moment), we lean on the reactions and support of our chosen others. We draw ideas and refine thoughts in concert with our collaborators. Collaboration in writing produces a whole that is larger and better than the sum of its parts.

10. *A writing community makes the concept of audience more visible.* Reading drafts for a regular group of respondents, particularly ones whom you trust and who know what you need, can bring the idea of audience to life. As you move your writing from draft to finished product, it is always best to envision a reader. Articulating what kind of response you need and creating a habitual writing community is the way to do it. Whether you begin that habit with formal classroom writing groups; informal evening groups of other writers with similar interests; a spouse, sibling, son, or daughter; or one friend, you "test out" your writing on an audience while it's still in draft—and move it toward effective revision.

◈ *Mindwork:* Read Research on Writing

Find an article or book written by a teacher about writing, one that's relevant to your discipline, grade level, or topic. It may be one of your all-time favorites. Or it may be something you've been wanting to read but haven't yet.

◈ What universal ideas about writing are mentioned?

◈ What data are used to illustrate these ideas?

◈ How—and over what period of time—did the author collect these data?

◈ How does the author share her or his own professional experiences with the reader?

◈ What is new for you?

◈ What did you already know?

◈ How might these ideas relate to your teaching of writing?

◈ How might these ideas relate to your own writing process as you construct the final product of your research?

And, Finally, Back to Praxis

We end this book by returning to *praxis*, an idea we introduced at its beginning and one we believe teacher inquiry is all about. Our friend and colleague Hephzibah Roskelly (2005) defines *praxis* better than anyone we know, as the movement between action and reflection:

> *Praxis* is really a theory about theories, in fact, a way of explaining how theories are derived, made workable and necessarily altered. Engagement in *praxis*, then, is crucial for teachers as they attempt to nurture the literacies of their students . . . to experience, to understand experience, and to use understanding to change and improve experience. It requires both the time to speculate, explore, and theorize and the ability to apply reflection to action. (289)

In this book we've emphasized the kinds of informed and thorough projects that allow you the authority to begin change or to work against mandated procedures already in place and to add your voice to the richly historical and long-lived chorus of educational reformers. Teachers who conduct classroom inquiry give themselves the validity, evidence, and documentation to make changes, whether personal, curricular, schoolwide, community-wide, statewide, regional, national, or international. Teachers who ask what works, gather data, and present what they discover in systematic ways are those we admire in classrooms and recognize as the leaders in our field. We hope this book helps you to be a teacher who asks, "What works?"

Frequently Asked Questions About Writing Research

Writing is a complex cultural act. No wonder it's fascinated people throughout history and that we continue to study and write about it. As we conclude, we want to present the sorts of questions that teacher-inquirers ask about writing. We've heard them many times. We've asked them ourselves about our own research writing, and they seem to echo consistent themes.

Although the term FAQs (Frequently Asked Questions) has become annoyingly commonplace in our Web-based culture, their real purpose is to summarize, anticipate, and offer helpful advice to a specific audience. Thus we compile these FAQs to help you navigate the specifics of "writing up" your work, a task that may be unfamiliar and feel somewhat unsettling but which, ironically, draws from the very topic we as teachers spend most of our time exploring—the fundamentals of writing.

Q: *How can I use what I already know as I draft my inquiry project?*

A: Think about what and how you write, and expand your definition to include all the paperwork you do in your professional life: anecdotal reports, memos, lesson plans, handouts for students, recommendations, notes to parents and administrators, emails to colleagues. It's important to include personal writing as well: formal and informal notes to your family, newsletters, toasts and eulogies, birthday poems, holiday letters to friends, log or daybook or journal writing and computer blogs, emails and chat rooms. How do you get ideas on paper? interest the audience you're addressing? revise for meaning? edit and polish your work? Don't treat your inquiry project any differently than you would any of these writing tasks. Lean on what you already know:

1. Brainstorming, mapping, listing, outlining, freewriting, are great ways to get ideas onto a page (Bonnie calls them "brain dumps"). These are just starter ideas, thrown together in a pile for recycling later.

2. You write even when you're not writing. Often, away from your desk—in the car, in the shower, cooking, walking the dog—your mind makes the important connections that it can't make when you're stuck inside a developing text. It's not a matter of being visited by the magical "muse" but more simply being receptive to the ideas lurking in the corners of your mind.

3. A "lead," or compelling opening, helps you set the tone, establishes your voice and authority, and most important, invites a reader into your text to meet your work. Working on a good lead can be a very good investment. On the other hand, a good lead might not come until after you've done the bulk of your writing.

4. Sharing writing at all stages is the best way to know whether you're making sense to an audience. Ask your partner the questions the responses to which will help you revise.

5. Sometimes the gaps in your writing can tell you more than what's already there. As you look at a draft, ask yourself what's missing, what you need to find out more about, what details someone might need who doesn't know as much as you do about the topic.

6. Outlining a draft after you've written it can help you locate imbalances of details and information. What do you have too much of? What doesn't fit? What might a reader find incomplete or extraneous? Use your outline to create a new draft or a new outline.

Q: *What distinguishes research writing from writing I've done before?*

A: Research writing is a unique genre; in a way, it is a blended form. It draws on experience, like the personal essay. It has alliances with journalistic or scientific reporting because its main sources are researched data. Its relatives are anecdotal records and school reports because we use a range of student voices to bring our classroom research to life. Teacher inquiry often includes images, so it requires the conciseness of poetry. Recapturing classroom talk demands the dialogue of a drama or a novel. And since teacher-research writing describes people in the context of their classroom culture, it often seems like good anthropology or compelling documentary film.

Since research writing is its own form, the work requires its own techniques and tools. Combining disparate data into a draft is like baking a meringue and trying to add nuts or chocolate chips. The goal is to fold the ingredients into the stiffly beaten eggwhite mixture, not to stir it, not to have it collapse. The meringue must remain strong and fluffy enough to hold the nuggets you drop into it. In research writing, you drop the multitextured data into your personal account of your classroom research so that it will blend with the narrative and not collapse either the story or the evidence. Similarly, by "folding in" your data nugget by nugget, piece by piece, you create a thick and strong mixture of data sources: descriptions, quotations, field notes, reflections, readings personal experience, charts, maps, visuals, and more. Your research finds its shape and texture from the data.

Q: How do I manage the disparate data sources I have collected?

A: While gathering your data, you've probably composed many useful pieces of text that can be grafted directly into your research writing. You may be able to quote from your own journal notes or use maps and visual displays. You may want to use direct quotations from your students' talk. You will want to excerpt transcripts. You want to share with your reader how your thinking changed over time. These ready-to-use chunks of writing by themselves will not make a smooth ready-for-audience draft, but they may suggest a framework as you look at them, analyze them, recombine them, and organize them into the story you want to tell.

Working with chunks of text might suggest a lack of focus in other forms of writing, but in research writing your project has already found its shape in your guiding question, which functions as a "thesis statement." That's the good news. The bad news is that once you begin to write, you'll see that you can't use all of the data you've collected. Although you have a focus and analytical themes, once you begin combining data to re-create a picture or confirm a point, you'll need to decide what's worth using and what you must give up. One solution is to present a "slice," a cross-section of your data, in order to create an image or support an idea. Sometimes a well-written slice, like a good image, can illustrate a much larger context.

Q: How do I interrogate my own thinking? How do I monitor how my thinking has changed?

A: For sure, your thinking will have changed during the course of your research. Ask the three analytical questions one more time to synthesize the changes in your thinking: What surprised you? What intrigued you? What disturbed you? As you've answered these questions throughout your study, you're giving yourself (and potentially your reader) an account of how your assumptions, positions, and tensions have altered. Including these insights in your account provides the underlife, the backstory, of your research, which is sometimes even more valuable than the data themselves. Once you understand and write about how your thinking has changed, your reader will have a better sense of how you've come to your findings.

Q: How do I revise from one draft to another? How do I make this mass of data hang together into a smooth narrative account, even if it's not chronological?

A: Revision in research writing is the slow process of making a smooth text out of all those piles of disparate data. Sticking with a piece of writing through draft after draft allows you to experiment and try out options. Remember that first drafts often have characteristics you don't want in final drafts. Knowing what these characteristics are helps you ask for assistance—from readers whose responses will prompt subsequent drafts or simply with yourself. Bonnie and her colleague Joan Dunfey have identified these "healthy habits" of first draft writing:

- ☀ *Chronological or narrative structure.* The human "default mode" is chronology: "First this happened, then this, finally that." Often, in order to understand the bulk of material, it's important to outline or write in a chronological narrative. But that's certainly not how you have to present your ideas to the public. In a final presentation of your research, your story may be arranged by theme, by character, by setting—just as it would if you were writing a story.

- ☀ *"Saturated" words.* Psychologist Lev Vygotsky describes words that are "saturated" with meaning—words that may be perfectly clear to the writer but need more explanation for the reader. Often, especially in research writing, you forget that the images or ideas that have become completely familiar to you might need background information. The term *metacognitive reflection*, for example, is part of a professional vocabulary that contemporary teachers understand—it's "saturated" with images of students looking over their work and telling us about what they've learned. But to an audience of town taxpayers or government funders, it might appear as snobby educational jargon. In a first draft, the term can act as a placeholder, something you'd return to as you revise, knowing that it requires a more accessible explanation.

☀ *Multiple points of focus.* Just as you expect your students' first drafts will include multiple themes and ideas, expect your own will. Eventually, you'll need to rein them in for the reader's benefit. But for now you haven't yet polished your ideas, you have images and data you're not yet willing to discard, and you want your readers to know everything you know and see everything you've seen. It's healthy to find multiple focuses in first drafts. When you peruse a first draft with the intention of sharpening the focus in later drafts, you allow yourself to exercise the writer's option to choose what's relevant, what fits with the whole, finished piece.

☀ *Telling rather than showing.* A long narrative telling what happened, what it looked like, and what it meant can be the way you first describe a scene full of important data. But to a reader, long strings of thoughts from the writer are lifeless and boring. Remember Mark Twain's advice: "Don't say the old lady screamed. Bring her on and let her scream." As you write about your research, draft to draft, you must find ways to "bring on" the characters and images you've found so interesting. To bring your data to life, you can't invent what happened, but you can scrutinize your transcripts, field notes, and other people's words for the scenes you'd like to show. Use a dynamic "movie camera" to tell your story: alternate the focus from close-up to midshot to panoramic view. Manipulate language for dynamic effect. Leverage muscular verbs to do the heavy lifting; adjectives and adverbs can work as placeholders in drafts but are often wimpy and ineffective. It's impossible to accomplish all of this in a first draft; each scene requires intricate inspection. The role of the first draft is to frame the whole; it is in later drafts that you can work toward bringing your data to life.

☀ *Ambiguities.* It's disconcerting to read ambiguities in published work ("Bonnie and Elizabeth went to the café. She bought her a cup of coffee."). But a first draft is full of ambiguities: of reference, of image, of angle and point of view. You can't possibly make everything clear the first time. Asking readers to look for ambiguities is a wonderful way to find them. Or you can take the role of "the writer's other self" (Donald Murray's term) and read your own drafts as a reader, looking for ambiguous references. It's hard to detect ambiguity when you've created it, but knowing to look for it in early drafts (or in someone else's) is the best way to find it.

Q: How do I find a reader/writing partner to respond to my drafts? And then how do I help the reader help me?

A: All readers are not equal, particularly when you want someone to respond to your work "in progress." Try to find a writing partner who is neither too critical nor too complimentary, who won't make a value judgment on a draft. You don't want to hear "Wow, that's really great" or "It doesn't work for me!" or "Why don't you start all over again?" while you are developing a draft. A draft is not ready for someone's assessment—whether criticism or praise—not even yours. What you need is: "I want to know more about . . ." (to expand or add more details); "What I think you're trying to say here is . . ." (to summarize the meaning); "What confuses me is . . ." (to direct attention to specifics or lines of argument); "This reminds me of . . ." (to get a sense of your overall tone or impact, or to recognize an influence).

But it's also important to articulate clearly what kind of help you're looking for: "I'm having trouble with my lead. What's good about it? Where do you think this paper/presentation *really* begins?" "I feel like I'm doing all telling and no showing. How can I bring this draft to life with more details? What's working for you?" "What images can you see in my text? What's murky?" "My voice sounds formal in some places and informal in others. Can you help me with making the tone consistent?" A good writing partner will be a "keeper"; you'll learn from the response you ask for, and as a partner yourself, you'll get better at both asking and giving.

Q: What's all this talk about tension? What do you mean by tension in writing and research?

A: All writers know that tension is a crucial element in storytelling. You can't have a plot without a conflict, and you can't investigate a topic without looking at narratives and counternarratives. In school-based research it's easy to depict our educational archetypes: the teacher-as-hero, the underachiever-with-hidden-brilliance, the beleaguered-student-who-makes-good, the negligent-parents-who-learn-from-the-school, the mean-teacher-who-gets-what-he-deserves. These are cultural stereotypes: you see them on TV, in movies and books, and often we want to believe them in our own teaching lives. But it's important always to be on the lookout—and to try to account—for the subplots, the counternarratives, and the thematic undercurrents that live below our accounts—and be creative about integrating them into our writing.

Q: *How do I manage my desire for control? my perfectionism? my dislike for chaos?*

A: Although everyone has different levels of tolerance, you probably have some need for control, a bit of perfectionism, and an eye for how much chaos you can handle before you "lose it." Don Murray has an apropos comment: "Perfect is the enemy of good." With long and intricate pieces of writing, it's difficult to let the "good" flow without getting caught up in wanting it to be perfect at the outset. *It never is!* A good organizational pattern can help eliminate chaos and keep you in control, can help you tell your readers the complex story of your research.

One way to organize is to locate a controlling symbol, metaphor, or theme and work with it for a portion of your text. The meringue metaphor in the answer to the second question is an example. Writing "thick" description and baking a meringue are different. But folding differently textured ingredients together without making everything collapse, to our minds as cooks and writers, is a useful way to describe that process.

Experimenting with point of view is another strategy for organizing. Like cropping photographs or finding the right angle from which to take a picture, choosing a point of view (or more than one) is a good way to determine how to tell a story. One informant's viewpoint, juxtaposed with yours or someone else's, can organize and validate an image or a theme.

Finally, creating section headings can help you organize—and explain some of your analysis. When we began this book, we felt chaotic and out of control. The task was daunting until we created the table of contents and the headings and subheadings.

Q: Okay, so what do I do about editing? Grammar is important!

A: Grammar and syntactical clarity, of course, make the ultimate difference to a reader. Strong nouns hold cultural meanings and create concise images. Verbs bring action to the page and free sentences of clutter. Adjectives and adverbs can be dangerous when we use them too frequently: they mask assumptions. As researchers, we have a special responsibility to use language precisely. Once your draft says what you want it to mean, try a few of these "precise language" strategies:

1. Clean up "word dust." Scan through your writing for words that don't need to be there: long strings of prepositional phrases, for example, hide weak verbs.

2. Find places in which a few lines of dialogue might replace your own description about what happened when there were people involved in a scene.

3. Comb through your text for the sole purpose of identifying the verbs. Circle each one and try to find alternatives that might bring more action to your sentences and hence to your research. Forcing yourself to find the right verb makes you look more closely at the action in your notes and at your field site.

There are many other ways to check on your clarity of grammar and syntax: length of sentences, complexity of sentences, awkward punctuation, use of jargon, and so on. We recommend keeping a good grammar handbook at your elbow.

Q: I don't want to write an article or an essay. No one in my school cares about that. What choices do I have for disseminating my findings? Who are my audiences? What do you mean by "genres"?

A: Disseminating your work beyond yourself gives you professional agency and the power to bring about educational reform. It is also a mark of your credibility and confidence and an affirmation of the hard work you've done. But often, writing a journal article or a book chapter has far less impact than sharing your information in other ways. Remember, though, that you'll still need to organize your data and write it up for yourself before you shape it for an audience.

Having evidence to pull out of your files when administrators, parents, or your colleagues call you on the time you've spent on a focused research project ("Hey, look what I found out!") is sometimes quite enough. Other times, it's exciting to take your work to a school board meeting or a conference, where townspeople and colleagues can ask questions, affirm the value of your work, invite you to join them in other projects, and welcome you into the professional community of committed teachers who do research in their classrooms.

We've seen as many creative uses of audience and genre as we've seen teachers who do research. It's always a surprise to find that there are new ways to present findings and new audiences eager to hear about what actually works in classrooms. Here's a list to get you started:

Audiences
In school: Yourself, your classroom, your colleagues, school departments, the whole school; district, regional, state, national, international educators; other people interested in schools.
Out of school: community organizations, historical societies, local libraries, newspapers, newsletters, magazines and journals, educational publishers, regional and national gatherings of educators.

Genres
Lesson plans, curriculum units, scope and sequence designs, media presentations (radio segments, computer presentations, videos, local television shows), dramatic and artistic exhibitions (museum displays, performance art, community events), websites, brochures, town kiosks and bulletin boards, inservice workshops or professional development courses, academic conferences (poster presentations, workshops, panels).

"Chasing Friendship: Acceptance, Rejection, and Recess Play" by Karen E. Wohlwend

Hey! Up here!" Jeff flashed a try-and-catch-me grin and ducked inside the white plastic turret, disappearing from view. Giggling at the confusion of his pursuer on the ground below, Jeff peered down through the diagonal slots that served as windows in the playground tower. Perched on top of the largest piece of equipment on the school grounds, the lookout tower was the perfect spot for dropping handfuls of soft, shredded wood onto the unsuspecting heads of friends and foes below. Jeff's target, Kevin, crawled under the protection of a nearby slide and began digging in the thick layer of mulch with his bare hands, shoving the dusty bark chips into soft rounded mounds, stockpiling ammunition.

Meanwhile, Jeff waited, nestled inside the tower, hidden from view and protected from the intermittent bursts of wind that swirled across the playground. From his vantage in the circular tower, Jeff could scan the entire playground for potential allies: at the center of the L-shaped playground, clumps of first graders swatted balls toward each other on various lettered or numbered four-square grids that dotted the large blacktop circle. Surrounding this expanse of grayed asphalt, wide patches of exposed dirt spread out into tawny grass not yet worn away by the erosive force of hundreds of sneakers. Squealing children twirled and dropped from steel and vinyl equipment sets that sprouted up out of islands of mushroom-colored wood chips. A few children seeking a private space or a hiding place tucked themselves in the nooks under plastic slides or, like Jeff, inside the protection of the lookout tower.

"Aaagh!" Jeff shrieked in mock distress as Kevin's smiling face bobbed above the top rung of the tower ladder. Quickly wriggling out of his hiding place, Jeff slithered down the adjoining slide and darted off to join another group of children. Kevin crawled inside the abandoned lookout tower and waited for Jeff to reclaim his spot, unaware that Jeff had abandoned him for another set of friends.

The tension in this game of hide-and-seek typifies the social flight and pursuit recorded in an ethnographic study of recess play during the author's weekly observations on an elementary school playground. Analysis of field notes revealed that first-grade children frequently blurred the line between acceptance and rejection while they worked through peer relationships within the complex social web of playground friendships. One body of research on childhood relationships indicates that children may suffer peer rejection or lags in their social development as a result of ineffective play behaviors (McCay and Keyes 2001; Yanghee 2003). Other ethnographic studies (Corsaro 2003; Fernie, Kantor, and Whaley 1995; Kantor and Fernie 2003; Scott 2003) expand interpretations of exclusion beyond individual deficits, situating peer rejection within the social context of children's culture and the institutional structure of schools. In this article, inclusion and exclusion are interpreted not as functions of individual developmental deficit but rather as socially constructed phenomena within the peer group, highlighting the need for teachers to intervene with the entire class rather than focusing on perceived social skills deficits of particular children. The following three sections describe how children in this study used play materials and themes to create play group affiliations, restrict or challenge group membership, and stretch peer social boundaries. The final section offers classroom implications and suggestions for teachers to help young children form more inclusive play groups.

Creating Play Group Affiliations

During play, children not only explore and reproduce cultural roles and expectations of gender, race, and class, but also test and resist these cultural conventions as they set up and break down boundaries in their play groups (Corsaro 2003; Thorne 1993). On the playground, the relative freedom of recess play and its uniquely autonomous zone of proximal development (Vygotsky 1978) affords children the time and space to work through issues of friendship, which matter greatly to them.

> The term free play suggests "openness" or a lack of structure, yet we believe that it is still structured in many ways: by the possibilities and limits of the physical environment, by the socially constructed peer culture of this event (a patterned history of who plays with whom,

around what themes, where, and with what materials), by the wider school culture (norms and expectations for materials use, appropriate and inappropriate behavior, etc.), and by participants' explicit and implicit understandings of this way of doing everyday life in their setting. (Kantor and Fernie 2003, 210)

Thus, the frame of peer culture offers broader explanations of social inclusion and exclusion. Social boundaries provide a means of protecting fragile or emerging play scenarios or maintaining friendship groups, as children explore multiple ways to manage their social interactions (Fernie, Kantor, and Whaley 1995).

Restricting and Extending Group Membership

As Kantor and Fernie (2003) suggest, the physical environment creates opportunities for structuring group affiliations through children's use of playground materials. For example, the author observed children using a domed climbing apparatus as a "dungeon" to which access or escape required negotiation. Children also guarded swings for particular friends, or hoarded balls and jump ropes to restrict membership in games of four-square, soccer, or basketball. Ethnographic research in preschools shows that children control distribution of play materials to indicate group affiliation "as a socially constructed signal of membership in a social network" (Fernie, Kantor, and Whaley 1995, 160).

Children also restricted or extended access through nonmaterial means, such as themed play. When enacting *Lord of the Rings* or *Pokemon*, children negotiated roles before beginning play. At times, play group members cited the lack of an available role as the reason for excluding a child; at other times, children wishing to join a group would offer ideas for roles or plot action as a means of gaining entry.

Verbal rituals expanded opportunities to join play groups. In an elimination chant such as "One Potato, Two Potato," children were included by merely placing a hand or foot in the circle. Although these chants ostensibly eliminated players to determine who would be "it" in a game of tag, all the children who participated in the opening chant also participated in the ensuing game. Kevin easily joined one play group in this way and even taught the children a new chant variant: "Blue shoe, blue shoe. Who's it? Not you!"

Stretching Play Group Boundaries

Children appropriated material from popular culture as a highly effective strategy for joining play groups. A newcomer could demonstrate competence in a group's shared play theme by describing a character's special features. On this playground, *Pokemon* cards or specific knowledge of Pokemon characters' powers constituted "entry vehicles" that children used to join an "affinity group" (Fernie, Kantor, and Whaley 1995, 164–65). In several instances, the author observed Kevin leveraging his knowledge of popular television cartoon shows, such as *Pokemon* or *Teenage Mutant Ninja Turtles*, to join groups that previously had rejected his overtures.

Implications of the Collective Nature of Inclusion/Exclusion in Children's Play

How does recognition of the collective nature of social inclusion/exclusion affect classroom practice? Individual children will continue to need adult help to cope with peer rejection and to learn strategies for gaining peer acceptance (Saracho 2002). However, a narrow focus on modeling and teaching strategies to excluded children overlooks the powerful influence of peer culture, with its emphasis on the playful testing of physical and social limits. A sociocultural perspective that looks beyond individual social development reveals how children enact their shared beliefs about their social worlds through play membership. This recognition clarifies the need to intervene with the whole class rather than simply offering social skills training to an excluded child. "You cannot just work with the child and his or her behavior, because it is a social construction by the group that has a social history that must be undone over time" (Scott 2003, 92).

To foster inclusion with the entire class, teachers can encourage children to bring unresolved recess problems to democratic class meetings (DeVries and Zan 1994) as a means to make visible play group restrictions. After problems were openly discussed in class meetings, the children in the author's study appeared more consciously aware of the effects of play group membership and more lenient in granting access to others. In this school, the ground rules for class meetings prohibited naming specific children, to avoid placing blame and instead focus on solving problems. Discussions resembled those in *You Can't Say You Can't Play* (Paley 1992): children expressed frustration over interruptions in their

play, pain over peer rejection, indignation over closed social groups, and concern over disparate play goals. At the core of these issues, freedom vied with friendship; the rights of children to choose their own playmates and direct their own play were pitted against other children's desire to belong. Solutions were proposed, discarded, revised, attempted, recalled, and agreed to as the children, with teacher support, worked together toward equitable play.

How Can Teachers Support Friendship Within the Framework of Peer Culture?

☀ Value diversity, recognize the influence of the teacher's role in shaping student attitudes toward difference (Manning 2000), and model unconditional acceptance of all children. Teachers should self-critically ask themselves: "Do I restrict activities for some children or allow more freedom for others? Do I follow up on tattling by certain children while ignoring others?"

* Create an observation checklist, using the dimensions in Figure B–1 (see page 202), to discover *the* local peer culture on the playground. Use the checklist to focus on one dimension at a time during recess observations.

* Provide a play environment that encourages children to share their personal expertise in popular culture by allowing children to bring in objects or enact themes that reflect children's interests. In Kevin's case, popular culture provided a shared context as a play base and proved to be an effective means of gaining entry into dosed play groups.

* Teach children the social language of friendship. William Corsaro (2003) compares children's peer culture to an adult cocktail party, with unstated expectations that set up appropriate ways to approach an established group. Children often successfully use direct references to friendship in their entry bids to play, announcing and confirming affiliations before proposing new play ideas. Teachers can smooth the way for children to join a new group by mediating with entry phrases that refer to friendship (e.g., "You're friends, right?") or a shared affinity ("OK, you both like soccer").

* Introduce activities that open up access to play, such as silly rhymes, jokes, and humor. The contagious nature of humor makes it a powerful entry vehicle for play. Yet, teachers tend to consider play a serious activity and tone down humor rather than encourage it (Bergen 2002). Instead, laugh with children at silly jokes, teach them nonsense songs, and curb the adult impulse to squelch the playground pratfalls that children find hilarious.

* Trust children to resolve their own conflicts. Whenever children seek adult help for peer conflicts, teachers can ask, "What have you tried?," and follow up with one or two suggestions, such as, "Listen to the other person" or "What can you do to make things better?" Misunderstandings are a common source of conflict. Among this group, children at odds with one another sometimes merely needed the chance to clearly explain their side of the issue to each other. Once they did, play would resume without further negotiation.

☀ Encourage children to address peer social problems (Adams and Wittmer 2001; DeVries and Zan 1994, 1995) through negotiation and perspective-taking (Piaget 1965), rather than by tattling or relying on adult intervention. When children meet to discuss conflicts, teachers can help children understand each other's feelings and clarify possible solutions by asking "How did that make you feel?" and "What do you want to happen now?" Children often think of solutions that are eminently sensible to them but that would not occur to adults (DeVries and Zan 1994); for example, the children solved the problem of "Whose turn is it?" by agreeing to simultaneously throw their balls at a basketball hoop.

☀ Empower children to challenge exclusion. One tool that children used to gain access to closed peer groups was a friendship meeting, a conflict resolution strategy that allowed children to protest exclusion or other wrongs by interrupting play to hold a meeting. Friendship meetings, usually called by the injured party, had three rules:
  - Only two children at time in a meeting; if more than two people have a problem, get an adult to help.
  - Children in a friendship meeting need to talk until they both feel better.
  - Anyone can call a meeting. If you are called to a meeting, you have to meet or stop playing until you are ready to meet.
The children needed help initially to work through the process of listening to the other child, offering ideas, and generating solutions. Soon, however, they were able to resolve the majority of their conflicts independently.

☀ Intervene in conflict resolution when children's physical or emotional safety is concerned, but do so in ways that keep children's dignity intact. Spend time listening and questioning, rather than placing blame or dispensing punishment. When describing a conflict to a mediating adult, children often begin with dueling accusations to deflect blame; ignore these and keep the tone solution focused by asking, "What would make you both feel better?"

☀ Work with the entire group in class meetings to create more accepting peer cultures. Class meetings in this school had three ground rules:
  - Anyone can call a class meeting, as long as the problem concerns the entire group.

- No names are mentioned when describing a problem to the class.
- Listen to and respect other people's ideas even when you disagree.

After a problem is aired, children can generate possible solutions. Children sometimes offer overly general strategies ("Everybody be nice") or punitive solutions ("Send them to time-out"). Teachers should ask questions that prompt specific suggestions ("What would that look like?") and positive outcomes ("Would that be fair to everyone?") (The Child Development Project 1996). Remember that the consciousness-raising generated by the discussion is as valuable as the potential solutions.

☀ Appreciate peer culture and the resilience of its socially constructed history—history created by children over time. Teacher mandates, and even rules voted on by the class, often just send prohibited activities underground within the peer culture. Teachers should take a participant role in class meetings, bringing up issues but also re-fraining from orchestrating the discussion or engineering group decisions. Open discussion that respects children's insights allows teachers and children to work together to build networks for friend-ship and cooperation.

Conclusion

Through their play, this group of first graders grappled with cultural conventions on their own terms. The playground problems raised by the children reflected not only personal social behaviors but also their concerns over gendered, classed, ethnic, and religious differences. Class meetings served as a forum for bringing problems to the children's attention. However, the children frequently discovered that the solution to recess exclusion lay not in discussions but rather within play itself. The dynamic nature of children's play groups created plentiful opportunities for shifts in membership tied to changes or innovations in play activities or themes.

Teachers should act with an awareness of how their prohibitions and interventions affect the social landscape of the playground. By discouraging children from bringing action figures or trading cards to school or from engaging in play about popular cartoon themes, we may be banning a powerful tool that children use to access peer play and thereby be inadvertently exacerbating excluded children's isolation. By appreciating peer culture and considering the collective nature of inclusion and exclusion, we reduce our tendency to assign deficit labels to already excluded individuals, while expanding our conceptualization of social development in ways that hold more promise for understanding children in their actual cultural context.

References

Adams, S. K., and **D. S. Wittmer.** 2001. "I had it first": Teaching Young Children to Solve Problems Peacefully." *Childhood Education* 78: 10–16.

Bergen, D. 2002. "Finding the Humor in Children's Play." In *Conceptual, Social-Cognitive, and Contextual Issues in the Fields of Play,* ed. J. L. Roopnarine, 209–20. Westport, CT: Ablex.

Child Development Project, The. 1996. *Ways We Want Our Class to Be.* Oakland, CA: Developmental Studies Center.

Corsaro, W. A. 2003. *We're Friends, Right? Inside Kids' Culture.* Washington, DC: Joseph Henry Press.

DeVries, R., and **B. Zan.** 1994. *Moral Classrooms, Moral Children: Creating a Constructivist Atmosphere in Early Education.* New York: Teachers College Press.

———. 1995. "Creating a Constructivist Classroom Atmosphere." *Young Children* 51 (1): 4–13.

Fernie, D. E., R. Kantor, and K. L. Whaley. 1995. "Learning from Classroom Ethnographies: Same Places, Different Times." In *Qualitative Research in Early Childhood Settings,* ed. J. A. Hatch, 156–72. Westport, CT: Praeger.

Kantor, R., and D. Fernie, eds. 2003. *Early Childhood Classroom Processes.* Cresskill, NJ: Hampton Press.

Manning, M. L. 2000. "Understanding Diversity, Accepting Others: Realities and Directions." *Educational Horizons* 78 (2): 77–79.

McCay, L. O., and D. W. Keyes. 2001. "Developing Social Competence in the Inclusive Primary Classroom." *Childhood Education* 78: 70–78.

Paley, V. G. 1992. *You Can't Say You Can't Play.* Cambridge, MA: Harvard University Press.

Piaget, J. 1965. *The Moral Judgment of the Child.* New York: Free Press.

Saracho, O. N. 2002. "Developmental Play Theories and Children's Social Pretend Play." In *Contemporary Perspectives on Early Childhood Curriculum,* ed. O. N. Saracho and B. Spodek, 41–62. Greenwich, CT: Information Age Publishing.

Scott, J. A. 2003. "The Social Construction of 'Outsiders' in Preschool." In *Early Childhood Classroom Processes,* ed. R. Kantor and D. Fernie, 63–98. Cresskill, NJ: Hampton Press.

Thorne, B. 1993. *Gender Play: Girls and Boys in School.* New Brunswick, NJ: Rutgers University Press.

Vygotsky, L. 1978. *Mind in Society.* Cambridge, MA: Harvard University Press.

Yanghee, A. K. 2003. "Necessary Social Skills Related to Peer Acceptance." *Childhood Education* 79: 234–38.

Note: All children's names used here are pseudonyms.

Play Groups: Track play group membership *Who plays together?* *Who plays alone?*	Large Groups	Small Groups	Pairs and Singles
Valued Activities: Tally numbers of children in each *Which activities are popular?* *Who plays?* *How do children control access to an activity?*	Sports/Games Ball Games Jump Ropes Chants/Games	Climbing Equipment Swings Slides Favorite Themes	Fantasy Play Chasing Walking/Talking Other
Valued Materials/ Areas: *What locations or materials are valued?* *Who has access to these?*	Scarce Materials in Demand	Crowded Locations in Demand	Who Gets Access? Who Does Not?
Rules and Routines: *How is friendship limited by rules?* *In conflict, are children separated, punished, or helped to talk?*	Handling Conflict: Tattling? Time-out? Forced apology? Negotiation?		Who Benefits? Who Loses?
Teacher Interaction: *What effects do my actions have on friendships?* *Whose play do I restrict, mediate, or expand?*	Restricting Access: How often did I . . . Ignore tattling? Separate players? Send a child to time-out?	Mediating Conflict: How often did I . . . Listen to both sides? Prompt children to talk it out? Settle an impasse?	Expanding Access: How often did I . . . Suggest roles that would allow a new player into play? Initiate a valued play activity with an excluded child?

Fig. B–I *Dimensions of Peer Culture on the Playground*

Works Cited

Atwell, Nancie. 1987/1998. *In the Middle: Writing, Reading, and Learning with Adolescents*. Portsmouth, NH: Boynton/Cook.

Barthes, Roland. 1977. "Writers, Intellectuals, Teachers." *Image-Music-Text*. Trans. Stephen Heath. New York: Hill.

Bishop, Wendy. 1999. *Ethnographic Writing Research: Writing It Down, Writing It Up, and Reading It*. Portsmouth, NH: Boynton/Cook.

Bissex, Glenda, and **Richard H. Bullock,** eds. 1987. *Seeing for Ourselves: Case-Study Research by Teachers of Writing*. Portsmouth, NH: Heinemann.

Bomer, Randy. 1995. *Time for Meaning: Crafting Literate Lives in Middle and High School*. Portsmouth, NH: Heinemann.

Brooke, Robert. 1991. *Writing and Sense of Self: Identity Negotiation in Writing Workshops*. Urbana, IL: National Council of Teachers of English.

Buber, Martin. [1947] 1970. *I and Thou*. New York: Charles Scribners' Sons.

Calkins, Lucy. 1986. *The Art of Teaching Writing*. Portsmouth, NH: Heinemann.

Calkins, Lucy, and **Shelley Harwayne.** 1991. *Living Between the Lines*. Portsmouth, NH: Heinemann.

Chiseri-Strater, Elizabeth. 1991. *Academic Literacies: The Private and Public Discourse of University Students*. Portsmouth, NH: Heinemann.

Coles, Robert. 1989. *The Call of Stories: Teaching and the Moral Imagination*. Boston: Houghton Mifflin.

———. 1997. *Doing Documentary Work*. New York: Oxford University Press.

Dewey, John. [1938] 1963. *Experience and Education*. New York: Collier and Macmillan.

Dillard, Annie. 1989. *The Writing Life*. New York: Harper and Row.

Eisner, Elliott W. 1991. *The Enlightened Eye: Qualitative Inquiry and the Enhancement of Educational Practice*. New York: Macmillan.

Elbow, Peter. 1980. *Writing with Power*. New York: Oxford University Press.

Freire, Paulo. 1986. *Pedagogy of the Oppressed*. New York: Continuum.

Fletcher, Ralph. 1992. *What a Writer Needs*. Portsmouth, NH: Heinemann.

———. 1996. *Breathing In, Breathing Out: Keeping a Writer's Notebook*. Portsmouth, NH: Heinemann.

Graves, Donald. 2003. *Testing Is Not Teaching: What Should Count in Education*. Portsmouth, NH: Heinemann.

Greene, Maxine. 1995, 2000. *Releasing the Imagination: Essays on Education, the Arts, and Social Change*. San Francisco: Jossey-Bass.

Gregory, Kathleen, Caren Cameron, and Anne Davies. 2000. *Setting and Using Criteria for Use in Middle and Secondary Classrooms*. Courtenay, BC: Connections.

Heath, Shirley Brice. 1983. *Ways with Words: Language, Life, and Work in Communities and Classrooms*. New York: Cambridge University Press.

Heinemann. 2002. *Write from the Beginning: The Heinemann–Boynton/Cook Author Guidelines*. Portsmouth, NH: Heinemann.

Holmes, Lynda. 2001. "What Do Students Mean When They Say, 'I Hate Writing?'" *Teaching English in the Two Year College* 29 (2): 76–89.

Human Subjects Office. 2005. "Hawk IRB," University of Iowa. www.research.uiowa.edu/hso/index. February.

Johnson, Susan Moore. 1990. *Teachers at Work: Achieving Success in Our Schools*. New York: Basic.

Kindler, A. 2000. "Art Education Outside the Search for Deep Meaning: Sometimes What Matters Is on the Surface." *Art Education* 53 (1): 39–43.

King, Stephen. 2000. *On Writing*. New York: Scribner.

Kohn, Alfie. 1993. *Punished by Rewards: The Trouble with Gold Stars, Incentive Plans, A's, Praise and Other Bribes*. Boston: Houghton Mifflin.

———. 2004. *What Does It Mean to Be Well Educated? And More Essays on Standards, Grading and Other Follies*. Boston: Beacon.

Kozol, Jonathan. 1991. *Savage Inequalities: Children in America's Schools*. New York: Crown.

Lane, Barry. 1992. *After "The End": Teaching and Learning Creative Revision*. Portsmouth, NH: Heinemann.

Lawrence-Lightfoot, Sarah. 1985. *The Good High School: Portraits of Character and Culture*. New York: Basic.

Lawrence-Lightfoot, Sarah, and Jessica Hoffmann Davis. 1997. *The Art and Science of Portraiture*. San Francisco: Jossey-Bass.

Merriam, Sharon. 1998. *Qualitative Research and Case Study Applications in Education*. San Francisco: Jossey-Bass.

Meyer, Richard. 1996. *Stories from the Heart: Teachers and Students Researching Their Literacy Lives*. Mahweh, NJ: Lawrence Erlbaum.

Murray, Donald M. 2002. *The Craft of Revision*. 5th ed. Boston: Heinle.

Newkirk, Thomas. 1998. *The Performance of Self in Student Writing*. Portsmouth, NH: Boynton/Cook.

Ogbu, John. 1974. *The Next Generation* 2. New York: Academic Press.

Ohanian, Susan. 1999. *One Size Fits Few: The Folly of Educational Standards*. Portsmouth, NH: Heinemann.

Paley, Vivian G. 1992. *You Can't Say You Can't Play*. Cambridge: Harvard University Press.

Perl, Sonda. 1980. "Understanding Composing." *College Composition and Communication* 31: 363–69.

———. 1983. "Reflections on Ethnography and Writing." *The English Record* 11.

Postman, Neil. 1995. *The End of Education: Redefining the Value of School*. New York: Knopf.

Postman, Neil, and Charles Weingartner. 1969. *Teaching as a Subversive Activity*. New York: Dell.

Powdermaker, Hortense. 1966. *Stranger and Friend: The Way of an Anthropologist*. New York: Norton.

Rief, Linda. "Reflections on Teaching Writing in 8 Workshops." www.learner.org/channel 6/workshops/middlewriting pl_/n.

Rose, Mike. 1984. *Writer's Block: The Cognitive Dimension*. Carbondale: Southern Illinois Press.

Rosenblatt, Louise. 1978. *The Reader, the Text, the Poem: The Transactional Theory of the Literary Work*. Carbondale: Southern Illinois Press.

Roskelly, Hephzibah. 2005. "Still Bridges to Build: English Education's Pragmatic Agenda." *English Education* 37: 4.

Schon, Donald. 1983. *The Reflective Practitioner: How Professionals Think in Action*. New York: Basic.

Sunstein, Bonnie Stone, and Elizabeth Chiseri-Strater. 2002. *FieldWorking: Reading and Writing Research*. 2d ed. New York: Bedford/St.Martin's.

Tobin, Lad. 1993. *Writing Relationships: What Really Happens in the Composition Class*. Portsmouth, NH: Boynton/Cook.

Tolstoy, Leo. 2004. "Are the Peasant Children to Learn to Write from Us?" In *Teaching Stories: An Anthology on the Power of Learning and Literature,* ed. Robert Coles. New York: Modern Library.

Van Maanen, John. 1988. *Tales of the Field: On Writing Ethnography.* Chicago: University of Chicago Press.

Van Manen, Max. 1990. *Researching Lived Experience: Human Science for an Action Sensitive Pedagogy.* London, ON: SUNY Press.

Vanderstaay, Steve. 1992. *Street Lives: An Oral History of Homeless Americans.* Philadelphia: New Society.

Vygotsky, Lev. 1978. *Mind in Society.* Cambridge: Harvard University Press.

———. 1986. *Thought and Language.* Cambridge: MIT Press.

Yancey, Kathleen. 1998. *Reflection in the Writing Classroom.* Logan: Utah State University Press.

Index

Oral language
  discussion techniques, studying, 93
  documenting, 92–93
Origination, behavior-disordered
  students and, 153
Outlining
  drafts, 111–13
  proposals, 111–13
Outsiders, The, 170